# Liminality
# Transitional Phenomena

Nathan Schwartz-Salant and Murray Stein, editors

Chiron Publications • Wilmette, Illinois

**The Chiron Clinical Series**
**ISBN 0-933029-29-2**





Printed in the United States of America.

Book design by Elaine Hill.

**Library of Congress Cataloging-in-Publication Data**

Liminality and transitional phenomena / Nathan Schwartz-Salant and Murray Stein, editors.
p. cm. — (The Chiron clinical series)
Includes bibliographical references.
ISBN 0-933029-29-2 : $15.95
1. Liminality. 2. Transitional objects (Psychology). 3. Jung, C. G. (Carl Gustav), 1875–1961. 4. Psychoanalysis. I. Schwartz-Salant, Nathan, 1938– II. Stein, Murray, 1943– . III. Series.
BF175.5.L55L56 1991
150.19'54—dc20

90-42229
CIP

# Contents

# The Muddle in Analysis

**Murray Stein**

> *When I was working on my book about the libido and approaching the end of the chapter "The Sacrifice," I knew in advance that its publication would cost me my friendship with Freud. For I planned to set down in it my own conception of incest, the decisive transformation of the concept of libido, and various other ideas in which I differed from Freud. . . . But Freud clung to the literal interpretation of it and could not grasp the spiritual significance of incest as a symbol.*
>
> C. G. Jung, *Memories, Dreams, Reflections*, p. 167

## The Muddle

A woman enters analysis and declares at the outset that she's a feeling/intuitive type, but she behaves, as it turns out, like a sensation/thinking type. This is compensatory to her natural functioning, an obsessive/compulsive defense, which both affords her protection in the "real world" and conceals her true inner being even from herself. In addition to this, in the early phase of analysis she shows evidence of developing a split transference, such that women (the "feminine") are taken to be the caretakers of feelings and relationships while men (the

---

**Murray Stein**, Ph.D., is a member of the Chicago Society of Jungian Analysts and has a private practice in Wilmette, Ill. He is the editor of *Jungian Analysis*, co-editor of *Jung's Challenge to Contemporary Religion*, and author of *In Midlife* and *Jung's Treatment of Christianity: The Psychotherapy of a Religious Tradition*.

"masculine") take care of the outer world. The male analyst is expected to respond a) to her true self-functioning and b) as a man with concrete, outer-world concerns and interests on her behalf.

Instead, the analyst responds with puzzlement and frustration. So many mixed messages pour out of this woman, beginning with her twisted typology. Frequently he feels maneuvered first into taking an obsessive amount of interest in her outer-world concerns, then toward giving up the analytic attitude and his neutrality, then toward counseling and instructing and advice-giving, all the while continuing to be expected to recognize her true, feminine core. Resisting these pressures, the analyst sometimes makes negative interpretations: she is resisting analysis by these "diversions," he thinks, and sometimes he says so.

The analysand, who at first felt uneasy at being in analysis, eventually comes to feel betrayed and complains that she's not being helped. At times she even feels she's being abused by interpretations, which feel demeaning and demonstrate to her a lack of understanding of her real needs for help. She dreams that men are betraying her, even that her own husband is going behind her back and consorting with the enemy.

Communications in analysis become fraught with misunderstanding; an undertone of suspicion and accusation gathers force. Meanwhile, the analysand has found a woman analyst with whom she wants to consult on her feminine parts, in addition to continuing (but less frequently) with the male analyst, to "balance out her growth process." The analyst feels abandoned and debased. He wanted to be a full-service analyst, not an adjunct.

This muddle derives from the transference, by which he is assigned the role of the father/masculine who takes care of outer-world concerns, *so that* the analysand can relax the compulsiveness of her sensation/thinking functioning in order to experience and eventually to become her true self. He is supposed to replace her obsessive/compulsive defenses. When he does not play the role of her extraverted sensation/thinking adaptation, he falls into her negative father complex and looks to her like her inadequate father: crippled, unable to assert himself in and through the world, ineffective in making a place for her in it. She's been trying to repeat her childhood, to make it right this time. Instead she's ended up simply repeating it and feeling no better off after the analysis than before.

Straightening out this muddle would involve both of them understanding this transference dynamic and relating to one another symbolically rather than concretely/projectively. If she could treat the analyst as though he were her defective father, then she could mourn him as well as her failed childhood and use the analyst as a symbolic carrier of her father problem. The ramifications of this problem in her life generally would be grasped and perhaps worked through to a resolution and change of transference expectations from men and from life generally. For his part, the analyst could, in the symbolic "as-if" mode, express his countertransference reaction, and these could be used to further unpack her totally compacted inner life. "I'm feeling like you're asking the impossible of me" in the countertransference would become "I put myself into impossible situations and feel frustrated and helpless," or "When I get put into impossible situations, I feel helpless, abandoned, betrayed, and angry at myself." "I feel like you want me to break the rules for you" would become "I feel like I want to break the rules and destroy everything so I can have it my own way, but without guilt." These kinds of statements, made in the symbolic as-if space of the analytic vessel, would be extremely useful in both elucidating and transforming this analysand's inner life. The meaning of the negative father complex would ultimately unfold into the image of the wounded Father, the suffering and helpless God.

## The Muddle as Betwixt-and-Between

This movement into psychic space—where the transference projections and the countertransference reactions can be taken up in the as-if attitude and made conscious, and where archetypal images can take form and their meaning be recovered—is the nub of the problem. This transition is exceedingly difficult with analysands whose transference interferes in the way described above. They want to keep everything concrete. The muddle, occurring in the space between the literal/contractual side of analysis and the psychic/symbolic as-if side, creates a hazard for the entire analytic enterprise. To get from concrete, literal communications and their univocal meaning to a symbolic as-if field of communicating with its multivocal meanings, one must often pass through the valley of the muddle, a state of confusion between these other two types of communication. Typically it is the transference that accounts for the hang-up in muddleland.

Naively, one would expect the transition from literal communication to the symbolic field of communication to be easy because this is what analysis is explicitly about, after all. Who would think otherwise? Who could possibly come to a Jungian analyst, of all types of therapists, for help in dealing with situational problems on the concrete level?

Jungian analysts are as far from vocational counselors, behavior modifiers, activistic social workers, evangelical preachers, drug-pushing physicians, or professional mentors in the world of work and taxes as one would expect to find in the spectrum of "mental health professionals." Surely anyone who consciously chooses a Jungian analyst would know, implicitly, that what we concern ourselves with is the inner world: images not people, memories not events, conflicts not family squabbles, fantasies not careers. And yet, transference is able to interfere with this conscious knowledge and to create the muddle. Jungian analysts are not immune from the muddle just because they explicitly state their way to be symbolic.

The muddle lies in the realm of "betwixt-and-between" (Turner 1969): between concrete communication ("waiting-room behavior," as Vin Rosenthal once aptly termed it) on the one side, and symbolic communication on the other. The analyst assumes that concrete communication is necessary but is for the "world out there" and for certain concrete aspects of analysis (time, place, fee, ethical matters), while the analytic area is filled mostly with symbolic communication. This difference is parallel to the distinction Jung made between signs and symbols: signs are univocal, referring to one thing clearly and explicitly; symbols are polysemous, cannot be defined exactly or interpreted completely, and create a bridge between consciousness and the unconscious. When we listen concretely, it is with only one ear, and what we hear are clear, enharmonic tones and signals; when we listen symbolically, it is in stereo and we hear resonances, reverberations, depths, dimensions, and we sense a mysterious core of meaning that remains elusive and unspeakable. Listening to the muddle, however, requires the "third ear," which can hear a latent signal dimly beneath a misleading and deceptive surface of static and disinformation.

The muddle is neither concrete nor symbolic communication, but both. It pretends to be concrete but is actually symbolic in disguise, and it therefore creates misunderstanding, puzzlement, and confusion. In the muddle, we ask questions like "What's going on here?" "I don't understand this; are we out of control?" Or we might defend against it: "This is nonsense; let it go." Yet, however we confront it, it opens into an abyss of liminality and generates an urgent demand for understanding the dynamics at work. It throws us into a desperate need to sort things out and to get to the bottom.

This experience of liminality is quite different from the kind one finds in the "secured symbolic field" (Goodheart 1980). There one experiences a kind of liminality that belongs to transitional space (Winnicott 1971), and the distinction between literal fact and symbolic meaning is not relevant; it is suspended. Illusion and reality are simply accepted as one and the same, allowing the ego to float in an attitude of play. This kind of liminality is much less confusing to the analyst, because it is what one looks for and expects in analysis. For the analyst at least, this is a comfortable sort of liminality. What Rosemary Gordon calls "the symbolic process" and William Goodheart "the secured symbolic field" are transitional spaces in which the as-if attitude has been reached (Gordon 1977, Goodheart 1980). The as-if attitude, Gordon says, "enables men to relate to inobservable realities in terms of observable phenomena" (1977, p. 336). This is what the analyst hopes will happen, for, as Witenberg points out, if the analysand "does not ultimately see the transference as an 'as-if' experience the analysis cannot work" (1979, p. 52). In fact, the whole analytic enterprise, *qua* analysis, hangs on the attainment of the as-if attitude because it is this that allows a relation between ego and unconscious to become a psychological reality. This attitude is a necessary condition for the transcendent function to operate. Without it, one is limited in range to ego-consciousness, and there is thus no penetration into depth, no emergent feeling for the self, no sense of the levels of psyche and their harmonic resonances, and little integration of unconscious material.

The muddle is therefore usually seen by analysts as far from ideal, at best as a transitional state from concrete to symbolic process. It is akin to Goodheart's complex-discharging field. It introduces liminality of a sort different from the liminality of the symbolic process, a kind much less comfortable for the analyst.

## Struggles with Muddles

I would like to explore the muddle for more promising potential than has generally been noted. This type of liminality in analysis may generate an opportunity for a kind of consciousness and integration not offered by either concrete or symbolic experience. The muddle is uncomfortable, threatening, and anxiety-provoking for both analysand and analyst, but this anxiety may allow them to bring to the surface hidden assumptions and to sort out transference and countertransference contents and dynamics.

The muddle calls ingrained assumptions ("projections") into question and may break *participation mystique* by forcing awareness of differences of agenda, inner processes, and archetypal patterns. When a muddle thickens the analytic interaction, it leads to an awareness of "otherness" and to the sense that analyst and analysand are not what they first appeared to be. They live in different psychological universes. This awareness, in turn, may move the analytic relationship toward the "achievement of a satisfactory therapeutic partnership . . . an environment in which therapeutic transformations occur" (Redfearn 1980, p. 3).

This outcome, much to be desired, depends however upon the ability of both partners, but especially of the analyst, to sort out the confusion, to recognize projections and interpret them, and to accept the differences or adjust to them until they can, perhaps, be dissolved. The muddle creates a crisis of confidence and understanding, and it can just as well lead to an impasse and to premature termination as to a more workable partnership.

> *Example 1*: An analyst tells her analysand, Mr. A, that she is taking an extended holiday of six weeks. Mr. A, who has been in analysis only briefly, reacts by saying he's had enough analysis for now and feels satisfied not to continue when she, the analyst, returns. The analyst accepts this and the analysis ends.

Here the muddle is that the analyst is communicating concretely while the analysand hears the message as symbolic: "I'll be out of my practice for six weeks" is muddled into "You're rejecting me, and before you can do so explicitly, I will reject you." The analyst makes the mistake of accepting the response on the same concrete level at which she delivered her vacation announcement, thereby most likely acting out a negative countertransference of her own. This muddle destroyed the analytic container.

> *Example 2*: Mr. B comes to the analyst asking concretely for psychological help in overcoming a negative transference to his previous analyst after that analysis had ended in mutual acrimony and misunderstanding (itself a muddle). The analyst accepts this and begins sessions. As things progress, the analyst begins sensing an unconscious request for a magical cure to a deeply disturbed condition and some concomitant rage for not delivering it quickly enough. The analysand will not confess to this wish or engage the transference symbolically, so the analyst abruptly terminates the analysis with the explanation that they cannot communicate and therefore cannot possibly work together.

The muddle here derives from the wide discrepancy between the analysand's conscious and unconscious expectations. The negative transference, unacknowledged or dealt with in an as-if manner, causes the analyst to feel battered and helpless. The analyst, in turn, cannot sort out the muddle, and he retaliates by communicating his rage in the form of a concrete termination. Again, the muddle destroys the analytic relationship.

The negative outcome of muddles is usually brought about by the refusal, on one or both parts, to enter the anxiety of its liminality and to experience it until the latent message can be deciphered. In the first example, the analyst might have confessed to being confused—"I'm only going away for six weeks; how does it follow that you're going to stop analysis?" The analysand might have replied, "Doesn't this mean that you're trying to get rid of me?" But this was too risky for both, and so the muddle, so rich in transference and countertransference allusions, was not used to create consciousness. In the second case, where the relationship was fraught with mutual hostility, the analyst was not willing to endure further the heat of an unacknowledged virulent negative transference. Perhaps, too, the analyst's grandiosity was offended when he could not help the analysand more expeditiously achieve the concrete aim set out at the beginning. Because the muddle was ignored in both instances, an impasse developed and neither party quite understood what happened. Premature termination affords few pleasures.

A successful passage through a muddle, however, can yield analytic gold.

> *Example 3*: The analysis began with high expectations on the young man's part. He came to his analyst initially as to one wise, learned, and experienced. After a brief first phase of idealization, he entered a long middle period of analysis in which he mostly complained that the analyst was not close enough, did not give useful advice, said little, taught little, and was not stimulating. This was not what he had expected, and he was confused because he was coming, concretely, for help. He felt that he was being left to do all of the work by himself. The analyst, for his part, had realized early on that his interpretations were consistently ignored or bettered, so in his frustration he chose to remain mostly silent and passive and to wait for the transference to clarify itself. He, too, was confused by the contradiction between concrete demands for help and the consistent refusal to be symbolically helped. After a long period of intense disappointment and much complaint on

> the analysand's part, he began to uncover all the ways in which the analyst resembled his father: silent, remote, passive, helpless, inarticulate, unempathic, and generally useless. Gradually he became able to use the analyst consciously as a negative transference (symbolic) object to sort out his massive father complex and its pervasive influence in his emotional life.

Here the muddle occurred and reoccurred many times, when the analysand would concretely ask for advice and help in gaining insight and would then find that no matter what the analyst said or did, it was unhelpful and insufficient. The analyst, for his part, felt trapped between the concrete demand for advice and helpful interpretations on the one hand and the young man's inability to accept them on the other. The analyst's sense of frustration lay in his inability to negotiate the distance between concrete demand for help and the as-if symbolic attitude that is needed to make use of his psychological services. He simply had to wait until the analysand could make this crossing for himself, which in this case worked out successfully. The muddle actually became the door through which the analysis of the father complex could take place, and only later, after the passage had been made under extremely trying circumstances while the negative transference was largely unconscious, could the analysis enter anything that approached the as-if symbolic space. Shortly after that space had been achieved, this particular analysis actually came to an end.

**Tracking the Muddle Maker**

Muddles great and small are nearly inevitable in Jungian analysis because it is a multilevel field of operations. There are, however, various strategies available for avoiding them. One is to stay concretely goal-oriented: you came to work on your unconscious, and all we will therefore consider are your fantasies and dreams; we will not deal with transference and will interpret resistance as only obstructionistic. Another strategy is to stay adamantly symbolic: all of your communications ("I have a cold today"; "my mother died yesterday"; "my car broke down and I couldn't get here on time") are symbolic, and that is the only level on which we will deal with them. Both of these are ego-dominated positions in that the analyst determines at the outset the appropriate, or the only, level on which communication and interaction will be considered. But if the ego-dominated attitude is put aside and the analyst remains open to every level of possible communication and interaction, muddles are inevitable.

The muddle may first crop up in the initial session (in one case it even occurred on the telephone when, in setting up the first appointment, the analyst became confused and could not give clear directions for getting to his office!). More likely, it occurs in subsequent sessions as the initial clarity of the case and the presenting issues and history became more complicated and opaque, and the outline of an ideal individuation process and line of development become submerged in the immediacy of a complex relationship. The dream series, often transparent and sharply delineated in theory and in retrospect, becomes Protean and illusive. Life experiences happen to analyst and analysand—deaths, births, divorces, weddings, graduations, crises—and the pure and clean treatment situation is inevitably affected. Jung's account of the transference/countertransference process as an alchemical combination of psyches is accurately descriptive. The mixture of conscious and unconscious elements from both sides creates a myriad of opportunities for falling into a muddle. And every analysis that goes at all deep, i.e., into the unconscious, will have to struggle with the muddle maker.

The muddle maker is the unconscious itself, Mercurius. And both partners in analysis have one of these spirits.

Muddles occur at those points where it is not clear whether concrete or symbolic communication is taking place (as in the examples above). The concrete then *feels* symbolic, overdetermined, driven by a complex; but a symbolic apprehension of its as-if quality has not been established. Mercurius is present but invisible. This is the liminality of the muddle.

*Example 4*: The analysand opens a session by pointing out that a mistake had been made on her monthly bill. The analyst receives this as a concrete communication and offers to check the records and confirm later. This does not end the discussion, however, for the analysand goes on to show in detail, using her calendar and a pencil and paper, *how* the bill was incorrect. The analyst feels a good deal of affect and pressure but does not know quite from where it's coming. He asks: "Are you angry? You sound like it." She replies: "No, I just wanted to point this out." He: "But there seems to be something more behind it." She: "No, I just don't want the confusion to continue, and I'd like to get it straightened out now rather than let it go into the next month when it will be harder to track down."

This scenario has the potential for turning into a full-scale muddle if the analyst pursues it by trying to probe for the underlying symbolic content. The muddle would form when the analysand clings tenaciously to the concrete level while the analyst tries to elicit some vaguely intuited transference content. Before long, neither would understand what the other was trying to say. The analyst could, on the other hand, see the problem coming and duck it altogether by accepting the concrete level and placating the analysand: "OK, I'll be sure to take care of it." But the feeling tone in the session by this time is such that this option seems unpalatable, if not irresponsible. Mercurius has struck and will not be denied. Is there some way to catch a glimpse of this "fugitive stag" more clearly?

The analyst would ideally like to use this moment to enter the symbolic process, so that he and the analysand together could explore the various psychological levels of this interaction: all the reverberations of being overcharged by a transference object; the feelings of confusion, guilt, and anger that derive from this; the archetypal dimension of human–divine reciprocity and its breakdown; the need for retribution and justice, for being seen and acknowledged. This would be rich material for exploration in true analysis. But what the analyst actually confronts is anxiety and a compulsive defense aimed at reducing the anxiety. It is this anxiety that prevents them from moving to the symbolic level, and the muddle comes about by the analyst not recognizing the anxiety itself before probing for deeper reasons. The anxiety is committed to maintaining the concrete level because this is where the analysand feels safe and where the problem seems to lie. The muddle maker, Mercurius, cannot be caught at work here because the anxiety produced in the transference will not allow it. Because of the anxiety, the muddle cannot be excavated for psychological gold.

There might be a chance to move this interaction to the symbolic process level, where Mercurius could be glimpsed, if the anxiety were first recognized and dealt with, and then deeper explorations were encouraged: "You feel anxious this won't be taken care of, that I will let it get out of hand, that you will be overcharged or have to continue struggling to get things straight in the future. I can assure you that I'll take care of it and we'll discuss it next time. But it might also be worthwhile to explore your associations to this kind of an experience, just to see what might be behind the anxiety." This might, of course, also go nowhere, but now the anxiety has been acknowledged and a way cleared to move into as-if territory. The analyst has actually addressed two levels: the concrete level of the bill, and the defensive level of the compulsiveness and anxiety. He has also introduced the possibility for yet another level, the as-if symbolic level, where the analyst is seen by the unconscious through the lens of the transference.

There is yet another way to move in this scenario. The analyst may gain some consciousness about the psychological universe inhabited by this analysand just because this particular muddle developed. In the analyst's mental universe, this mistaken bill is no great cause for alarm. The more important matters are the psychological dynamics underlying such a concern. This (more or less standard analytical) attitude may truly misread the needs and concerns of this particular analysand. The analysand's insistence on holding to the concrete level may be as real and genuine as this person can possibly be. Such an analysand would be faking it should she begin taking everything on the symbolic process level. It would be disingenuous and simply adaptive to the analytic context and to the wishes and attitudes of the analyst to play the symbolic process game about the bill. The muddle might therefore rebound another way. Instead of trying to open the way to a symbolic as-if attitude, the analyst might adopt the concrete approach. This need not be seen as a mere capitulation to the analysand's anxiety and compulsiveness. It could be a clearer recognition of the psychological world in which she lives and out of which she operates. This kind of clarification of the analyst's view of the analysand—where and who she actually is, as different from him—can also move the therapeutic partnership to a more effective level "where ego boundaries are dissolved and transcended" (Redfearn 1980, p. 3). They may decide to meet on the concrete level to work out problems, such as the billing problem, and in working out something together, they may experience the "healing factor that we encounter in the good womb and the good mothering experience" (ibid.). The anxiety that drove the compulsion to solve the problem concretely would, of course, be allayed, but more importantly, the muddle would have led to a clearer understanding, on the analyst's part, of how *this person* must be treated. For this person, the as-if experience may come only through the concrete and never apart from it.

In making this latter adjustment in his attitude, the analyst is not actually giving up on attaining the symbolic process level with this person, but is rather changing the strategy for getting there. Rather than achieving symbolic process by reflecting upon events and persons as symbols or experiencing the many dimensions of an event or person, one narrows the doorway leading to the symbol to concrete events, objects, and tasks. The feeling of being in a symbolic field may not be present, or only minimally so, in the consciousness of the analyst, although it should always be there theoretically. And while it does not feel or seem like this is an as-if experience, it is! Working out the muddled bill in concrete terms resonates on the symbolic level—what has been divided comes together; there is a unity of focus and purpose; the outcome is mutually arrived at and defined. The *coniunctio* is actually experienced, but not as-if, not as a symbol but as a concrete event that has symbolic overtones. For this particular analysand, this is a more effective experience of the *coniunctio* than a more self-consciously symbolic as-if experience would, or could, be. Here Mercurius is trapped in the concrete.

Muddles are of course meant to be resolved in one way or another, otherwise they harden into impasses and stalemates. But it is a mistake to escape the liminality of the muddle too cheaply or too quickly. Mercurious is behind the muddle and may be glimpsed at work behind the scenes. Muddles can therefore be one of our most effective teachers, leading the way to a more conscious therapeutic partnership, if dealt with creatively and courageously.

## References

Goodheart, W. B. 1980. Theory of the analytical interaction. *San Francisco Jung Institute Library Journal* 1/4:2–39.

Gordon, R. 1977. The symbolic experience as bridge between the personal and the collective. *Journal of Analytical Psychology* 22/4:331–342.

Jung, C. G. 1946. Psychology of the transference. In *Collected Works*, vol. 16. New York: Pantheon, 1954, pp. 163–323.

______. 1948. The spirit Mercurius. In *Collected Works*, vol. 13. Princeton, N.J.: Princeton University Press, 1967, pp. 191–250.

Redfearn, J. W. T. 1980. Romantic and classical views of analysis. *Journal of Analytical Psychology* 25/1:1–16.

Rosenthal, V. 1986. Personal communication.

Turner, V. W. 1969. *The Ritual Process*. Chicago: Aldine.

Winnicott, D. W. 1971. *Playing and Reality*. London: Tavistock Publications Ltd.

Witenberg, E. G. 1979. The inner experience of the psychoanalyst. In *Countertransference*, L. Epstein and A. H. Feiner, eds. New York: Aronson, pp. 45–57.

# Ritual, Sacred Space, and Healing: The Psychoanalyst as Ritual Elder

Robert L. Moore

## Introduction

At a recent session of the American Academy of Religion focusing on cross-cultural ritual studies, I was reminded once again why, after a long immersion in the Freudian and Adlerian schools of psychoanalysis, I became an enthusiastic proponent of Jungian analysis. One of the speakers was a bright, much-published Freudian psychoanalyst who, in a *very* self-confident manner, assured the gathering that the ritual processes which they were studying were essentially defenses against painful reality and, while understandable, certainly represented symptoms of pathological states and not a means to a cure. If any of us have gotten the idea that recent developments in the Freudian tradition have led Freudians to a deeper understanding of ritual and religious processes, then this scene should remind us that *metatheoretical assumptions in psychoanalysis really matter*. This Freudian psychoanalyst was prevented by his metatheoretical assumptions from seeing the ways in which he functions as a ritual elder in a quasi-religious movement providing "spiritual direction" to secularized modern individuals.

---

**Robert L. Moore**, Ph.D., is a professor of psychology and religion at the Chicago Theological Seminary. He is author of *Anthropology and the Study of Religion* and *The Magician and the Analyst: Ritual, Sacred Space, and Psychotherapy* (forthcoming).

Jungians should do better than this. Yet I am convinced that both pre-Jungians and many of the so-called post-Jungians have failed to understand the radical significance for both cultural and psychological hermeneutics of Jungian concepts of the collective unconscious and the objective psyche. The discussion that follows assumes, with Jung, that research into cultural anthropology and the history of religions is, for the analytical psychologist, empirical psychoanalytic research into the structure and dynamics of the psyche, into the very deep structures of the collective unconscious. Understanding the ritual role of the psychoanalyst should not be seen as negating psychoanalysis as a human science. Rather, coming to terms with this interpretive task can show the way in which psychoanalytic conceptuality can help us understand the most basic processes of human transformation and healing. While Jung did not have access to the resources discussed below, the very structure of his thought anticipates these later developments in anthropology, phenomenology of religion, and psychoanalysis. In a day when some are de-emphasizing the importance of studying the deep structures of human personality, ideation, and behavior, studies in the field of psychoanalysis and ritual process once again give us an opportunity to appreciate not only the genius of Jung's own thought, but the power of his theoretical contributions to make sense of the latest developments in scientific anthropological and psychological research. The following discussion is offered in that spirit.

## Space and Transformation in Ritual Process

For some time I have been convinced that the next important agenda in the psychology of religion in general, and in studies of the relationship between religious and psychotherapeutic processes in particular, is to devote much more of our effort to understanding not only the psychology of ritual processes, but also the ritual processes fundamental to psychotherapeutic practice.[1] There is no better example of the negative impact of Protestant cultural biases on the field than the manner in which the psychosocial role of ritual has been typically either neglected or viewed as somehow regressive. We are currently at the beginning of an exciting new era in ritual studies which is forcing us to reexamine our most fundamental assumptions about ritual processes in human life (Moore, Burhoe, and Hefner 1983). Psychoanalytic practice will be one of the fields that will benefit most from this new focus on the importance of ritual process.

Victor Turner, of course, is one of the most important theorists responsible for the current renewal of interest in ritual. In the following essay, I will examine some of the ways in which his concepts of the *liminal* and the *liminoid* have begun to help us move beyond Van Gennep and Eliade in our reflections about the relationship between space and transformation in ritual process and analytical practice.

*Eliade on Space and Transformation*

In any discussion of the importance of the concept of sacred space in understanding religion in general and ritual process in particular, the seminal work of Mircea Eliade on this topic must be a key reference point. Many of Eliade's most fundamental insights into the nature and dynamics of human religious life are based on his assumptions about the heterogeneity of space in human experience.[2] In the following reflections I will examine these assumptions and show how they are extended by the work of Turner.

For Eliade, the human experience of the world is divided into two fundamentally different modalities. In his influential monograph, *The Sacred and the Profane*, he characterized the differences between the human experience of sacred space and time and profane space and time (Eliade 1961). In profane space and time there is no fixed point or center from which one can gain orientation. There is no contact with the really real, with the power that alone can renew life and through which regeneration can occur. Profane space is a formless expanse, homogeneous in its fundamental unreality. It is a space essentially devoid of creativity. Rather than persons and things being created or renewed in profane space, it is in fact the locus of the deterioration of the cosmos as ordinary temporal duration, profane time, runs its course.

*Homo religiosus*, however, has periodic contact with a totally different kind of space:

> For religious man, space is not homogeneous; he experiences interruptions, breaks in it; some parts of space are qualitatively different from others. "Draw not nigh hither," says the Lord to Moses; "put off thy shoes from off they feet, for the place whereon thou standest is holy ground" (Exodus 3:5). There is, then, a sacred space, and hence a strong, significant space; there are other spaces that are not sacred and so are without structure or consistency, amorphous. Nor is this all. For religious man, this spatial nonhomogeneity finds expression in the experience of an opposition between space that is sacred—the only *real* and *real-ly* existing space—and all other space, the formless expanse surrounding it. (Eliade 1961, p. 20)

It is this break in ordinary profane space that allows the world to be regenerated. Because of this break, a center for orientation, a fixed point grounded in absolute reality, is revealed. The sacred has manifested itself in a hierophany, and this irruption of the sacred "results in detaching a territory from the surrounding cosmic milieu and making it qualitatively different" (ibid., p. 26). Discussing Jacob's dream at Beth-el, Eliade elaborates:

> The symbolism implicit in the expression "gate of heaven" is rich and complex; the theophany that occurs in a plane consecrates it by the very fact that it makes it open above—that is, in communication with heaven, the paradoxical point of passage from one mode of being to another. . . . Often there is no need for a theophany or hierophany properly speaking; some *sign* suffices to indicate the sacredness of a place. . . . This amounts to an evocation of sacred forms or figures for the immediate purpose of establishing an *orientation* in the homogeneity of space. A *sign* is asked, to put an end to the tension and anxiety caused by relativity and disorientation—in short, to reveal an absolute point of support. (Ibid., pp. 26–28)

Once the sacred breaks into the profane realm and sacred space is constituted, an irrevocable change has occurred. The sacredness of the place will continue, even through major changes in the dominant religious tradition of the area. The hierophany continues to repeat itself in that place.

> In this way the place becomes an inexhaustible source of power and sacredness and enables man, simply by entering it, to have a share in the power, to hold communion with the sacredness. This elementary notion of the place's becoming, by means of a hierophany, a permanent "center" of the sacred, governs and explains a whole collection of systems often complex and detailed. But however diverse and variously elaborated these sacred spaces may be, they all present one trait in common: there is always a clearly marked space which makes it possible (though under very varied forms) to communicate with the sacred. (Eliade 1958a, pp. 367–369)

Although sacred space cannot be generated by a simple act of will on the part of human beings, they do have important responsibilities in the consecration of the space and in the stewardship of its boundaries. Whether the space was directly generated by a hierophantic event or the result of the application of traditional techniques for provoking a sign, the creation of an enclosure, a clear boundary between the two realms, was always important. "The enclosure, wall, or circle of stones surrounding a sacred place—these are among the most ancient of known forms of man-made sanctuary. They existed as early as the early Indus civilization" (ibid., pp. 369–371).

The importance of the establishment and maintenance of the

boundaries of a sacred space can hardly be overemphasized. Not only does the boundary serve notice that entry into a radically different mode of human existence is near, but the recognition of and proper respect for the boundary is the *sine qua non* for a proper relationship to sacred space and the primary condition for being benefited and not harmed by contact with it.

> The enclosure does not only imply and indeed signify the continued presence of a kratophany or hierophany within its bounds; it also serves the purpose of preserving profane man from the danger to which he would expose himself by entering it without due care. The sacred is always dangerous to anyone who comes into contact with it unprepared, without having gone through the "gestures of approach" that every religious act demands. . . . Hence the innumerable rites and prescriptions (bare feet, and so on) relative to entering the temple, of which we have plentiful evidence among the Semites and other Mediterranean peoples. The ritual importance of the thresholds of temple and house is due to this same separating function of limits, though it may have taken on varying interpretations and values over the course of time. (Ibid.)

The recognition of and respect for the boundary, then, is the most fundamental affirmation in praxis of the reality and importance of the heterogeneity of space in human life. This relationship between boundary and space is one of the key elements in understanding the relationship between space and transformation in both religion and psychotherapy, and we will return to this repeatedly as we examine different theorists. At this point, it will suffice to note that for Eliade, archaic *homo religiosus* understood clearly that sacred space was the indispensable locus of all the paradigmatic transformations fundamental to human existence. Without it, there would be no access to the powers of creativity and renewal, no access to the primordial patterns that are the source of all correct order, no access to a transhistorical center which can give orientation and structure in a time of deterioration and impending chaos.

For Eliade, not only is sacred space linked to the myriad transformations of archaic experience of cosmos and culture, more specifically it is closely linked to phases of transition in that experience. Certainly, while one can argue that all religious transformation involves transition of a sort, the relationship between space, transformation and transition stands out most clearly when one examines Eliade's treatment of rituals of initiation.

> Broadly speaking, the initiation ceremony comprises the following phases: first, the preparation of the "sacred ground," where the men will remain in isolation during the festival; second, the separation of the novices from their mothers and, in general, from all women; third, their segregation

in the bush, or in a special isolated camp, where they will be instructed in the religious traditions of the tribe; fourth, certain operations performed on the novices, usually circumcision, the extraction of a tooth, or subincision, but sometimes scarring or pulling out the hair. Throughout the period of the initiation, the novices must behave in a special way; they undergo a number of ordeals, and are subjected to various dietary taboos and prohibitions. Each element of this complex initiatory scenario has a religious meaning. (Eliade 1958b, pp. 4–5)

As in other rituals for renewing the cosmos, initiation rituals include a reenactment of the cosmogony. Here, the individual's return to origins offers the initiand himself an opportunity for regeneration. In the symbolism of initiation, the sacred space that is the locus of initiation is often identified with the place of the individual's origin, the womb.

First and foremost, there is the well-known symbolism of initiation rituals implying a *regressus ad uterum*. . . . We will limit ourselves here to some brief indications. From the archaic stages of culture the initiation of adolescents includes a series of rites whose symbolism is crystal clear: through them, the novice is first transformed into an embryo and then is reborn. Initiation is equivalent to a second birth. It is through the agency of initiation that the adolescent becomes both a socially responsible and culturally awakened being. The return to the womb is signified either by the neophyte's seclusion in a hut, or by his being symbolically swallowed by a monster, or by his entering a sacred spot identified with the uterus of Mother Earth. (Eliade 1963, pp. 79–82)

In rituals of initiation, then, the relationship between space and transformation stands out in bold relief. Because of the heterogeneity of space, the initiand has an opportunity to undergo a return to origins, a *regressus ad uterum*, to touch once again the creative powers and to be reborn into a new mode of existence. "The basic idea is that, to attain to a higher mode of existence, gestation and birth must be repeated; but they are repeated ritually, symbolically" (ibid.). The context of this symbolic action is always sacred space, and according to Eliade one of the primary tasks of archaic technicians of the sacred was to be able to locate and utilize effectively the properties of this extraordinary transformative milieu. For archaic society the importance of this ability to help initiands enter and leave this transformative space effectively can hardly be exagerated.

From a certain point of view it could almost be said that, for the primitive world, it is through initiation that men attain the status of human beings; before initiation, they do not yet fully share in the human condition precisely because they do not yet have access to the religious life. This is why initiation represents a decisive experience for any individual who is a member of a premodern society; it is a fundamental existential experience because through

> it a man becomes able to assume his mode of being in its entirety. (Eliade 1958b, p. 3)

On the basis of the above discussion, it is easy to see why Eliade views human existence under the conditions of modern industrial culture to be so radically impoverished. In his view, the fall into modernity brought an end to the availability of transformative access to sacred space. Space in modernity is homogeneous and therefore relative.

> No *true* orientation is now possible, for the fixed point no longer enjoys a unique ontological status; it appears and disappears in accordance with the needs of the day. Properly speaking, there is no longer any world, there are only fragments of a shattered universe, an amorphous mass consisting of an infinite number of more or less neutral places in which man moves, governed and driven by the obligations of an existence incorporated into an industrial society. (Eliade 1961, pp. 23–24)

For Eliade, the only traces left in modern life of the truly religious experience of nonhomogeneous space consist of mere vestiges that cannot offer a milieu for fundamental transformation.

> Yet this experience of profane space still includes values that to some extent recall the nonhomogeneity peculiar to the religious experience of space. There are, for example, privileged spaces, qualitatively different from all others—a man's birthplace, or the scenes of his first love, or certain places in the first foreign city he visited in youth. Even for the most frankly nonreligious man, all these place still retain an exceptional, a unique quality; they are the "holy places" of his private universe, as if it were in such spots that he received the revelation of a reality *other* than that in which he participates through his ordinary daily life. (Ibid., p. 24)

Still, it is clear that for Eliade, the experience of space in modern industrial society is fundamentally characterized by homogeneity. Certainly, he is correct in his assumption that human transformative experience requires heterogeneity in the experience of space. But his assumption that such heterogeneity is *never* available in modernity has undoubtedly been a key factor in limiting the impact of his thought on attempts to understand contemporary cultural and personality processes. It is here that the work of Victor Turner has made its greatest contribution to our understanding of the human experience of space. Turner has shown that even under the conditions of modern industrial culture, the human experience of space is anything but homogeneous. Let us now turn to an examination of the impact of Turner's work on our understanding of the relationship between space and transformative process.

*Turner on Space and Transformation*

Like Eliade, Turner has devoted much of his research to the task of understanding the nature and significance of the heterogeneous forms of space which may be discerned in human experience. Indeed, while reflections on the relationship between space and transformation constitute an important component in Eliade's approach to human religious process in archaic culture, in Turner's work the issue is more central and receives a more sustained focus. Deeply influenced by his intellectual progenitor, Arnold van Gennep, Turner has based many of his insights on van Gennep's pioneering monograph, *The Rites of Passage* (1960). Van Gennep, of course, was a pioneer in describing the ways in which time and space are altered during a psychosocial transition. His distinguishing of the three phases in a rite of passage—separation, transition, and incorporation—was fundamental for the development of Turner's understanding of ritual process. *Separation* was the phase in a ritual that served to draw a clear distinction between sacred space and time and profane or ordinary space and time. During this part of the ritual, a cultural realm is created that is clearly out of ordinary space and time and is to be the locus of the activities of the intervening phase of *transition*. This phase was called "margin" or "limen" ("threshold" in Latin) by van Gennep. During this middle phase, the ritual subjects pass through a period of ambiguity in which they are stripped of the statuses and attributes characteristic of their previous state, undergo ordeals, and receive instruction from ritual elders. The final phase van Gennep called reaggregation or *incorporation*. Here ritual actions returned the subjects to ordinary space and time prepared for the new demands of a different cultural location.

Turner's great contribution to our understanding of the relationship between space and transformation has been his extensive elaboration of the significance of the cultural realm of the middle transitional phase of liminality. For Turner, it is the presence of liminality that clearly distinguishes ritual from ceremony. "Ceremony *indicates*, ritual *transforms*, and transformation occurs most radically in the ritual 'pupation' of liminal seclusion—at least in life-crisis rituals" (Turner 1982, pp. 80–81). Turner goes on to characterize the cultural significance of this special space.

> Ritual's liminal phase, then, approximates to the "subjunctive mood" of sociocultural action. It is, quintessentially, a time and place lodged between all times and spaces defined and governed in any specific biocultural ecosystem (A. Vayda, J. Bennet, and the like), by the rules of law, politics, and

> religion, and by economic necessity. Here the cognitive schemata that give sense and order to everyday life no longer apply, but are, as it were, suspended—in ritual symbolism perhaps even shown as destroyed or dissolved. Gods and goddesses of destruction are adored primarily because they personify an essential phase in an irreversible transformative process. All further growth requires the immolation of that which was fundamental to an earlier stage—"lest one good custom should corrupt the world." (Ibid., p. 84)

Turner emphasizes that while this "liminal space–time 'pod' " can sometimes be dangerous to the *liminar* or ritual subject, it is important that we see that much more than destruction of the previous life-world is taking place in liminality.

> Nevertheless, the danger of the liminal phase conceded, and respected by hedging it around by ritual interdictions and taboos, it is also held in most culture to be regenerative, as I mentioned earlier. For in liminality what is mundanely bound in sociostructural form may be unbound and rebound. . . . New meanings and symbols may be introduced—or new ways of portraying or embellishing old models for living, and so of renewing interest in them. Ritual liminality, therefore, contains the potentiality for cultural innovation, as well as the means of effecting structural transformations within a relatively stable sociocultural system. (Ibid., pp. 84–85)

While many parallels can be drawn between Turner's views and those of van Gennep and Eliade, it is not difficult to discern the extent to which he has surpassed them in the subtlety of his understanding of the relationship between the heterogeneity of space and psychocultural processes. By focusing his attention in both field work and theoretical reflection on the differences between ordinary and transformative social space, he has been able to offer us a far more adequate "mapping" of the geography of the existential space of human lived experience. Turner is quite conscious of the extent to which he has accepted the enormous task of helping us formulate a geography of human space—and not just that, as in van Gennep and Eliade, of premodern cultures.

> I am frankly in this exploratory phase just now. I hope to make more precise these crude, almost medieval maps I have been unrolling of the obscure liminal and liminoid regions which lie around our comfortable village of the sociologically known, proven, tried and tested. Both "liminal" and "liminoid" mean studying symbols in social action, in praxis, not entirely at a safe remove from the full human condition. It means studying all domains of expressive culture, not the high culture alone nor the popular culture alone, the literate or the nonliterate, the Great or the Little Tradition, the urban or the rural. Comparative symbology must learn how to "embrace multitudes" and generate sound intellectual progeny from that embrace. It must study *total* social phenomena. (Ibid., p. 55)

Turner's distinction between liminal and liminoid phenomena has itself grown out of his willingness to examine complex modern societies as well as tribal and early agrarian ones. For Turner, liminal phenomena are more characteristic of transitions in tribal societies. They tend to be collective and to be related to biological, calendrical, and other sociostructural rhythms as well as to social crises resulting either from internal adjustments or external adaptations. They characteristically appear at the natural breaks and disjunctions in the ongoing flow of natural and social processes. Usually integrated into the total social process of the culture in question, liminal phenomena are usually organized around symbols that have a common intellectual and emotional meaning for all of the members of the group. The symbols and behaviors reflect the history of the group over time and, in order to represent the negativity and subjunctivity of the group, often are in the form of reversals, negations, disguises, inversions, and so on. For example, under the conditions of *structure* in a preliminal or postliminal status system, social space permits distinctions of rank, clothing, sex, and degrees of autonomy. In liminal space, on the contrary, such distinctions are minimized. Turner has shown that where liminality is fully developed and unfragmented, the properties of liminality form a relatively consistent set of binary oppositions to the properties of life in structure, of course expressed in the dominant symbolic forms of the group (Turner 1969, p. 106).

Liminoid phenomena, more characteristic of complex modern societies, are usually individual products, although they may have a widespread effect on the society. Not cyclical in nature, they develop independently of the central political and economic processes of the culture. Marginal to the dominant cultural institutions, they are more fragmentary, plural, and experimental in character than liminal states. Associated with leisure time and therefore with play, liminoid phenomena are more idiosyncratic and are usually generated by individuals or groups who are competing for recognition. Liminoid phenomena, Turner suggests, can be seen as representing the "dismembering of the liminal" for in them "various components that are joined in liminal situations split off to pursue separate destinies as specialized genres—for example, theater, ballet, film, the novel, poetry, music, art, both popular and classical in every case, and pilgrimage" (Turner and Turner 1978, p. 253).

In seeking to develop a more nuanced approach to the differences in expressive culture between societies before and after the Industrial Revolution, Turner has emphasized the importance of this distinction between liminal and liminoid. He has gone so far as to suggest that the use of the term "liminality" properly belongs only in interpretations of tribal systems. "When used of processes, phenomena, and persons in large-scale complex societies, its use must in the main be metaphorical" (Turner 1979, p. 23). But elsewhere, he moves away from this stark contrast and affirms that in "modern societies both types coexist in a sort of cultural pluralism. But the liminal—found in the activities of churches, sects, and movements, in the initiation rites of clubs, fraternities, masonic orders and other secret societies, etc.—is no longer society-wide" (ibid., p. 54).

Here we confront the major limitation of Turner's theory in relation to issues of space and transformation. By limiting, or appearing to limit, the application of the category of liminality to tribal systems, Turner has led us away from the question of whether or not there may be forms of liminality manifest in modern culture that—although different from those in tribal culture—are far more liminal than liminoid. That Turner vacillates a bit on this issue is a testament to his characteristic openness and willingness to view his system as an open one. Still, the stark way in which the liminal/liminoid distinction has come to be viewed as paralleling premodern/modern or tribal/industrial in contemporary appropriations of his work is an unfortunate reification of an important theoretical contribution.

Certainly, both liminal and liminoid space have clearly distinguishing characteristics. His mapping of these differences is a major part of his contribution to our understanding of the heterogeneity of space in human social life. Turner has not, however, given enough attention to the importance of the relationship between boundary and space in his reflections. Rather than basing distinctions between liminal and liminoid on the totality and comprehensiveness of ritual involvement in the social system, I suggest that this judgment should be made on the basis of how the boundaries that delimit the space are constituted and maintained or "stewarded." The issue should not be drawn as whether the practice is "society-wide" or not; it should be focused on the nature and permeability of the boundaries of the space involved and on the relative importance of the leadership of ritual elders or "technicians of the sacred" in making judgments as to the appropriate utilization of the space.

Ritual leadership, then, is the key variable that Turner has not highlighted in his distinctions between liminal and liminoid space. The central point may be phrased simply as follows: while liminal space *requires* ritual leadership, liminoid space does not. A ritual leader *may* be present in liminoid space, but *must* be present for liminal space to exist. Liminality can occur at or near the center in tribal society not just because the social processes are relatively "simple," integrated, or totalistic—but because of the availability of knowledgeable ritual elders who understand how transformative space is located, consecrated, and stewarded. In modern culture knowledgeable ritual leadership is so lacking that a quest for transformative space together with a lack of ritually created boundaries usually leads to the boundaries provided by the socially marginal or by actual movement through natural or sacred geography. Liminoid space is, then, not so much constituted by boundaries as it is *on the boundary*. This is, of course, one reason for the association of leisure with seashore and mountains, and for the popularity of deserts as a location for liminoid phenomena. In the case of sacred geography, the space of pilgrimage shrines is usually liminoid precisely because the structure of pilgrimage does not require the existence of ritual leadership.

The point can be made in another way: one can participate in liminoid space without there being present in any social actor conscious intentionality as to the psychocultural purposes of the activities involved. Liminal space cannot properly be said to exist without the existence of such conscious intentionality on the part of its stewards. The unstewarded boundaries of liminoid space are permeable and hence cannot sustain or "hold" the intensity of transformative process characteristic of liminal states. It is a commonplace among ritual specialists that transformative processes in liminal states go awry when the leaders do not prevent such permeability of boundaries from developing. Turner's interest in the promise of some forms of theater as a postmodern recovery of cultural transformative modes should be seen in this context: knowledgeable directors can function as ritual elders and dramatic forms may be able to create a "liminal space–time 'pod' " where human beings may experience transformation (Turner 1982, pp. 86, 120).

It is indeed the presence of observable liminal "pods" in contemporary culture that necessitate the above amendments to Turner's understanding of transformative space. I have for some time been analyzing the special forms of space that appear in contemporary psychotherapy in light of Turner's theories. I have become convinced that much of the phenomena observable in a wide range of therapies cannot be adequately designated as liminoid, but rather should be viewed as a contemporary expression of liminal space. Let us turn now to some evidence of this sort of space from contemporary psychotherapeutic theory and practice.

## Space and Transformation in Contemporary Psychotherapy

Reflection on ritual processes and psychotherapy to date has been dominated by the tendency to view preindustrial tribal healing rituals as "primitive psychotherapy" (Frank 1963). Since ritual process is characteristically not valued by the culture of modernity, little effort has been made to understand the ritual processes involved in contemporary psychotherapeutic practice. The time has come for us to recognize that contemporary psychotherapy provides a narrow spectrum of our population with important ritual leadership in times of crisis. In a recent survey of ritual dimensions in psychotherapy, I sought to draw attention to some of the ways in which these therapies offer individuals an opportunity to engage in what Turner has called transformative performances (Moore 1983).

In the course of my research and reflection on this topic, I realized that most genres of contemporary therapy manifest within their process ritualized submission, containment, and enactment (ibid., pp. 292–293). In order to facilitate a needed deconstruction of the old personality structure of the individual, the individual is offered an opportunity to surrender autonomy temporarily, to submit to a total process which has an autonomy of its own and which can enable the individual to maintain needed orientation and structure during this time of deconstruction. Built into the therapeutic process is the creation of a relatively safe psychosocial space in which this deconstruction and surrender of autonomy can occur. It is in this ritually constructed space that the enactment, both playful and painful, of innovative new behaviors and styles of thinking can be tested experimentally before returning to the world of structure and its merciless demands for adaptive effectiveness.[3] While many other ritual dimensions in therapy exist and merit careful research, it is this creation of the therapeutic container or "vessel" that is most salient to our discussion of space and transformation.[4]

We should be clear here that few clinicians would see their construction and stewardship in the therapeutic space as a ritual process in Turner's terms. Ritual process has characteristically received such a negative evaluation in modernity that when a psychotherapist is told that he is providing ritual leadership, the remark is often taken as an insult! A similar lack of awareness exists among many therapists with regard to the actual nature and dynamics of the special space that is constituted in the interpersonal field of the therapeutic milieu. This is not to say that the therapist lacks a "conscious intentionality" directed toward the creation of a therapeutic space and the maintenance of its boundaries. Yet often these concerns are understood in the language of professionalism, including the emphasis on the professional contract between therapist and client and other concerns of professional ethics which are viewed as a means of protecting the client from unprofessional behavior on the part of the therapist.[5] There is usually also an awareness of the need to put limits on the kinds of expectations the client may have of the therapist. The therapeutic contract is usually the means of spelling out these limits and expectations in an attempt to avoid inappropriate behaviors on the part of either therapist or client.

Only recently, however, has there been focused and sustained attention to the nature of the therapeutic environment as a special space created by the therapeutic contract and other agreements and behaviors of both therapist and client. Current attention to issues relating to space and transformation in depth psychology suggests that a revolution may be beginning in our awareness of the importance of the heterogeneity of space in the therapeutic environment. Nowhere is this increase in interest in the nature and dynamics of space more pronounced than in contemporary Freudian and Jungian psychoanalytic theory and practice. Psychoanalyst Simon Grolnick recently characterized this new emphasis in psychoanalysis:

> At this writing, psychoanalysts are beginning to realize that given the contemporary patient, the psychoanalytic situation evokes far more than an interpretation of unconscious conflict. It is more than simply a place to deal with the analyst's or therapist's role as an oedipal-level transference figure. We are finding that the dramatic, illusionary nature of analytic interplay and the manifestations of the transference must take place within a facilitating environment, a facilitating analytic *setting*, to provide a fertile ambience for the ultimate building, or rebuilding, of the self, and its capacity to create a richness of symbolic meaning. The more traditional function of psychoanalytic treatment, the interpretation of hidden or repressed meanings from the unconscious and the past, can proceed concurrently and dialectically. Without *both* processes, there is danger of substituting dead, affectless and nonsynthesizing symbols (intellectualized new understandings or reconstructions) for the often incapacitating "sick" or "neurotic" symbols (symptoms) developed by the patient. (Grolnick and Barkin 1978, p. 538)

The healing process of innovative and creative symbolization in psychoanalytic process, then, has begun to be viewed as being dependent upon the presence of a very special therapeutic space *which may or may not be manifest at any given time in the process of analysis or therapy*.[6] Many contemporary analysts are addressing these issues in their clinical work and research. Two of the most influential currently are Freudian analyst Robert Langs and Jungian analyst William Goodheart.[7] Let us turn now to an examination of the deepened insight into the heterogeneity of space in analysis shared by these theorists.

First, both Langs and Goodheart emphasize that the securing of a stable *frame* or boundary for the therapeutic space is more than just an expression of professional ethics. For them, it is the *sine qua non* which must be present for the facilitation of any truly transformative therapeutic space. It is the establishment and maintenance of the frame which makes possible the evocation of the kind of interpersonal field that can allow the unconscious materials to manifest without unnecessarily terrorizing the analysand. This containment, in short, does not guarantee that a transformative field will be constituted—but its absence will either inhibit the emergence of materials from the deeper levels of the unconscious or make such an emergence more dangerous for both analyst and analysand.[8]

Second, both emphasize that several types of space may be discerned through close observation of the therapeutic interaction.[9] If the analyst does not pay close attention to the maintenance and stewardship of the boundary or frame, the space—while it could certainly not be called ordinary—does not become a truly transformative field. If the frame is broken and the boundary becomes too permeable, then analyst and analysand unconsciously collude in avoiding the truths about themselves which might become manifest if the boundaries were maintained.[10] In effect, the intensity and depth of the process are truncated. From a Turnerian perspective, this would suggest that inadequate stewardship of the frame constitutes an interpersonal field that is liminoid in nature. We have noted above that the mere presence of a ritual leader does not in itself guarantee the constitution of liminal space. Here we see that those interpreters of psychotherapy who consider it to be liminoid in nature are at least partially correct.[11] *Psychotherapy in our culture is always at least liminoid*. However, by adhering to Turner's criteria for understanding the nature of liminality and by neglecting, with Turner, the critical importance of the relationship between boundary and space, these interpreters do not grasp the fact that liminal space can be—and often is—manifest in the therapeutic environment.[12]

We should be clear here that neither in tribal culture nor in contemporary psychoanalysis is the ritual leader the *master* or *controller* of transformative space. Such space, ritual leaders have always understood, cannot be commanded—it can only be invoked. It is a mistake, for example, to conclude that the rigorous attention to detail characteristic of ritual elders reflects a sense of mastery of sacred space. On the contrary, such care is an indication of the ritual leader's awareness of the fragility of regenerative space and the ease with which it can be spoiled. The leader can facilitate the right conditions by avoiding the kinds of behavior that clearly destroy the possibility of its appearance. Even the most knowledgeable tribal elder or analyst, nevertheless, cannot generate it or sustain it *on demand*. Here again, in Langs and Goodheart we see the critical emphasis on the creation and stewardship of the boundary without which there is no possibility of a secured, truly transformative space.

We noted above that individuals, when sensing the need for a liminal space, will seek out boundary and containment wherever they can. If knowledgeable ritual elders are not present to invoke liminal space and lead them through it, then they gravitate to the liminoid and try to find containment or generate it on their own. The attraction of geographical boundaries such as seashores to those in transition states is a striking example of this intuitive quest for the boundary. Finding a natural boundary is, of course, relatively simple. Locating an appropriate transformative container, however, is much more difficult.

Both Langs and Goodheart note that analysands always are aware at an unconscious level of failures of the analyst in stewarding the boundary of the therapeutic space. Close observation of the analysand's materials, they believe, reveals that the analysand is constantly commenting on whether the boundary is being maintained in an appropriate manner (Goodheart 1980, p. 28–32). The unconscious psyche, we might say, is aware of the radical difference between the liminoid and the liminal. Albeit in an unconscious manner, the individual notes that the therapeutic space is merely liminoid and gives the analyst clues about how the process is failing and what is needed to repair the boundaries and thereby to invoke the liminal space that is needed for transformation.

This turn to a new sensitivity to the heterogeneity of space in psychoanalysis has had the unexpected effect of making Jung's own understanding of the analytical relationship seem much less esoteric and incomprehensible. Jung, of course, viewed the alchemical vessel or *vas* as a parallel to the appropriate therapeutic relationship. In his words, the

> *vas bene clausum* (well-sealed vessel) is a precautionary rule in alchemy very frequently mentioned, and is the equivalent of the magic circle. In both cases the idea is to protect what is within from the intrusion and admixture of what is without, as well as to prevent it from escaping. (Jung 1944, par. 219)

In a manner anticipating this recent turn in psychoanalytic theory, Jung emphasized that the transference was more than just the compulsive repetition of old object relationships in the present—for him it was a transformative container.[13] Only recently, with the new attention to the heterogeneity of space in analysis, has the importance of Jung's references to the significance of the study of alchemy in understanding transference begun to be positively reassessed.[14]

## Conclusions and Implications for Analytic Practice

First, the word *liminality* has been used far too loosely in discourse by both analysts and specialists in ritual studies. We must examine much more closely the necessary and constituent elements in the formation of the extraordinary psychosocial space that we designate by this term. Turner's own usage should not be taken as normative in this task because of the limitations of his understanding noted above.

Second, we must attempt to draw more careful distinctions in analytic practice between those phenomena which are *liminal* and those which are merely *liminoid*. Fragmentation phenomena and related derivatives do not constitute the necessary and sufficient evidence to call a psychological state a liminal one. In other words, the appearance of deconstructive processes and related symptoms in ideation and behavior do not automatically mean that a liminal state has been entered (e.g., the onset of a mid-life crisis) or that an initiatory transformation has begun. Symptoms are clearly invitations to ritualization—but in the absence of containment marked by carefully stewarded boundaries, liminality with its deep structural transformations will not be present. *Liminality, in short, is always within a context of containment in which the boundaries are not tended by the ego of the individual involved.*

Third, in light of the above, so-called "acting out" and related symptomatology should be designated liminoid in nature. This would, of course, support the views of those who believe that acting out on the part of an analysand is often a symbolic commentary on inadequate stewardship of the boundaries by the ritual elder/analyst.

Fourth, the time has come for an extensive, careful, and systematic study of the ritual context of the phenomena of psychopathology. Our long-held intuitions that symptoms are symbolic communications which contain messages necessary for deep healing are clearly accurate. Cross-cultural and interdisciplinary studies of healing ritual are entering a new era today. These studies clearly constitute for us an important resource for deepening our understanding of the ritual context of psychopathology.

Fifth, transference and countertransference phenomena must, of course, be brought under the same conceptual perspective. As noted above, Langs's and Goodheart's positions on the nature and dynamics of "frame" management in analytic practice can be both affirmed in part and systematically criticized from a ritual perspective. Archetypal dimensions in these phenomena stand out when examined as ritual process. In this context we must give far more attention to the nature and significance of the archetype of the Magus in analytic practice—especially its role in archetypal transference and the problems it causes in managing an archetypal countertransference.

Finally, we should spend more time in reflection on what may constitute some guidelines for interpreting images of sacred space when they appear in dreams both in and out of an analytic context. For example, if such dreams are seen as commentaries on conditions within the analytic vessel, what guidelines do we use in interpreting their meaning?

## Epilogue: Toward a Geography of Inner Space

I began this essay with a note on the importance of continuing in Jung's tradition with regard to using materials from anthropology and the history of religions for research into the deep structures of the human psyche. Nowhere is this dictum more relevant than in psychoanalytic inquiry into the nature and dynamics of the human experience of space. Through recent research into the archetypal configurations of the King, Warrior, Magus, and Lover as they are manifest in masculine psychology, I have come to believe that these patterns in comparative mythology represent distinct yet interrelated "spaces" in masculine experience. I am convinced that further research will document that the experience of and attention to transformative and healing space is located in a sector of the human personality, both male and female, which operates in an inner space dominated by the potentials and constraints of the archetype of the Magician. The next agenda in the psychoanalysis of space will be to map the different phenomenological and psychological "worlds" that open out under the auspices of each of these archetypal configurations and to describe what happens when these worlds collide.[15] In the language of this essay, inner worlds may be said to collide when there is no knowledgeable ritual elder to show one where to find the passages between worlds when such transits are needed and appropriate. It may be that current Jungian interest in shamanism is an anticipation of research into inner geography only just beginning.

## Notes

1. Excerpts of Robert L. Moore's *The Magician and the Analyst: Ritual, Sacred Space, and Psychotherapy* (forthcoming from CSSR, 1991) are published by permission from the Center for the Scientific Study of Religion.

2. Few concepts in Eliade's work are as important as that of the heterogeneity of space in relation to human ritual and religious experience. It is therefore strange that so little attention has been given to elaborating the many implications of this characteristic of the human experience of space.

3. I am using the word *structure* in Turner's technical sense. See the definition of the term in *Image and Pilgrimage*, p. 252.

4. For an interesting recent discussion of ritual elements in psychotherapy, see Onno van der Hart, *Rituals in Psychotherapy: Transition and Continuity* (New York: Irvington Publishers, 1983).

5. See the discussion of the rise of professionalism in Burton J. Bledstein, *The Culture of Professionalism* (New York: W. W. Norton, 1976). Professionalism in modern industrial culture carries many unacknowledged ritual functions in secular forms.

6. There is an increasing realization in psychoanalysis that technical virtuosity on the part of the analyst does not in itself assure that healing will result in the analysand. A healing interpersonal field can be facilitated by certain behaviors of the analyst. It cannot, however, be guaranteed—even by the most competent analysts.

7. The influence of D. W. Winnicott has been a key factor in this new attention to therapeutic space. See Madeleine Davis and David Wallbridge, *Boundary and Space: An Introduction to the Work of D. W. Winnicott* (New York: Brunner/Mazel, 1981); William B. Goodheart, "Theory of Analytical Interaction," *San Francisco Jung Institute Library Journal* 1/4 (1980), 2–39; and Robert Langs, *The Bipersonal Field* (New York: Jason Aronson, 1976), and *Technique in Transition* (New York: Jason Aronson, 1978).

8. See Alexander McCurdy III, "Establishing and Maintaining the Analytical Structure," in Murray Stein, ed., *Jungian Analysis* (LaSalle, Ill.: Open Court, 1982), 47–67.

9. See Goodheart's "Theory of Analytical Interaction" for a careful discussion of the heterogeneity of space in the analytical setting.

10. Langs has referred to such unconscious collusion of analyst and analysand as "lie therapy."

11. See Volney P. Gay, "Ritual and Self-Esteem in Victor Turner and Heinz Kohut," *Zygon* 18 (September 1983), 271–282.

12. It should be clear here that I am not suggesting that psychotherapy is the *only* locus of liminal experience in modern industrial culture. See, for example, J. Gordon Melton and Robert L. Moore, *The Cult Experience: Responding to the New Religious Pluralism* (New York: The Pilgrim Press, 1982), 47–64.

13. See the discussion of the transference in C. G. Jung, *The Practice of Psychotherapy, Collected Works*, vol. 16 (Princeton, N.J.: Princeton University Press, 1954).

14. Jung's views of the transference as resembling an alchemical process in a sealed vessel have often been dismissed as vague, mystical, and without any practical significance. There is now an increasing realization that Jung's emphasis on the transference as a transformative space was in fact one of his most creative contributions.

15. I have elaborated some of my work on this topic in a paper presented to the International Congress in Paris, entitled, "The Magician and the Analyst." A series of five

books (co-authored with mythologist Douglas Gillette) based on my research into the archetypes of King, Warrior, Magician, and Lover will soon be forthcoming. The introductory volume will be published by Harper and Row and the quartet on the four archetypes by William Morrow Press.

## References


Bledstein, Burton J. 1976. *The Culture of Professionalism*. New York: W. W. Norton.

Davis, M., and Wallbridge, D. 1981. *Boundary and Space: An Introduction to the Work of D. W. Winnicott*. New York: Brunner/Mazel.

Eliade, M. 1958a. *Patterns in Comparative Religions*. New York: Sheed and Ward.

______. 1958b. *Rites and Symbols of Initiation: The Mysteries of Birth and Rebirth*. New York: Harper and Row.

______. 1961. *The Sacred and the Profane: The Nature of Religion*. New York: Harper and Row.

______. 1963. *Myth and Reality*. New York: Harper and Row.

Frank, J. D. 1963. *Persuasion and Healing: A Comparative Study of Psychotherapy*. New York: Schocken Books.

Gay, Volney P. 1983. Ritual and self-esteem in Victor Turner and Heinz Kohut. *Zygon* 18:271–282.

Goodheart, W. B. 1980. Theory of analytical interaction. *San Francisco Jung Institute Library Journal* 1/4:2–39.

Grolnick. S. A., and Barkin, L., eds. 1978. *Between Reality and Fantasy: Transitional Objects and Phenomena*. New York: Jason Aronson.

Jung, C. G. 1944. *Psychology and Alchemy. Collected Works*, vol. 12. Princeton, N.J.: Princeton University Press, 1968.

______. 1946. The psychology of the transference. *CW*, vol. 16. Princeton, N.J.: Princeton University Press, 1954.

Langs, R. 1976. *The Bipersonal Field*. New York: Jason Aronson.

______. 1978. *Technique in Transition*. New York: Jason Aronson.

McCurdy, A. 1982. Establishing and maintaining the analytical structure. In *Jungian Analysis*, M. Stein, ed. LaSalle, Ill.: Open Court, pp. 47–67.

Melton, J. G., and Moore, R. L. 1982. *The Cult Experience: Responding to the New Religious Pluralism*. New York: The Pilgrim Press.

Moore, R. L. 1983. Contemporary psychotherapy as ritual process: an initial reconnaissance. *Zygon* 18:283–294.

Moore, R. L., Burhoe, R. W., and Hefner, P. J. eds. 1983. Ritual in human adaptation. *Zygon* 18:209–325.

Turner, V. 1969. *The Ritual Process: Structure and Anti-Structure*. Chicago: Aldine.

______. 1979. *Process, Performance and Pilgrimage: A Study in Comparative Symbology*. New Delhi: Concept Publishing Co.

______. 1982. *From Ritual to Theatre*. New York: Performing Arts Journal Publications.

Turner, V., and Turner, E. 1978. *Image and Pilgrimage in Christian Culture*. New York: Columbia University Press.

van der Hart, O. 1983. *Rituals in Psychotherapy: Transition and Continuity*. New York: Irvington Publishers.

van Gennep, A. 1960. *The Rites of Passage*. Chicago: University of Chiago Press.

# The Watcher at the Gates of Dawn: The Transformation of Self in Liminality and by the Transcendent Function

James A. Hall

When the Inter-Regional Society hosted, for the first time, the national meeting of what was to become CRSJAA—the Council of Representatives of Jungian Societies in America—the central activity was a visit to the Green Corn Dance at the San Ildefonso Indian Pueblo just outside of Santa Fe.

At the dance, I sat on the edge of the central plaza watching the dancing Indians, who were grouped in families and dressed in their traditional ceremonial costumes. Their dance progressed in slow, rhythmic concentric circles, making a large mandala form that filled the central square of the pueblo. I noticed the rhythm of their bouncing turquoise earrings, the slower waving of feathers, and the dull background rhythm of drums and feet.

But the most memorable personages were *outside* the rhythm of the dance and moved either with or against the unidirectional circling

---

**James A. Hall**, M.D., is clinical associate professor of psychiatry, Southwestern Medical School, Dallas, and a founding member of the Inter-Regional Society of Jungian Analysts.

of the dancers. In fact, these unusual dancers might move in any direction at all!

These were the "clowns," smeared with what seemed to be white chalk or mud. While other dancers wore jewelry and feathers and were very finely costumed, the clowns dressed primitively in animal skins with deer-hoof rattles about their ankles. They moved independently of the collective rhythm of the family groups. It was the clowns, I noticed, who retrieved fallen earrings, a symbol of protecting (so it seems to me) the personal values of the dancers who never once broke the rhythmic collective dance.

Facilitating the dance of the dancers, the clowns themselves seemed outside the dance, remnants of an older, more basic order. The clowns were on the *margin* of the dance, moving in the *interstices* of the dancers, with none of the signs of social rank worn by the turquoised Indian women, devoid of the man-made ornamentation and badges of rank, lower than the dancers—or were they "higher"? In the language of anthropologist Victor Turner, the clowns were *liminal*—yet their liminality served to maintain the community of the dancers, their *communitas*. The clowns were "outsiders" who were more "in" than the dancers themselves.

There is an essential grace in these liminal figures, the clowns. They are officially outside the power and structure of society, yet essential to its order and continuity, to its humanness. But who (or what) can remind us of these liminal truths in the midst of the vanities and forgetfulness of everyday life? The answer to that question, the thesis of this paper, is the *transcendent function*, a mode of activity of the Archetypal Self.[1] I hope to show that what Turner's concept of social *liminality* does for status in a society, Jung's psychological concept of *transcendent function* does for the movement of the person through the life processes of individuation.

## Liminality

As a term of discourse, *liminality* began in 1909 as the middle of three stages of primitive initiation ceremonies defined by Arnold van Gennep in *Rites of Passage* (van Gennep 1960). The classical three stages are 1) *separation*, 2) *liminality* (or *transition*), and 3) *incorporation* (or *aggregation*). They describe the manner in which a person (often in early adolescence) is separated from one status in the society, placed in an intermediate state of liminality "betwixt and between," and finally returned, after initiation, for reincorporation into the social structure in a newly achieved role-status.

The state of the ritual "passenger" or *liminar* is ambiguous, neither here nor there, not described by the usual points of social classification, devoid of the status insignia of both the old state and the not-yet-acquired new state (Turner 1974, p. 232). The new status is usually ritually "higher" than the pre-liminal state, but may be lower in some cases (ibid.). Varying emphasis on the three stages may be seen in various social situations (Turner 1982, p. 2): funerary rites emphasize the separation stage, marriages emphasize incorporation, while the liminal transition stage is accented in pregnancy, betrothal, and initiation rites. Liminality is imaged as "a place that is not a place, and a time that is not a time" (Turner 1974, p. 239). Liminality is "cunicular"—like being in a tunnel between the entrance and the exit (ibid., p. 231). Liminality traditionally denotes the stage of initiation in which the identities of the initiates have been reduced to the most basic human level, with a concomitant sense of the communitas with one's fellow initiates in the liminal state. Institutionalized forms of the liminal state, persisting over time, also deemphasize the usual persona and ego roles, even in dress, as the saffron robe of the Buddhist priest or the stark black and white of traditional Christian religious orders.

Van Gennep's definition of liminality, according to Turner, removed a major stumbling block in the development of sociological and anthropological theory—the previous almost complete identification of the social with social *structure*, a sort of homo hierarchicus (Turner 1974, p. 269). When "society" is reduced to merely "social structure," the loss of structure would seem to cause *anomie* or *angst* (ibid., p. 250). But when liminality is considered, the social is seen to have both an unbound as well as a bound dimension. The breakdown of social structure, like the breakdown of physical systems described by Prigogine (1983), does not lead to pure chaos, but rather to "dissipative structures," smaller units that retain their own order and purpose. In psychological parallel, the breakdown of normal ego functioning does not head to random events, but to discrete "fields" of psychological complexes, such as (in Jungian terms) the shadow or anima/animus, that have a coherence and purposiveness of their own, although fragmented and partial when compared to a more fully integrated personality.

Turner and Turner enlarged van Gennep's concept thusly: liminality may be institutionalized as a state in itself, rather than a temporary stage of transition; it "cannot be confined to the processual form of the traditional rites of passage in which he [van Gennep] first discovered it" (1978, p. 2). Increasingly institutionalized and specialized societies and cultures often retain traces of the "passage" origins of liminality in such expressions as "the Christian is a stranger in the world, a pilgrim" (Turner 1969, p. 107). In fact, pilgrimage was early Christianity's own form of institutionalized liminality for the laity (Turner and Turner 1978, p. 4). The unbound social dimension, outside usual persona roles, is the "place" of liminality, but it is also a major source of what Turner called *communitas*.

### *Communitas*

Three types of communitas are cited by the Turners (1978, p. 252):

1. Spontaneous, existential communitas
2. Normative communitas
3. Ideological communitas

Spontaneous, existential communitas tends to be generated between individuals who for a time share the same liminal situation. Examples are: fraternity or sorority pledges, military recruits in basic training, persons who share hardship together, and (I would add) participants in extended process-oriented group psychotherapy. Normative communitas, however, can lead to persona forms which can be a basis for strong negative judgments against others if not outright shadow projections. I remember, for example, a situation in which an older woman said threateningly to a younger woman as they engaged in a heated discussion about religion:

> "God is *good*, honey, and YOU BETTER BELIEVE IT!"

Her *non*communitas meaning was quite clear.

The third form of communitas, ideological communitas, can lead to a utopian blueprint for the reform of society (Turner and Turner 1978, p. 252). But attempts to maximize either communitas or social structure to the exclusion of a balanced enantiodromia between them can lead to instability in society. Social structure maximized to the point of rigidity leads to the twin problems of either violent revolution or uncreative apathy while maximization of communitas produces totalitarianism in its drive to suppress individual independence and difference (Turner 1974, p. 268). Turner's words quickly bring to mind recent events in the U.S.S.R. and Eastern Europe.

In this second danger—communitas tending toward totalitarianism—one hears echos of Jung's recurrent concern about the danger of submersion of the individual in collective consciousness. Turner seems aware of the danger of misusing the leveling and cohesive aspect of communitas to impose totalitarian rule on a population, although the traditional intention is to induce in the neophytes through liminality a tabula rasa state prepared for the inscription of the traditional knowledge and wisdom of the group (1969, p. 103). Turner also notes the mistake of such thinkers as Marx, who confuse communitas, a quality of any society, with an archaic and "primitive" form of society (ibid., p. 130). There are also overtones of Polanyi's analysis of "dynamo-objective coupling," which he also called "moral inversion," the linking of a hidden moral purpose with an alleged scientific objectivity—Marxism being one of Polanyi's examples (Polanyi 1953, pp. 236–237).

The communitas produced in a liminal ritual or religious state permits cooperation for maintenance of cosmic order by persons who would be deeply divided in the nonreligious secular world. A "mystical character" is often associated with the sentiment of human kindness in liminality (Turner 1969, p. 105). I am told by a museum expert on Korean pottery that the aesthetic Japanese tea ceremony, so strongly the product of Zen, once served a practical necessity—it permitted the Emperor of Japan to speak with wealthy merchants who alone could supply ships needed for the invasion and annexation of Korea. Without the liminal aesthetic focus of the tea ceremony, rigid court protocol would not have permitted even an introduction of the merchants to the Son of Heaven who needed the loan of their ships.

Communitas is a state in which persons confront each other not as players of persona roles, but as "human totals," as "integral beings who recognizably share the same humanity" (Turner 1974, p. 269). It is an equal and human relationship between "concrete, historical, idiosyncratic individuals" (Turner 1969, p. 131). This approaches the millennial Christian imagery of the Kingdom of God and also suggests the vow of the bodhisattva in Mahayana Buddhist tradition. The essence of this vow is that the bodhisattva, who has attained the right to enter into nirvana, refrains from doing so until all sentient beings have been saved.

Turner believes that no society can adequately function without communitas as a counterpoint to structure (1969, p. 129). Communitas breaks into social structure through "the interstices of structure, in liminality . . . at the edges of structure, in marginality; and from beneath structure, in inferiority" (Turner and Turner 1978, p. 251). By separating the person from the persona role, liminality, at least in principle, offers the possibility of obtaining a total view of the value of human society (Turner 1974, p. 259).

A society tacitly asks its mature members for both conformity and initiative (Turner 1974, p. 256). Serious shifts in self-image involve liminality, but there may be "liminoid" states that are playful. An exclusive "club," for example, may produce a *liminal* rite of passage into a *liminoid* space. "One works at the liminal, one plays with the liminoid" (Turner 1982, p. 55).

## Lowermost, Outsiderhood, and Marginals

In enlarging van Gennep's concept of liminality, Turner's purpose is to locate the origins and functions of communitas as a counterpoint to fixed social structure. In this he seems to be moving toward an understanding of the function in society of paired archetypal opposites, such as structure and liminality. Through their mutual function in a conscious or unconscious enantiodromia, they contribute toward maintenance of a stable but oscillating society, one that moves from presently defined social structure, through contained liminal experiences, to renewed and renovated social structure.

Turner's view of liminality in stabilizing social structure is analogous to a goal of individuation in Jungian analysis—the stabilization of an ego-self "axis" that bears the fluctuations of the individuation process without major disruption of the personality. In mythological and archetypal images this pattern of integrated liminality and structure suggests the cyclic stability of the Egyptian kingship: the living Pharaoh (Horus) begets a son, who on the death of Pharaoh becomes Horus (Pharaoh) in his own turn, replacing his deceased father (who then becomes Osiris, pharaoh of the underworld). One of the most striking scenes in Egyptian mythology, found in the contendings of Horus and Set, illustrates the dual-value system, the state of liminality, and the alterations that occur in self-image after the liminal period. It should be viewed from the point of view of Isis as ego.

Isis is standing on the bank as her son Horus and her brother Set struggle in the water. Horus calls to her for help, but she is paralyzed by her dual commitments, unable to choose whether to honor the social system that emphasizes her duty to her brother Set (who also murdered her brother/husband Osiris, the father of Horus) or to honor the cry of Horus, her own son by Osiris. She does not intervene, being unable to resolve the dilemma. This so angers Horus that he beheads her, perhaps the most complete image of loss of usual values. She is restored, but in altered form, by Thoth, the Hermes of the Egyptians, who gives to her the cow head of Hathor, after which both she and (to some extent) Set become supporters of Pharaoh's throne. It is interesting that Thoth, the reconciler, is himself considered the son of both Horus and Set, having been conceived by Set from the sperm of Horus that had been homosexually consumed by Set through the trickery of Isis (TeVelde 1977, pp. 43–46).

A less violent image of liminality and change can be seen in the traditional Zen ox-herding pictures, an analogy of the interaction of the ego with the natural mind (Miyuki 1985). The overall movement of the pictures is a transformation of the original "boy" into a sage who returns to the community with "gift-bestowing hands." In between the identity of the boy and that of the sage occurs a most striking image of liminality. It is simply a circle, indicating a state in which the boy has already caught and tamed the ox and now "they are both gone away."

Lowermost status refers to the lowest strata of a stratified society, and yet lowermost status may carry religious or ritual meaning (Turner 1974, p. 234), like Gandhi's calling the lowest caste of Indian society the "children of God"—illustrating the way in which the lowermost can stand for basic human alikeness (which is the communitas experience occurring during a state of liminality). The concept of the lowermost carrying special religious or cultural meaning can be applied to ethnic and national identities as well (Turner 1969, p. 109)—for example, the politically insignificant nations as upholders of religious or moral values—the Hebrews in the ancient Near East and the Swiss in modern Europe. Both Gandhi and Tolstoy tried to remove marks of social distinction from their own persons (Turner 1974, p. 243). Marginals may have social or ritual status in one or more groups other than that group in which they are outsiders; their various social identities may even be opposite to one another. While liminality is an intentional loss of status during a period of ritual transition, *outsiderhood* refers to relationships which do not flow from recognized status.

Turner discusses outsiders as including shamans, diviners, mediums, priests, monks in seclusion, hippies, hoboes, and gypsies (1974, p. 233). Might one add psychoanalysts in our culture? Marginals include migrant foreigners, second-generation citizens, persons whose racial origin is mixed or ambiguous, downwardly mobile persons, those moving from one milieu to another (usually rural to urban), and women or men in nontraditional social sexual roles (ibid.). Liminality is a midpoint of transition between two status positions within a fixed society; outsiderhood originates outside a recognized social position; and lowermost status is the lowest recognized rung in a hierarchical social system.

Although communitas may be carried by the liminal, the outsider, and the lowermost, the term *liminal* has seemed to catch the imagination and the ear of psychology and literature. Perhaps its metaphor is more easily portable to other fields of inquiry. Firmat calls liminality "less a concept than a conceptual archetype," preferring "liminality" to "marginality" because of its ready etymological connections with "nouns like limit, limb, limbo, limbus, lintel; with verbs like limn, delimit, and eliminate; and with adjectives like preliminary, sublime, and subliminal" (1986, p. xiv). Liminality is rich in folklore figures such as "holy beggars," "third sons," "little tailors," and "simpletons," as well as the classic Western image of the "homeless and mysterious 'stranger' without wealth or name who restores ethical and legal equilibrium" (Turner 1969, p. 110). Some of my own generation will at this point involuntarily hear the thundering hoofbeats of the great horse Silver and, as the moment passes, may ask nostalgically, "Who *was* that masked man?"

The gods partake of liminal behavior as they "slay or unman their fathers, mate with their mother and sisters, copulate with mortals in the form of animals and birds," while their human representatives in various rites may symbolically or literally reenact these "immortal amoralities" (Turner 1974, p. 257). A classic example of the liminal image is the demigod *Chiron*, the inspiration for the name of the conference at which this paper was originally presented and its sponsoring publisher. Both man and stallion, and fully neither, he lived in a cave. Outside, marginal, and liminal, with no fixed social status, Chiron nevertheless taught the sons of kings and princes the arts of civilization and healing. Himself liminally outside, he was a source and strength of social order. Such theiranthropic figures are frequent in liminal situations (ibid., p. 253).

### *Liminality and the Structure of the Psyche*

What might be the psychological equivalents of these sociological distinctions of *liminality, marginality*, and *lowermost* in the traditional structural terms of Jungian theory? It seems to me that these terms indicate parts of the personality that are not well integrated. Abilities may exist that cannot reliably be seen, even by the ego, although they may be quite useful when constellated.

*Lowermost* would perhaps suggest the shadow, the structurally despised alter-ego, dissociated from the dominant self-image by innumerable childhood decisions. Yet all analysts know that the shadow often contains the healing quality needed for the completeness of the personality. *Marginality* suggests qualities that are on the same plane as the dominant ego-image, but marginal to its identity; perhaps lesser integrations of the persona would be marginal.

*Liminality*, however, has a different quality. It would seem to involve significant changes in the dominant self-image, including at times even the basic body-image. Unlike marginal qualities, which are visable but not emphasized from the view of the stable self-image, the liminal identity is one that involves a shift of identity from the usual sense of self toward an identity that is known to be different from the persona, is feared to be the shadow, and actually moves, if successful, toward a more comprehensive dominant self-image than the one transiently abandoned in the liminal state. As images of psychological liminality, we might picture a person in meditation, lifted up in prayer, drifting off to sleep, slightly (or greatly) intoxicated, lost in sexual passion, divided in conflicting roles and responsibilities at a family reunion, standing naked in a strange hospital gown before a diagnosing physician or lying in the impersonal chamber of a CAT or MRI scanner—all situations in which the usually stable props of self-identity are suspended and a new identity status may emerge.

## *Liminality and the Archetypal Self*

Jung's most diagrammatic representation of his concept of the Archetypal Self appears in *Aion* (1951, par. 347–421). Although clearly indicating that he is speaking of structural relationships rather than specific examples, Jung did use parts of the biblical story of Moses to indicate the type of meaning that could be attached to the diagram. The four horizontal nodes at the base of each double pyramid represent a quaternity, while the apical nodes in the central vertical axis seem to indicate images transcendent to the quaternity that pull toward a unity "above" or "below" the quaternity (see Hall 1986). Nodes of the two upper double pyramids, above the central nodal point of the *serpens*, are assigned person roles. The uppermost pyramid represents what Jung calls the Moses Quaternio or the Anthropos Quaternio. The double pyramid just below it he calls the Shadow Quaternio. The base of the Moses Quaternio is represented by four relationships: Moses is opposite his wife Zipporah, and his sister Miriam is opposite his father-in-law

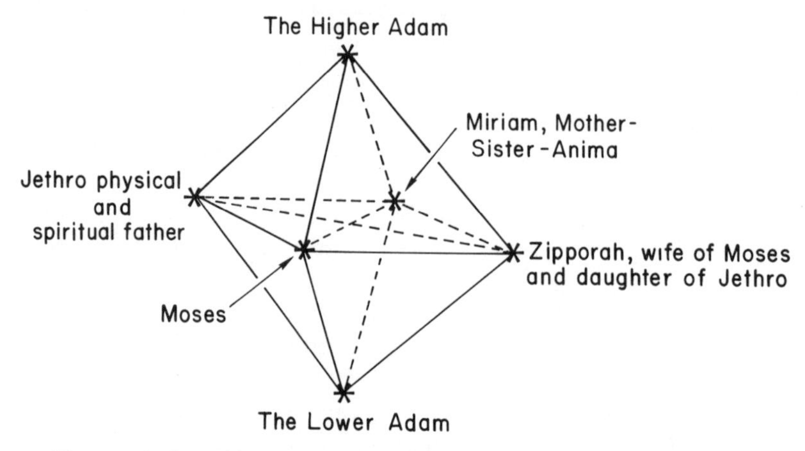


**Figure 1. Anthropos Moses Quaternio (from C. G. Jung, *Aion, CW* 9ii, p. 231)**

Jethro. The incest motif and tensions of the cross-cousin kinship system are indicated in this arrangement (Jung 1951, par. 363).

In the Shadow Quaternio, Moses as Carnal Man marries the Ethiopian Woman, the Kushite. Miriam speaks to God against Moses and is made leprous and cast out of the camp. Jethro, the father of Moses's official wife Zipporah, is then seen as a heathen priest. Thus not simply Moses but all roles in the Shadow Quaternio partake of the shadow.

As in a fairy tale, each figure may be seen as the nucleus of a self-identity, the self-identity chosen determining the relationship of other figures to the ego-image (the uncapitalized *self.*) The structure of the four double pyramids as a whole, of course, represents the Archetypal Self in Jung's metaphor. If the ego's self-image (self) is identified with the Moses node of the Anthropos Quaternio, then Jethro as priest of "God most High" is a numinous marginal figure, since his status as priest comes from another culture. Lowermost status describes all the figures in the Shadow Quaternio (as they are seen from the Anthropos Quaternio). Outsiderhood is a quality of Jethro as heathen priest.

The higher central node of Anthropos and the next lower central node, Homo, are difficult to conceive in terms of outsidership, marginality, and lowermost—all terms that seem to imply relationship between analogous states at the same level of conceptualization,

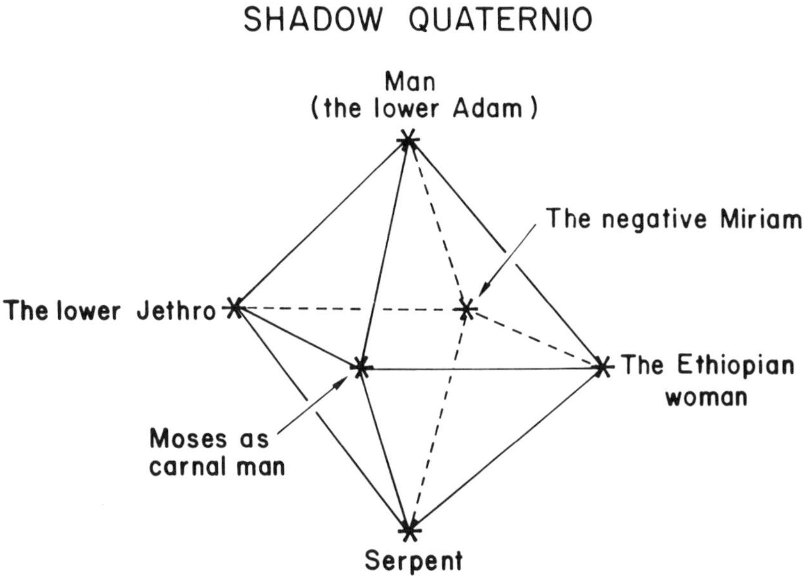

SHADOW QUATERNIO

Man
(the lower Adam)
The negative Miriam
The lower Jethro
The Ethiopian woman
Moses as carnal man
Serpent

Figure 2. Shadow Quaternio (from C. G. Jung, *Aion, CW* 9ii, p. 231)

whereas the central node of Anthropos transcends the entire plane of meaning where the terms outsiderhood, marginality, and lowermost are applicable. The lower node Homo perhaps has a similar transcending meaning, but in a "lower" direction—clinically suggesting a numinous pull toward the shadow. For a self-image that is established within the Anthropos Quaternio, movement toward either central node would suggest the experience of liminality for the whole relational structure of that quaternio.

Liminality thus can be a property of any movement from any relatively fixed identity, as, for example, the identity of Moses in the Anthropos Quaternio. But horizontal movement within the quaternio structure can be of a marginal and outsider nature, as toward the identity of Jethro as father-in-law outside the tribal boundaries. It can be liminality of a lowermost type if the self-image movement is toward an identity in the Shadow Quaternio. But *any* movement of self-identity that involves the quality of liminality can produce a sense of communitas, a feeling of basic oneness with humanity outside the usual social (persona) identity.

In addition to producing a social bonding with others, the experience of communitas seems to convey an experience of the *relativity of the ego's self-image*, so that the post-liminal ego has experienced communitas and can no longer so easily identify itself only with its basic social role, nor perhaps even with the shadow form of that role. This outcome of the liminal experience can produce an inner function similar to the Pueblo clowns—a constant reminder not to identify too completely with any of the various images of the self.

To designate as liminal any move from a self-identity within a quaternio to any position outside the plane of that quaternio, however, implies that the move is part of a larger, more extended process whose eventual outcome is a restoration and confirmation of the self in a renewed and transformed self-identity. This is what Jung seems to mean by suggesting that his diagram of the Self has analogy to self-renewing atomic processes. From an archetypal viewpoint, liminality does not imply the universal archetypal experience of death, but rather the more complicated archetypal patterns of death and transformation, death and rebirth, or death and resurrection. Considered clinically, liminality implies regression of the self in the service of the Self.

In short, marginality and outsiderhood imply aspects of a fixed ego structure, although they are far from the point of being integrated into the dominant self-image in such a structure. If the psyche is looked upon as fixed, identities not integrated into the persona will seem marginal, the shadow will take on qualities of the inferior lowermost including some of its numinous appeal, but liminality requires that the ego-centrum itself disidentify from the dominant self-image, undergo the experiences associated with the liminal state, and then reidentify with a self-image that is usually more comprehensive and inclusive than the original image.

Thus the ordinary result of a liminal transition is enlargement of what might be called the *personal sphere* of the psyche, that "area" in which the ego can move in a relatively conflict-free manner. The personal sphere of the psyche would be bounded externally by collective consciousness interfacing with the persona, and inwardly by the objective psyche or collective unconscious, interfacing through the function of the anima/animus.

Jung also shows an uroboric form of the Archetypal Self (1951, par. 391) in which *all* relationships in the hierarchical form of the Self are relativized. In a sense, the Uroboric Self is a liminal form of the entire Hierarchical Self. It is shown here as the rotating round form contained within the formula form of the Archetypal Self. These two forms are equivalent.

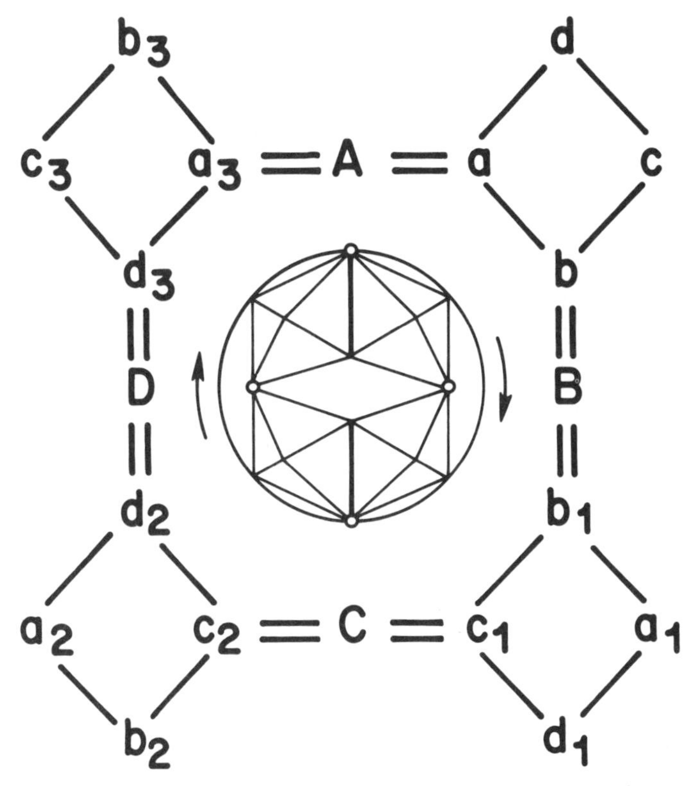


Figure 3. Uroboric form of the Archetypal Self within the formula form (modified from C. G. Jung, *Aion*, *CW* 9ii, pp. 248, 259)

## The Empty "I"

The more fluid sense of psychological liminality, lying too close to everyday life to earn diagnostic attention and definition, has been well described by Stein:

> In liminality the "I" 's standpoint is not fixed, and it occupies no clearly defined psychological location. It floats; it is not sharply delineated as "this" and "not that"; boundaries between "I" and "not-I" blur. . . . The ego is a has-been and a not-yet. . . . The "I" is not anchored to any particular inner images, ideas, or feelings. . . . Inner ground shifts . . . liminality is the realm of Hermes. (1983, pp. 9–10)

Psychologically, liminality is the sense of crossing and re-crossing borders. These may be the structural borders of the psyche: a lapse of the persona, a sly intrusion of the shadow, possession by the anima or animus. At unexpected moments there may arise an epiphany of the Self or of an archetypal image dormant behind the screening device of everydayness.

The actual emptiness of "I" is seldom experienced and perhaps must be classified as a mystical experience when it occurs (Roberts 1982). What is experienced frequently, however, is the "emptiness of I" in the sense of "I" referring to a *fixed* content. This is most evident when moving into and out of liminal states, although it is a common experience in many dreams and in emotional shifts during waking life. Such liminal movement across fixed borders occurs nightly with sleep and awakening, perhaps rarely accentuated by the marked liminality of hypnogogic or hypnopompic hallucinations. In all human sleep the cycle of dreams, based on the 90-minute rapid-eye-movement (REM) cycle, precipitates the sleeping subject into a dream-ego assigned to some point of reference within a dream scene that is not of its own choosing. The actions and inactions of the dream-ego in the liminal state of dreaming seem to affect the structure, emotion, and focus of the subsequent waking ego (Hall 1977, pp. 141–162). This is equivalent to asserting that the process of individuation proceeds in dreams, as in waking life, by the action of the ego in relation to the complex structures with which it is tacitly identified. It now seems likely that the 90-minute REM cycle continues during waking life, but is obscured by the activity of the waking cortex, so that this process may be part of normal assimilation of imaginal images into the tacit structure of the waking ego.

### *The Transcendent Function and Liminality*

In summary of the above discussion of Turner's *liminality* and Jung's *transcendent function*, it would appear that transcendent function refers to the ability of the Archetypal Self to produce a unification of opposites which cannot be done by the conscious ego alone.[5] The action of the transcendent function can, at times, be stimulated by such techniques as active imagination. Whether induced intentionally or occurring naturally and informally, it consists of 1) a stage in which the ego experiences itself as in contact with an activated complex from the unconscious, producing an affect-ego state, after which 2) intentional conscious reflection and understanding is needed in order to integrate the new symbolic material into consciousness, a process in which making a representation of the unconscious symbolic material may be helpful.

During the action of the transcendent function, the self-image undergoes a more or less marked stage of liminality, betwixt and between, as its identity is altered by the transcendent function of the Archetypal Self. When successful, the transcendent function unites conscious and unconscious, producing a unification of opposites. This both "expands" and "deepens" the range of the personal sphere in which the ego can move, often with less attachment to any self-image and a sense of communitas with mankind and communion with the Archetypal Self.

Serious psychological conflicts often are not solved on the level at which they are posed. Instead, they are transcended. Of what does the transcendence of a conflict consist? I suggest that Jung's model of the Archetypal Self suggests a possible answer for the mode of transcendence and the action of the transcendent function. Transcendence of a conflict of opposites often consists of a change in the self-image from which the conflict is perceived. The most striking change, in Jung's model, would be for the self to be established on the uroboric model of Self, rather than upon any of the possible nodes, such as the role of "Moses," within the heirarchical model of Self. Nevertheless, there also would be transcendence of conflict (constellated, say, upon the "horizontal" plane of the Moses Quaternio) if the self instead were established at the node of the Anthropos, which is "above" conflicts at the base level of the Moses arrangement of roles.

The transcendent function, therefore, is the ability of the Self to bring symbolic solutions to conflicts of opposites that are insolvable in their original form. There are two moves in the action of the transcendent function. First, a symbolic solution is presented from the unconscious. Second, the self must take an attitude toward the symbolic solution, an attitude that often exemplifies and/or produces a change in the tacit self-image from which the conflict is viewed.

This change in self-image is initiated, mediated, and contained by the transcendent functional activity of the Archetypal Self. In this manner, the transcendent function parallels in the intrapsychic realm the change in role described by Turner within societies.

### *Symbols/Images*

In spite of all discussion, the sense of psychological liminality is best conveyed by literature and poetry, not by prose. T. S. Eliot produced memorable short descriptions of liminality in "The Hollow Men" (1971, pp. 58–59). To emphasize the liminal quality in a neutral way I have omitted the refrain, "Falls the Shadow," from these three selected verses:

> Between the idea
> and the reality
> Between the motion
> And the act . . .
>
> Between the conception
> And the creation
> Between the emotion
> And the response . . .
>
> Between the desire
> And the spasm
> Between the potency
> And the existence . . .

Farther back in my mind are more images of the return, renewed, from the liminal mode of night through the imagery of dawn:

> In ancient Greece, the goddess Aurora, the Mother of the Winds, slowly draws open with her rosy fingers the many-hued curtains of the dawn. All is transformed and new.
>
> In classical Egypt, the enduring land, the baboon of Thoth arouses himself from slumber to salute the first rays of the sun as Kephera, the divine scarab, rolls the golden ball over the eastern horizon, illuminating the gilded top of the Great Pyramid—and all living things rejoice.
>
> Again closer to our own time, at the foot of Mt. Kenya, stands the unknown Elgonyi man whom Jung silently watched as he spit upon his open palms and offered them solemnly to the sun arising in the East at the time the world returns from the liminality of night.

And yet, the literary image that comes with most force into my mind is a less grand one. It is a scene from a children's book, *The Wind in the Willows*, from the chapter "The Piper at the Gates of Dawn," although I wish to emphasize not the piper, who was the great god Pan, but the watchers, who are closer to our own identity and named simply "Mole" and "Rat." Mole and Rat have gone in search of Portly, the missing son of Old Otter. Out in their boat they searched and searched for the missing child.

> Then a change began slowly to declare itself. The horizon became clearer, field and tree came more into sight, and somehow with a different look, the mystery began to drop away from them. A bird piped suddenly, and was still; and a light breeze sprang up and set the reeds and bullrushes rustling. Rat . . . sat up suddenly and listened with a passionate intentness. (Graham 1969, pp. 99–112)

"It's gone!" sighed the Rat, who had been listening to a strange, new sound that was so beautiful he wished he had never heard it now that it was gone, so much did he yearn to hear it once more. But it came again, and Rat was "transported, trembling . . . possessed in all his senses by this new divine thing that caught up his helpless soul and swung and dandled it, a powerless but happy infant, in a strong sustaining grasp." At last Mole heard the music also, and was as enraptured as his friend the Rat. Together they approached the sound, as if pulled by an ancient summons, until they were in a rich meadow in the morning freshness.

> The suddenly the Mole felt a great Awe fall upon him, an awe that turned his muscles to water, bowed his head, rooted his feet to the ground. It was no panic terror—indeed, he felt wonderfully at peace and happy—but it was an awe that smote him and held him and, without seeing, he knew it could only mean that some august Presence was very, very near. (Graham 1969, pp. 99–112)

Finally, he looked up and "raised his humble head" and found that he "looked into the very eyes of the Friend and Helper." He saw

> the backward sweep of the curved horns, gleaming in the growing daylight; saw the stern, hooked nose between the kindly eyes that were looking down on them humorously, while the bearded mouth broke into a half-smile at the corners; saw the rippling muscles on the arm that lay across the broad chest, the long supple hand still holding the panpipes only just fallen away from the parted lips, saw the splendid curves of the shaggy limbs disposed in majestic ease on the sward; saw, last of all, nestling between his very hooves, sleeping soundly in entire peace and contentment, the little, round, podgy, childish form of the baby otter. (Graham 1969, pp. 99–112)

And then in a moment the vision vanished. Mole rubbed his eyes and stared at Rat. It had been like a moment in and out of time, a lost moment in the rose garden. And then they awakened the sleeping Portly, and took him home to his parents. Only Rat lingered briefly, looking long and doubtfully at certain hoof marks deep in the sward.

## Notes

1. In 1916 Jung wrote an essay on the transcendent function. It was discovered in his files in 1953 and, in 1957, was published by the Students Association of the Jung Institute

(Zurich) in an English translation by A. R. Pope. In 1958 a revised German original was published. The English translation based on both the revised German publication and on Pope's translation appears in Jung's *Collected Works*, volume 8, paragraphs 131–193. In this essay, Jung speaks of the transcendent function, of active imagination, and of potential dangers in the use of active imagination. "Transcendent function" is also referenced throughout the works of Jung.

2. For example, a haiku whose authorship I have been unable to verify seems to speak of both the "I" that performed action and the "I" that observes, but remains ambiguous as to whether they are the same "I":

A peach tree blossoms
Planted there by someone, seen
From here by someone.

3. For a particularly clear example of this see Hall 1977, pp. 174–177.

4. Von Franz is citing this dream from M. K. Fortier's dissertation *Dreams and Preparation for Death*. Ann Arbor, Mich.: University Microfilms International, 1972.

5. Turner (1969) presents an extensive list of opposites that describe the tension of structure and liminality. Selected examples include transition/state, totality/partiality, homogeneity/heterogeneity, communitas/structure, equality/inequality, absence of prosperity/property, absence of status/status, absence of rank/distinctions of rank, unselfishness/selfishness, foolishness/sagacity, simplicity/complexity.

The unification of opposites in the psyche is anything but a mean between them or a mere alteration of one and then the other. See my essay "Enantiodromia and the Unification of Opposites: Spontaneous Dream Images" (Hall 1983) for examples and discussion of this question of "unification" of opposites. In essence, when "unified" both opposites, and the ranges between them, are available to the ego.

## References

Eliot, T. S. 1971. *The Complete Poems and Plays*. New York: Harcourt Brace and World.

Firmat, G. 1986. *Literature and Liminality: Festive Readings in the Hispanic Tradition*. Durham, N.C.: Duke University Press.

Graham, K. 1969. *The Wind in the Willows*. Burgenfield, N.J.: New American Library.

Hall, J. 1977. *Clinical Uses of Dreams: Jungian Interpretations and Enactments*. New York: Grune and Stratton.

______. 1983. Enantiodromia and the unification of opposites: spontaneous dream images. In *The Arms of the Windmill: Essays in Analytical Psychology in Honor of Werner H. Engel*, D. Young, ed. New York: C. G. Jung Foundation.

______. 1984a. Dreams and transference/countertransference: the transformative field. In *Transference/Countertransference*, Chiron Clinical Series, Nischwartz-Salant and M. Stein, eds. Wilmette, Ill.: Chiron Publications, 1984, pp. 31–51.

______. 1984b. Pseudo-objectivity as a defense mechanism: Polanyi's concept of dynamo-objective coupling. *Journal of the American Academy of Psychoanalysis* 12(2):199–209.

______. 1986. *The Structure of Collective Shadows: Why They Endure*. Presented at the 10th Congress of the International Association for Analytical Psychology, West Berlin, September 9, 1986.

Jung, C. G. 1951. *Aion*. In *CW*, vol. 9ii. Princeton, N.J.: Princeton University Press, 1959.

Miyuki, M. 1985. The Zen ox-herding pictures. In *Buddhism and Jungian Psychology*, J. Spiegelman and M. Miyuki, eds. Phoenix: Falcon Press, pp. 29–42, 103–108, and 109–113.

Polanyi, M. 1953. *Personal Knowledge: Toward a Post-Critical Philosophy*. Chicago: University of Chicago Press.

Prigogine, I. 1983. Man's new Dialogue with nature. *Perkins Journal* 36 (4):4–14.

Roberts, B. 1982. *The Experience of No-Self*. Sunspot, N.M.: Iroquois House.

Stein, M. 1983. *In Midlife*. Dallas: Spring.

TeVelde, H. 1977. *Seth, God of Confusion*. Leiden: E. J. Brill.

Turner, V. 1969. *The Ritual Process: Structure and Anti-Structure*. Chicago: Aldine.

______. 1974. *Dramas, Fields and Metaphors: Symbolic Action in Human Society*. Ithaca, N.Y.: Cornell University Press.

______. 1982. *From Ritual to Theatre: The Human Seriousness of Play*. New York: Performing Arts Journal Publications.

Turner, V., and Turner, E. 1978. *Image and Pilgrimage in Christian Culture Anthropological Perspectives*. New York: Columbia University Press.

van Gennep, A. 1960. *Rites of Passage*. Chicago: University of Chicago Press.

von Franz, M. L. 1984. *On Dreams and Death*. Boston: Shambala.

# Liminality and Animus in *Blue Velvet*

**Florence Wiedemann**

Although analytical psychology has long recognized important differences in the psychologies of men and women largely on the basis of anima and animus differences, we have much to do to clarify a legitimate female psychology. The development of a female sense of self in relation to animus over the course of individuation was initially explored by Neumann (1959) and later Toni Wolff (1956) elaborated feminine typologies. Other writers in the area of animus were reviewed by Claire Douglas (1986)—such writers as Emma Jung, Esther Harding, Barbara Hannah, Irene de Castellejo, Florida Scott Maxwell, Marie-Louise von Franz, Hilda Binswanger, Ann Ulanov, and Edward C. Whitmont. These writers stressed the archetypal aspect to animus, and often the "nastiness" of the negative animus. Mary Ann Mattoon (1981) questioned whether the concept was necessary at all. Our work in analysis and psychotherapy with adult women has led to a developmental understanding of a woman's current gender identity and the function of her animus.

Polly Young-Eisendrath and I have described, in *Female Authority: Empowering Women Through Psychotherapy* (1987), the stages

---

**Florence L. Wiedemann**, Ph.D., is president of the C. G. Jung Institute of Dallas, and has a private practice in Dallas, Texas. She is co-author, with Polly Young-Eisendrath, of *Female Authority*.

through which a woman goes as she individuates in relationship to the animus complex. By animus, we mean the tendency in women that directs attention toward actuality, an enterprising spirit of courage, determination that moves ahead with authority and forcefulness. These qualities of animus allow a woman to be effective, powerful, and competent in the world. In addition, animus signifies a woman's feeling relationship to a man, to men in general, to the patriarchal culture, and to spiritual life. This animus functioning occurs intrapersonally and intrapsychically, affecting how a woman judges herself, and in relation to the wider culture. My article, "Mother, Father, Teacher, Sister: Transference and Countertransference Issues with Women in the First Stages of Animus Development" (Wiedemann 1984), dealt with a woman in the first stage. This paper will take a look at the two women in *Blue Velvet*. Dorothy as a first-stage woman who develops into the second stage, and Sandy, a woman in the second stage developing into the third stage.

The five stages of animus development, as derived from clinical observation, correspond to mythological themes; each stage is also associated with a particular developmental arrest or psychopathology. The first stage is called "animus as alien other." In this stage a woman's relationship to her own masculine figures and authority is filled with threatening possibilities. She responds to this with mistrust, fear, and masochism. The animus often appears as abusive in this stage, which is seen mythologically in the story of the rape of Persephone, the young daughter of Demeter, who was taken by Hades, god of the underworld and brother of Zeus, and abducted into the underworld.

The second stage is called "animus as father, god, and patriarch." Here the woman experiences herself as sacrificed to the world of the father or men. She may be "the father's daughter." She sacrifices her individuality by living for masculine approval in a collective way or by living out traditional patriarchal values. Her life is designed to meet the requirements of and to please the father, god, or patriarchy. She feels sanctioned by powerful male authorities, but has no power of her own. Predictably, such a woman will become depressed if she remains fixated at this level of development all of her life. Sad to say, it is the modal consciousness of women today in our culture. The mythological theme that best fits this stage is the story of Pandora, with Zeus and Hephaestus for a supporting cast. (For the purpose of this paper, I need not discuss the final three stages of animus development.)

*Blue Velvet*, a film written and directed by David Lynch, illustrates my points about the first two stages of animus development. This film is so full of liminal images we can see how the changes take place in the characters. David Lynch is a master of liminality—a homegrown surrealist who combines peculiar moods of dread with comedy and apple-pie-good detail. He shows us the images in a dreamlike style with slow dissolves, extreme close-ups, and figures who emerge out of darkness. He confuses details, brand names, and cars from different eras, taking us to the liminal edge.

Dorothy Vallens, the masochistic nightclub singer in *Blue Velvet*, is an example of a woman caught at the first stage of animus development, and Sandy, daughter of Detective Williams, is a woman at the second stage. Through the film storyline, we will observe the transitional process through which they go.

Van Gennep (1909) has described the "liminal phases" of rites and passages as the rites accompanying every change, of place, state, social position, or age. I hope to show how liminality is betwixt and between the place where changes occur. I hope to show how the transformation experiences with Frank and Jeff as animus figures affected Dorothy's and Sandy's development. The whole story of *Blue Velvet* is a liminal state "in and out of time." It takes place in Lumberton, an archetypal small sleepy town in an indefinite mythic present that feels like the past.

*Blue Velvet* has many mythological analogues, such as those reviewed by Stein, Stein, and Wiedemann (1984). Jeff can be seen as a hero such as Perseus or Theseus, who heroically faces the monstrous and kills it to redeem the maiden. He also appears to be a Parsifal—the young fool who seeks a cure for the ailing king and consequently the ailing culture—whose quest represents the urge to discover the inmost core of the world (Goethe 1952). It can be seen as the sadistic use and abuse of the feminine by the masculine in our culture, a case study in perversion, or as a young man's initiation into sexuality and manhood. The title *Blue Velvet* refers to the sash of Dorothy's bathrobe (which seems to symbolize the union of infant and mother). This sash, the fetish in an elaborate sado-masochistic ritual of Hades and Persephone (Frank and Dorothy) entangles not only them but us. This transitional object contributes to an intermediate area of experiencing in which inner reality and external life both contribute (Winnicott 1986). Winnicott argues that the area, transitional between fact and fantasy, where the infant half-creates, half-discovers the objects in its world, is the same area in which adults play and from which acting and art spring. The mother enables the infant to experience omnipotence by actually finding what the infant imagines or creates, to link this fantasy to what is actual. But when this early creativity goes wrong, Winnicott believes the individual must go on pushing omnipotence and control, like trying to sell unwanted shares in a bogus company. Dennis Hopper's villainous performance as Frank is so authentically perverse that the film takes on an extra chilling dimension. He is a worthy Hades, deeply disturbing and ferociously uncontrollable. He truly represents the darkest, most twisted depths of personality gone awry. Isabella Rossellini's performance as the lady of the night, Dorothy Vallens, reminds me of the victimized and haunted women I have seen in therapy, who continue to return to various kinds of mental, emotional, and physical abuse at the hands of men.

From Winnicott's picture of goodness we can infer its opposite, evil, as sterility, constriction, cruelty, and envy. He sees good things as always in danger from the envy of those who feel deprived of them. Frank's horrific energy as the abusive animus certainly spoils Dorothy's goodness. He can be seen as representing the masculine's fear of and need to control the feminine which limits and spoils the feminine goodness in our culture.

In *Blue Velvet*, we are under the strain of relating inner and outer reality. I do not feel the film is pornographic, but rather that it depicts an inner reality. The movie has an eeriness about it, a timeless quality which suggests a prolonged state of liminality. I see it as a story of Tom's comatose experience in the hospital, or Jeff's descent into the underworld as a rite of passage into manhood in which he redeems the maiden while heroically slaying the dragon. The film is also about our culture's shared reality of the persona world in Lumberton, and the shadow world that lives below with the denigration and subjugation of the feminine. The oft-repeated problems of our culture have reached a critical period. The resources of the earth are being exhausted as we see trucks of felled trees go down the streets of Lumberton. Mother Earth is poisoned, exhausted, and threatened ecologically—suffering, oppression, and starvation prevail. We are alienated from nature, and women have been denigrated, devalued, and deprived of their individuality (Whitmont 1982).

The fascinating, nightmarish, intensely disquieting story is an exploration of voyeurism and incestuous allusions which pushes the boundaries of what we can tolerate on the screen while the rich visual humor and poetry juxtapose to give the film depth and tension.

The bucolic images of bright flowers against a picket fence topped by a blue sky, underscored by Angelo Badalamenti's disturbing score in the background, lets us know that the persona world of Lumberton, USA, is in for a shadow visit.

The father of the story is Tom Beaumont. All the names appear to be symbolic, with Beaumont alluding to the beautiful mountain or Mont Salvat, the place where father gods appear and salvation takes place. Tom keels over from a stroke while gardening at the opening of the film. His mid-life crisis (which also could symbolize the crisis of the patriarchal culture) consists of losing his persona and experiencing the unconscious. In a prolonged liminality state, he discovers through the actions of his son, Jeff, the evil shadow, Frank Booth, and his tortured anima, Dorothy Vallens.

Lynch has the camera move from Tom's stricken body to the lawn abruptly beneath it, while the sound track swells to a frightening death battle between warring insects. We hear the roaring violence and rage in the underground, and we suspect the unconscious is about to erupt. Bugs are a repetitive theme throughout the film, from the diseased, rotting ear to Jeff's posing as an exterminator to gain entrance into the mysterious and suspect Dorothy's apartment.

Enter Jeff (Kyle McLachlan), Tom's son, an innocent Parsifal, the naive young fool who knows there's a mystery around the old king's sickness and who, with healthy curiosity and a bit of his father's shadow (Frank, the sado-masochistic pervert), wants to get to the bottom of it. He "asks the questions," even though he is warned not to further his quest. He wants to know what ails his father and his culture, and how he is to relate to the feminine (i.e., serve the grail). When Jeff's girl friend, Sandy (Laura Dern), says, "I don't know if you're a detective or a pervert," even Jeff doesn't know the answer. It's ambiguous to the viewer how much of Jeff's actions are heroic and how much are shadow, also. After discovering his strange find, a dismembered ear, Jeff determines to get to the bottom of the mystery which necessitates a descent into the unconscious. Jeff represents the part of the patriarchy and the part of Tom who recognizes the dismemberment, i.e., men in our culture only hear what they want to hear, are not receptive, and thus are not able to communicate in relationship. Lynch seems to have a penchant for looking through things to view the monstrous (see *Eraserhead*, an earlier film)—wounds, organs, holes, receptive but diseased ears, slats in the closet—all image his view of knowledge as dangerous, but irresistible and redeeming, and perhaps suggest Lynch's own fear of the feminine.

Finding the dismembered left ear starts Jeff's journey to discover what's hidden beneath the red, white, and blue peaceful beauty of

Lumberton. Despite being set in 1950, Jeff wears a Hermes-like earring in his left ear, suggesting the sixties and seventies, cars switch from fifties to eighties models, all indicators that we are in the land of liminality.

Detective Williams is the father of Sandy, our second stage of animus development representative. Detective Williams is an archetypal upholder of law and order. Trapped in his collective role, supported by his preppie-looking wife, his self-protective nature and his fear are evident as he wears his gun even at home. For Sandy, he is the idealized father figure (Zeus), for he functions to keep the shadow elements out of the persona of Lumberton. The film implies, however, that he has one foot in the shadow, i.e., what gives him his power is his connection to Frank (Hades) and the world of crime, drugs, and violence. Zeus and Hades were brothers, you know.

Sandy is connected to the light, as she is inspired by traditional religious beliefs, and speaks naively and sweetly of the robins coming from the sky bringing a redeemed world of goodness and love. Sandy, as a Pandora-type woman, has idealized her father as a representative of the patriarchy. She has sacrificed herself, her individuality, to the world of the Father's. She has become an obedient father's daughter, getting her beliefs, values, and judgments from the father and the patriarchal institutions such as church, school, and law.

As such, she has sacrificed her authenticity gaining masculine approval by her appearance (a beautiful, thin princess). While dining at Arlene's Cafe with Jeff, she's never seen eating food, while Jeff enjoys several meals. A woman at this stage experiences herself as trying to please the patriarchal powers—in Sandy's case, serving a patriarchal church obedient to her father. Sandy also has a collective high-school boyfriend, a football player, when the movie begins. Her persona meets with approval of her father's. But she will not be able to claim her uniqueness, goodness, and truth. She has the power of the fathers to protect her as long as she conforms to the appearance they choose, but she has little power and authority of her own. Intense identity relationships are the hallmark of women at this stage, with severe identity crises following break-ups with males who give them identity. The spiritual aspect of the animus complex for Sandy takes the form of robins, the patriarchal god-spirit, who will end the darkness, bringing only love. The Pandora woman's self-worth is merged with men's view of her, and consequently she is dependent on their praise and positive reflection. She looks to them for guidance, knowledge, and protection and believes that being female implies weakness, so she fashions herself as Pandora was fashioned, to meet the standards of the masculine order. Such a woman feels a self-loathing for her body, unless it is fashionably thin.

Like Brunnhilde, another father's daughter of the Norse/ Germanic god Wotan, Sandy facilitates the development of the story and the development of all the characters, including herself. By doing the *true* unconscious will of her father, not what he tells her to do, she detects, uncovers, and gets to the bottom of things. Sandy leads Jeff to the dark anima, Dorothy, and thus to the monstrous Frank just as Pandora's insistent curiosity led her to open a box or remove the lid of an earthenware jar. All evils, sickness, and death were in the container which Pandora released from the underground darkness into the world, just as Sandy activated the revelation of the evils underground in Lumberton. Pandora's (Sandy's) desire to penetrate the power of appearance results in her lifting the lid off the contained forces of the buried and suffering matriarchal culture.

In the process of the film, Sandy develops from a girl with a football hero boyfriend and a collective idealized dependent relationship with her father to a young woman with Jeff, the questor, as her boyfriend. Her animus now is a seeker of understanding who is capable of transforming the culture. She protects Jeff against the dangers of the underground voyage, as he goes down to slay the monster (Frank) and free the enslaved aspect of femininity (Dorothy). As a result of his chilling experience and through the influence of Jeff, Sandy becomes more dynamic and self-confident.

The major theme of this second stage of animus development is the woman's experience of herself as being sacrificed to the world of men, father, and animus. Animus is projected onto powerful, supposedly benign, masculine figures who have all the control, power, authority, truth, and validity of the world. A woman may identify her animus with her father, with a male god, or with a representative of the patriarchy, such as a powerful political figure or a professor.

Most women we see in private practice enter therapy at this stage. Although validation and love by a father figure is essential for movement forward, it also may occur through the validation by the animus side of a female therapist.

The task of this stage is to "re-fashion" oneself in terms acceptable to patriarchal power. In her desire to identify herself with the "superior" person, the female takes up the challenge of her development with a sense of loss of her own authenticity. Penis envy, which is more accurately labelled phallus envy, is the crucial issue at this stage. A girl wants the power and freedom phallic power promises, not because it is inherently and obviously better to be masculine, but as a step in her liberation from her mother. This turning away from one's own identity as inferior and turning toward the man's identity as legitimate and validating is the initial "fall" from perfection as a woman and can be unconsciously imagined to be a sin or flaw. This is true especially if the girl acts out her loss of self-worth in terms of accommodation of men's abusive sexual desires (e.g., incest with father or brother) or in terms of stealing away supplies (e.g., shoplifting) or resources that belong to the world of the feminine. Losing self-worth to the masculine superiority can be endlessly repeated throughout a lifetime of seeking validation, for example, by years of therapy with an authoritative, depressed man who the daughterly client seeks to repair.

With the introjection of Jeff as a more individual and conscious animus, Sandy has a stronger identity and a more vital life. She can experience herself as voluntarily surrendering to animus and relationships with men or the masculine, rather than feeling passively sacrificed. Such a woman now feels more involved in her projects and life. "She may surrender to a man in marriage, a male-dominated institution (e.g., the church or graduate school), or to an ideal or even an abstraction (e.g., principles of existentialism) designed by men. She is swept away and actively wanting to give in" (Young-Eisendrath and Wiedemann 1987).

Sandy surrenders to this project with Jeff, but is still not his partner or equal. She makes a leap forward that is both exciting and frightening, but she fears that nothingness or sheer darkness is the real target of her leap. She commits to something, not at all sure she can carry herself through.

In the process she makes a journey to the place of her own pain, rage, and suffering—to the buried feminine within herself and her society. She enters into this underground exploration by her own initiative and experiences it as an initiation ritual before an angry goddess. The angry goddess may be imaged either as a rageful female deity or as her own mother complex, enraged and violent, demanding obedience. In the confrontation with Dorothy, Sandy can see her own and her mother's abuse and the oppression of other women.

At Jeff's request, Sandy takes Jeff to The Slow Club, where we first hear *Blue Velvet* sung by Dorothy, the trashy nightclub singer. Her poignant rendition of the song suggests a nostalgic longing. Frank appears transfixed and tearful, apparently longing for his sad, depressed, yet comforting mother.

Jeff is committed to the heroic quest now. Following Dorothy to her sleazy apartment seven flights up, Jeff becomes involved in and possessed by a brutal, highly sexually charged world that he can barely comprehend. Sandy's blond innocence is contrasted with Dorothy's ghoulish, masochistic allure. Dorothy's tacky wig reminds me of the Gorgon's snakelike hair. She can be seen as the negative aspect of the feminine—the raped Persephone, the horrible Gorgon, or the dreadful Orgeluse or Morgana la Fey of the Grail. She symbolizes the suffering, terrible, and dark aspect of the Goddess, the loathesome maiden, Medusa, Erishkigal, and Kali. All these stories have the chief elements of the angry, insulted feminine kept captive or hidden in a painful and grim underworld, waiting to be redeemed by the questor. To redeem her, the questor must reverence her in her hideous form and feel pity and compassion for the pain, as well as love for her beautiful aspect.

Dorothy lives on Lincoln Street, suggesting the sexual and emotional bondage to an abusive animus of a woman at this first stage of development. Both within, and without, the battle for freeing the enslaved feminine is fought on Lincoln Street. Jeff, son of Tom (Thomas Jefferson, author of the Declaration of Independence), is in mortal combat with enslaver Frank Booth (J. Wilkes Booth, assassin of Lincoln, liberator of slaves).

Dorothy's archetypal need to venerate the masculine is seen in its shadow side—masochism, the other side of worship (Gordon 1986). Dorothy's pain, suffering, and self-abasement can be seen as an early prefiguration of a surrender to the transcendent function—the sacrifice of the little self to the higher self. Her sacrifice was sacred, although forced, for it was made to insure the safety of her husband, Donald, and son, Donny. Donald's dismembered ear relates him to Adonis, beloved of Aphrodite, and to the mystery of death and resurrection, of disunion and reunion of the psyche. Adonis was often identified with the ancient Near Eastern deity Tammuz, consort of the great goddess, Ishtar, and as such belongs to the son/lovers of the Great Mother. Adonis's death was attributed to a boar, symbol of the negative Mother. Donald also has allusions to Van Gogh, the artist who is driven to self-destructiveness through lack of being understood. Arlene's Cafe is a sly reminder of Arls, where Van Gogh painted for a period.

Frank, the thug drug dealer, is a truly shocking symbol of evil. His cruelty, obscenity, and disturbing perversity which combines sado-masochism, fetishism, foul language, and murderous rage make him a perfect candidate for Hades, the alien animus to Dorothy's Persephone. Frank's sado-masochistic attacks on Dorothy make irrational sense when seen as his envy and rage at the hated creative mother. The patriarchal male's abuse and denigration of women is, of course, internalized by women, which then sets women up to constellate, expect, and tolerate such abusive encounters. The title of the film, *Blue Velvet*, refers to a blue sash used in the perverted and sadistic sex act of Frank on Dorothy. I suggest it is Frank's transitional object. The transitional object is an infant's first symbol. It stands for confidence in the union of the infant and mother based on the experience of the mother's reliability and capacity to know what the infant wants (Winnicott 1971). Was Frank's mother depressed, blue, and so overwhelmed that she couldn't provide Frank with a good experience? Did she comfort (blue velvet) him the best she could?

Dorothy for her part must have experienced near suicidal despair that she could ever become free and be her own authority. She must have despaired that a belief in her goodness could be achieved and that she could ever rid herself of her shameful self-evaluations. Her sacrifice of herself, her submission to Frank's perversions, were actions forced upon her. She turns the tables on Jeff when she forces him to disrobe and kneels in front of him to perform fellatio. In her mind, this humiliating activity has become associated with bowing before a man, before God himself, and making herself humble. Perhaps she found meaning and gratification in humiliating herself before the superior male. Perhaps she finally internalized some masculine power and delighted in ordering Jeff around as she has been commanded. Her development is ambiguous, and, later, Persephone (Dorothy), returning from Hades, finds not Demeter's arms waiting but Jeff's, there to protect her. She is battered and naked like a white apparition rising out of a chaotic hell into an ordered surburbia. Exposing her bruised body to all in a pathetic plea for help, Dorothy exposes the abused and battered feminine.

Countless numbers of women who are in this first stage of animus development abase themselves to their fathers, their employers, sacrifice themselves for their husbands, lovers, and children, and are abused physically, raped and beaten by men. More than 50 percent of wives, all shapes, sizes, ethnic backgrounds, and incomes, it is estimated, will at some point in their lives be subjected to domestic violence. And many of them stay around for more, even whole married lives of abuse, according to a *New York Times* magazine article (Fleming 1986).

For many women the price of "love" and "protection" is the surrender of their personal identity, and sometimes submission to sadistic demands or demeaning control by abusive men in their lives. The liminal image of Dorothy being raped by Frank (like Persephone being raped by Hades) is the result of the repression and devaluation of the feminine in the culture. Dorothy has actively taken on the largely unconscious suffering and rage of Jeff's mother about her life situation. Jeff's mother's rage at her husband, Tom, is seen in a projected form only as a blazing gun on the TV screen which she watches avidly as the film opens.

A Persephone woman is caught in the matriarchal realm, in an undifferentiated symbiosis with her mother and the world of children and kitchen, with no relationship to the father, or the masculine. For her, a transition away from the world of the mother into the patriarchal culture may feel like a rape. For the young Persephone, the ego must become unmoored from its former fixities as a daughter—as she is dragged down into the underworld of Hades. This area of psychological liminality is necessary for Dorothy as a separation from an earlier pattern of ego organization. After the ordeal is over and she is in the ambulance, Dorothy cries, "I'm falling, I'm falling." She has fallen completely apart and with her reappearance at the end of the film, in which she is reunited with her son in the woods, we are led to suppose that the transformation has occurred. The alien animus has moved into a fatherly patriarchal complex that would signal her second stage of animus development. Now she can experience thc morc positive connection to a male and feel his power protecting her. In this film, the protective male would be in the form of a therapist, a hospital, or halfway house for Dorothy.

Through Sandy's opening of Pandora's box, looking into the suffering, shame, loss, and anger at having lived primarily through masculine approval and through a false self, a change now occurs in her. After Dorothy's wraithlike reappearance from underground, Sandy can no longer ignore the suffering of the buried feminine. Opening the lid on her internal life in a patriarchal society is the beginning of the third stage of animus development for Sandy. Now she will have to commit voluntarily to her own development and perform many tasks (Amor and Psyche is the myth representing the third stage of animus development).

*Blue Velvet* is a film of liminality for it makes the archetypal depths palpable, opens the visible surface of consciousness to the invisible presence of the archetypal extensions, according to Stein (1983), and shows us the images of two women at differing stages of animus development in a bizarre but psychologically true scenario of the borderlands.

The end of the movie finds Jeff awakening from a nap, with the earring now in his opposite ear. Father is home from the hospital. Mother is in the kitchen watching a robin with a beetle in its mouth and Sandy is there. Dorothy is seen in a wooded park, with her son, Donny, running toward her, wearing his little wizard hat complete with whirling propeller, into her arms, and we hear the theme song, "I'll always remember *Blue Velvet* in my dreams," as the camera pans the white picket fence, red roses, and blue sky. We wonder that although the surface appears the same, perhaps a transformation has occurred. If so, there would be hope that a reversal of the patriarchal trend and a renewal of life has occurred through the dismemberment of Donald and Jeff's psychological act of courage and commitment to releasing the suffering feminine. We hope that creative possibilities can win in our culture against the regressive forces of destruction. With her redemption, Dorothy has opened Jeff to his weakness, fears, and his ambivalence. He can no longer maintain his heroic image. He now knows the split between his ideals and his unacceptable wishes. Perhaps Lumberton now can live in the consciousness of darkness, destruction, horror *and* of love, beauty, and truth. The film leaves us questioning, hoping, and wondering.

As women develop their animus, giving expression to their goodness, strength, power, and beauty, they will have full authority to bring to the world. *Blue Velvet* has shown how this develops in early stages of development, giving us hope that men and women can face their shadows and develop their strengths resulting in a more integrated life.

## References


Douglas, C. 1986. A review of animus. *The San Francisco Library Journal*. San Francisco, Calif.

Fleming, A. 1986. The American wife. In *New York Times Magazine*, October 26, 1986.

Goethe, J. 1952. In *Encyclopaedia Brittanica*. William Benton (publisher).

Gordon, R. 1986. *Masochism and the Need to Worship Shadow in the Split War*. Paper presented at the Ninth International Congress of the International Association for Analytical Psychology, Berlin. Mary Ann Mattoon, ed.

Mattoon, M. A. 1981. *Jungian Psychology in Perspective*. New York: Free Press.

Neumann, E. 1959. the psychological stages of feminine development. *Spring*.

Stein, M. 1983. *In Midlife: A Jungian Perspective*. Dallas: Spring Publications.

Stein, J., Stein, M., and Wiedemann, F. 1984. At the Movies: *Blue Velvet*. *The San Francisco Library Journal*, pp. 49–55.

Turner, V. 1966. *The Ritual Process. Structure and Anti Structure*. Ithaca, N.Y.: Cornell University Press.

van Gennep, A. 1909. *The Rites of Passage*. London: Routledge and Kegan Paul.

Whitmont, E. 1982. *The Return of the Goddess*. New York: Crossroads Press.

Wiedemann, F. 1984. Mother, father, teacher, sister: transference/countertransference issues of women in the first stage of animus development. *Chiron: A Review of Jungian Analysis*. In N. Schwartz-Salant and M. Stein, eds. Evanston, Ill.: Chiron Publications.

Winnicott, D. 1971. *Playing and Reality*. London: Tavistock Publications.

______. *Home Is Where We Start From: Essays by a Psychoanalyst*. New York: W. W. Norton and Company.

Wolff, T. 1956. *Structural Forms of the Feminine Psyche*. Zurich: C. G. Jung Institute.

Young-Eisendrath, P., and Wiedemann, F. 1987. *Female Authority: Empowering Women Through Psychotherapy*. New York: Guilford Press.

# Winnicott's Area of Freedom: The Uncompromisable

**Michael Eigen**

Why did Winnicott's paper, "Transitional Objects and Transitional Phenomena" (1953), become his most popular work? "Mind and Its Relation to the Psyche-Soma" (1954), read two years earlier at the British Psychoanalytic Society, was at least as important, and Winnicott expressed even more satisfaction with some later papers.

One reason is that the transitional object paper gave practitioners something to hold on to. Discussion of processes could be anchored to observation of behavior, e.g., attachment to a doll or blanket. For many practitioners, Winnicott's paper became a kind of transitional object itself, a me-yet-not-me possession, a vehicle to aid expression and orientation. It offered something more or less concrete to dig into and rally around.

Papers on the transitional object proliferated. They were part of the new Age of the Mother in psychoanalysis. Early mother–infant interactions came to center stage. Winnicott's speculations were refreshing because they were not couched in dogmatic language. Practitioners

---

**Michael Eigen** is senior member and control/training analyst at the National Psychological Association for Psychoanalysis and the Institute for Expressive Analysis, and has a private practice in New York City and Brooklyn. He is author of *The Psychotic Core*, co-editor of *Evil: Self and Culture*, and has many published papers.

from any school could use them. They were especially welcome to those who felt inhibited by Melanie Klein's and Margaret Mahler's concepts, yet were receptive to a depth-psychological approach to intersubjectivity.

Winnicott's work is a breath of fresh air. He makes his way through the claustrophobia of psychoanalytic mine fields and gives voice to his sense of freedom as a psychoanalytical person. I do not think Winnicott's work can be understood without reference to the importance he placed on "feeling free." Even practitioners who view the transitional object in a most reduced sense, merely as "mother substitute," understand that it represents a growth of freedom for the self.

## Objects, Phenomena, and Area

Winnicott's formulations allow themselves to be taken in many directions. Transitional objects may be soothing, insofar as they stand for the breast or mother. They may be used to deny separation. However, in certain instances they emphasize separation and stand for an endless gap they forever try to fill. Transitional objects may carry forward the richness of experience or be a place marker for an experience never had. They may stand for rich or unreal mothering and mediate a rich or unreal self.

Transitional objects are important for what they are not, as well as for what they are. They are not mother or self, although feelings of mother and self are invested in them. They are "something else"—something other than mother and me, although filled with the latter two. They are something less than mother and me, and something more. They are objects that can be handled, cared for, abused, lost, and rediscovered. They can be controlled.

Above all, they are *mine*. Winnicott describes them as first not-me "possessions." Not the first object of object-relationships, but "the first possession." The importance of possession is already a sign, a premonition, of all that cannot be possessed, of the vast claims I will have to abandon, of the vast claims I will have to discover, new, unknown worlds ahead in which possession and freedom clash and play.

Winnicott introduces his concept with the term "objects" but quickly enlarges it to "transitional phenomena" and "transitional area." He speaks first about concrete objects because it is easier to see an object than to grasp an area of experience. People know what he means when he calls attention to an infant's addiction to a blanket or doll. Winnicott uses this as a lever to open up an area of experience which is neither quite inner nor outer. The first bit of not-me possession is neither wholly other, nor simply part of self. It is not a hallucination, but an actual object filled with meaning, meaning for me: it is my *own* with bits of me and mother and itself blended in a way that does not fit any single category.

Transitional phenomena may include an infant's babbling or a child's repeated songs while preparing for sleep. The transitional expands into art, science, religion, and culture in general, or contracts into addictions and fetishes. Winnicott's concept covers a lot of ground. It is no wonder he has been criticized for being vague. Vague but useable. It is no wonder that many practitioners have tried to tie him down.

## The Intermediate Area

Winnicott pointed to the area that "felt free" by noting that it was not Klein's internal object world and not Freud's reality object world. Winnicott did not want to be trapped by subjectivity nor by the claims of objective perception. The terms "inner" and "outer" were buzzwords for Winnicott. In psychoanalysis they were tied to dogmas related to "internal fantasy," "reality testing," and the like. He did not find enough room in Klein and Freud for the sort of *experiencing* that felt free.

Inner and outer also had broader connotations clinically and culturally. In informal clinical terms, "internal fantasy" called up the specter of being stuck in one's own world, entombed in a fantasy bubble. Idealism seemed to be mired in various (often productive) solipsisms. The attitude embodied in Hobbes's saying, "The mind knows nothing but what the mind creates," was mathematically fruitful. The various German egologies drilled wells of subjectivity. Nevertheless, there were casualties (eg., the premature deaths of youthful explorers of subjectivity, as well as madness). The subject entrapped by his own webs began to feel unreal to himself. The split between the internal subject on the one hand, and his body as object linked with the material universe on the other, became too much to bear. Human personality collapsed under the strain. Everything inside and outside began to feel alien.

With Freud, the last bastion of personal unity—the ego—was undercut. Freud succeeded only too well in his will to celebrate the mortification of the Western ego, no longer master in its own house. Germanic egology recoiled on itself and the backlash set in. For Jung, subjectivity was an archipelago of centers orchestrated by a grand Self synchronous with the World Spirit, which included materiality in its unfolding project. Winnicott's touch was lighter. He did not want to be boxed in even by Jung's open-ended schemas. No psychoanalytic language that he knew of enabled him to feel free or did justice to the freedom feeling. At the end of his life, Winnicott was still shedding language skins.

The problem pressing on him was how to develop an account of experience that was not boxed in by inner and outer. One gambit was to develop the category of "between" or the "intermediate." Existentialism and phenomenology were well on their way by the time Winnicott began searching for a voice. Martin Buber had developed his own "between" in *I and Thou* (1958). His saying, "All real living is meeting," catches something of the tone Winnicott was searching out.

Nevertheless, Buber was not a pediatrician who became a psychoanalyst. He was not obsessed with the birth and growth of the infant self or the hairbreadth twists and turns of psychosomatic tonalities in sessions. For Winnicott, the "between" was a developmental concept. He was concerned not only with the moment of meeting, but the meeting's biography and evolution. He was concerned with an area of experience that felt free. But the freedom feeling, too, has its developmental movement, its unfolding. Winnicott described a succession of homes for it. The "transitional area" was one of his attempts to let freedom ring, but not his last. Winnicott's attempts to offer a developmental account of personal freedom also underwent development, as he became freer.

## The Subjective Pool and Linking with Experience

Winnicott associated transitional objects and phenomena with *illusion*, which he described as "at the basis of initiation of experience" (1953, p. 14). Transitional objects were also signs of "progress towards experiencing" (p. 6) and signs of an "area of experience." The emphasis here is on *experience* and *experiencing*. What is crucial for Winnicott is linking up with one's own experiencing, that which makes one feel true and real.

When one is most alive and real, can one locate experiencing as simply inside or outside? Inside and outside contribute to aliveness, but is this most precious *x* localizable? I think of St. Paul not knowing where he or mind or body was during a moment of grace. At such a moment, inner and outer did not seem to be relevant categories. Either and both would be too confining.

Winnicott uses the term "illusion" in a positive sense to signify the continuity or lack of rupture in the me-yet-not-me moment, in which self and object are not located in opposition to each other. The infant is not asked to decide whether he has created or discovered the object. The need to objectify or locate self and object would rupture or put the brakes on linking and dispel illusion.

Winnicott was concerned about avoiding promiscuous use of the term "symbol." *X* as a symbol of *Y* (or of *W, Y, Z, A, B, C*) is a form of thought overused in psychoanalysis. Actual experiencing is swallowed up by symbol hunting. Thus while the transitional object may have symbolic meanings, Winnicott insists that "the point of it is not its symbolic value so much as its actuality" (1953, p. 6). Whatever it may stand for, it simply is. The *being* of the transitional object is what counts most. In its being, it stands beneath distinctions that support use of symbol.

In an important sense, "being" is a developmental concept for Winnicott. Whatever being is, it is involved in a process of becoming. A clearer sense of distinction between inner–outer grows in the process of development. For Winnicott, "the term transitional object . . . gives room for the process of becoming able to accept difference and similarity" (ibid.). What is important here is the process of becoming, of developing a sense of division rooted in the unity of being. He speaks of "giving room," of making space for what is not overly restrictive, room to breathe and move, an area of freedom. One *comes through* union, distinction, distinction-in-union, in order to link up with the experiencing that is fed by, yet transcends, dualistic categories.

Winnicott uses organic growth terms, like root and core. "I think there is use for a term for the root of symbolism in time . . ."—*the root of symbolism* (ibid.). He is concerned with an area that underlies and gives rise to the growth of symbolism. His focus is not the symbolic end products themselves, but processes that give birth to symbols.

He finds it important to point out that the term "symbolism" changes meaning, that our understanding of symbolic processes is limited and open, that use of symbols is not uniform. For one group, the wafer in communion *is* the body of Christ, for another it is "a *substitute*, a reminder. . . . Yet in both cases it is a symbol" (ibid.). And in both cases there may be a heightening of experiencing, an intense sense of the meaningfulness of life, a healing of divisions. Whatever the ratio of symbol:real may be, the *experience itself* contributes to the sense of life's holiness.

We may enter into various relationships with illusory experience as it branches into art, religion, or madness. "We can share a respect for *illusory experience*" (1953, p. 3) or form groupings on the basis of such shared experiences. Winnicott calls similarity of illusory experience "a natural root of grouping among human beings." Again, root, a growth term. Winnicott tries to feel his way toward the roots of personality or self and social groupings. He rides experience like a gentle surf board, as far as he can. He wants to live his way toward where we come from, to a growing place or places out of which personality branches. Roots grow throughout the life of a plant and remain vehicles of nourishment for upper areas.

Winnicott does not like being tied down to his own terms. He means to use them flexibly, although there is a gentle fierceness in his writing, something rigorously uncompromising. He is concerned that the experiencing he so values may get compromised or swallowed up by terms. It is growth of experiencing, especially freedom, that concerns him. Terms are pointers and expressive vehicles which may further experiencing, but they are dangerous helpers, easy to solidify or pervert.

It is thus important for him that entrance to the transitional area may take many forms. The vast area between subjectivity and objectivity teems with possibilities. One may link up with transitional experience even from a split-off sliver of self, a self lost in unreality. As an example, Winnicott describes a case in which the only thing that was real for a woman was the unreality of her life (1953, pp. 20–25). Her transitional area of experience masked and gave voice to a sense of something missing at core and roots. *She* was missing. *Real* parenting was missing. Yet she and her mother could appear marvelous. They had so much to offer around the blank core, including real goodness and good intellect.

Her transitional objects in childhood supported her sense of the basic goodness of life and tried to convince her that things were going well, that life was as it should be. In this case, transitional objects supported a lie. They maintained her but threw her off the scent. Insofar as they functioned symbolically, they symbolized something that was not real. They themselves were a reality manqué. What was most real about them was their maintenance of a false self. They blotted out what was missing. The very goodness of her parents made repeated loss of them devastating, until what became most real was the loss that could not be represented and lived. The sense of loss became buried in an image of goodness. It had to be discovered in the patient's inability to live, in her loss of real experiencing.

The patient sank into a "pool of subjectivity" and discovered how she tried to maintain herself over the underlying sense of no-life or no-thing. She hoped the analyst would join up with the inner mother who buoyed her up and protected her from the null dimension. She hoped the analyst would be there as she wished her parents were, so that the missing reality would stay out of reach. If this tendency won out, the analyst would sink into "the general pool of subjectivity" (p. 25) and join up with her mother to protect her from the gap or absence.

Instead she was able to make use of the analyst's silence and his destruction of silence to recognize the silence at her core, the no-parents and no-self. She could experience her need to use the analyst's life to stay above the deadness. She could taste the freedom that recognition of lack provides. She began to treasure the space made possible by real absence, a gap not stuffed by falseness. She could do this because of the real support the analyst gave her to experiencing what was not there. At last the missing real, the no-thing or thing that was not there, became part of real existence. In what was missing, she found room to link up with herself, stretch, and begin to grow.

## From Object to Missing Function

What a distance traversed in Winnicott's paper on transitional experiencing! From discussion of concrete objects clung to by infants to a missing sense of realness in an adult patient. In pathology, objects are used as substitutes for missing functions. In a healthy infant, use of objects carries the real self forward. Winnicott focuses attention on both health and pathology in transitional experiencing.

His example of an adult woman's missing sense of realness announces the central theme of his mature clinical writings: the search for a real or True Self. What he is most vexed with in his adult patients is their missing sense of realness, their failure to link up with, sustain, and live from True Self feeling. Some live in a fantasy world, some in a world that is too realistic. The link between attitudes or functions is missing. The experience of the between, the intermediate area, the wonder of illusion, is deficient. *The first possession* with which Winnicott was concerned was the patient's own, most real and True Self.

His earlier clinical studies tended to emphasize the patient lost in his or her own world, the pool of subjectivity, a fantasy bubble. His later writings tended to emphasize individuals trapped in an overly sane, realistic, objective attitude. In both instances, he laid increasing stress on the developmental function of rage in clearing away obstructions and restrictions. In this effort, "The Use of an Object and Relating Through Identifications" (1969) was a high point (see also Eigen 1981a; 1986, Chapters 4 and 5).

### Use of Object

The apparent simplicity of Winnicott's formulations masked a burgeoning complexity. The simple presence or absence of an object tells little about how the object is used. What is missing in an object may be used to reject what is available. What is present can be used to hide what is missing. One can build a case for or against self or object with whatever is or is not there. Complexity itself can become maddening, a source of rage. How good it is to clear the air of all the directions in which our complicated unrealness can take us. How good it is to explode and clear the air of our oversimplified one-sidedness. Both complexity and one-sidedness can be stultifying.

In his "use of object" paper, Winnicott emphasizes the use of rage or fury or destruction in feeling and becoming free. The personality explodes in reaction to its sense of unreality. The self tries to break out of its fantasy bubble, its one-sidedness or aimless complexity. Rage, fury, destruction burst forth. Everything hinges on the response of the object. If the object survives the attack well enough, the patient gains a new sense of realness and tastes the joy of making use of others for real growth purposes. Genuine appreciation grows. A new dimension of object relating opens.

> From now on the subject says: "Hullo object!" "I destroyed you." "I love you." "You have value for me because of your survival of my destruction of you." "While I am loving you I am all the time destroying you in (unconscious) *fantasy*." (Winnicott 1969, p. 90)

A real sense of contact emerges. The impossible happens. I can really use another for my own true growth. I do not have to falsify myself in order to be with another person. All the destruction in me did not destroy what counts most, but actually made relating more possible. I do not have to develop along the line of false appreciation. I do not have to feel like an ungrateful monster for biting the hand that feeds. We survive each other. We grow with and through each other.

Winnicott emphasizes the importance of the object not retaliating or otherwise collapsing under the onslaught. In face of a bombing, the other acts naturally, remains himself, sees what is happening and is responsively supportive without loss of integrity. The result is subject-to-subject contact and the freedom of using true properties of another for personal growth. In this context, fantasy elaborations of what we take from others is productive, since we keep returning to the place of meeting, clear our minds, start again.

We live between aloneness and intersubjective aliveness. "Between" is not killed by "making use of." These dimensions extend each other. They carry the real self to more and more worlds, more openings, more experience, from light to light.

Winnicott's message certainly sounds like an idealization, a wish. Can such interactions really happen? Is communication without compromise possible? Is such flexible benevolence on the part of another under attack possible? I will answer a qualified yes by making use of Winnicott's concept of "unintegration."

## Unintegration

There is gentle light in Winnicott's writings but also soft darkness and what cannot be called simply light or dark, the intermediate area beyond clear-cut categories. What supports the emergence of the transitional area and objects that shine in transitional experiencing, and what supports the emergence of self facing a useable other, is the hidden capacity of the personality to give itself up and drift.

Freud spoke of "free association" for the patient and "free floating attention" for the analyst. In his letters to Fliess, the capacity to drift is an essential element of his method and language of creativity. In spite of many differences, Winnicott and Freud both felt that creativity made life worth living: "life is worth living or not, according to whether creativity is or is not a part of an individual person's living experience" (Winnicott 1970a, p. 39; also, Eigen 1983a). Freud spoke of riding on the unconscious and letting the horse go where it will. Winnicott emphasized drifting with experiencing or lack of experiencing, the importance of just being ("Be before Do. Be has to develop behind Do" (1970a, p. 42), "Creativity is then the doing that arises out of being" (1970a, p. 39)).

Winnicott shared Freud's belief in the critical importance of unconscious feelings. His emphasis, however, was not the "repressed unconscious" but the fact and feeling of existing "as a basic place to operate from" (1970a, p. 39). He meant existing in a highly personal way, as one's own self. The fierce personalism that stamps Winnicott's work is deeper than and provides relief from one's official personality.

At the end of his life Winnicott was more concerned than ever with new beginnings, with working and living from scratch. *Experiencing* for him meant *creative experiencing*, newness, freshness, aliveness, coming into life for the first time, finding, allowing, stretching, turning oneself over. He dreaded becoming addicted to some official version of himself, let alone someone else's version of selfhood.

> Evidently I must be always fighting to *feel* creative, and this has the disadvantage that if I am describing a simple word like "love", I must start from scratch. (Winnicott 1970a, p. 41)
>
> By creative living I meant not getting killed or annihilated all the time by compliance or by reacting to the world that impinges; I mean seeing everything afresh all the time. I refer to apperception as opposed to perception. (Ibid.)

To see everything afresh all the time, to incessantly start from scratch, meant letting built-up versions of self go so that one can drift. Winnicott likened this to a time in infancy before there were built-up versions of self. He pictured a time of "primary unintegration" when the baby drifted through a variety of states without organizing them in line with specific ego scripts (Winnicott 1945, pp. 149–155; Eigen 1989, 1986, Chapters 4 and 8; Phillips 1988, pp. 78–81). At times the baby "came together" in more unified ways. Integrated units of experience come and go. The baby did not yet feel pressured to harden itself into one or another integrated mold. he did not yet develop the need to rigidly cling to and use integrated moments in chronically defensive ways.

The mother's job was to support responsively the infant's being, so that it could follow its own impulsive doing and its own interests and rhythms, as it passed through unintegration to integration and back again. "In order to be and to have the feeling that one *is*, one must have a predominance of impulse-doing over reactive-doing" (Winnicott 1970a, p. 39). This "impulse-doing" meant acting out of unintegration, forming oneself anew out of the drift, coming together freshly, seeing things with new intensity, throwing oneself into the fullness of experiencing, being gripped by doing that will make life meaningful because it grows out of "a basic place."

We can see how thoroughly Winnicott's commitment to freshness has undergone distillation in his final positive emphasis on unintegration. Much earlier he referred to unintegration as resulting from "failure of technique of child care" (Winnicott 1952, pp. 98–99). At the end of his life, he writes, "It is only here, in this unintegrated state of personality, that that which we describe as creative can appear" (Winnicott 1971a, p. 64). Even earlier Winnicott distinguished unintegration from disintegration, a radically terrifying, catastrophic state. In his later paper, he also warns that creative use of unintegration hinges on sensed environmental support, otherwise it may go on too long and pass into disintegration.

### *Unintegration and Madness*

In a sense, unintegration refers to an innate capacity to unhinge oneself, to let links that become chains drop away. when Winnicott introduced the notion of primary unintegration, he mentioned in passing how sanity can be imprisoning.

> There is . . . much sanity that has a symptomatic quality, being charged with fear or denial of madness, fear or denial of the innate capacity of every human being to become unintegrated. (1945, p. 150)

A posthumously published paper, "Fear of Breakdown" (1974), represents the most definitive and beautiful crystallization of Winnicott's mature views on madness. Adult fear of breakdown refers to breakdown that already happened. The infant undergoes agonies which its equipment cannot process. Experiencing is life for Winnicott, but it also may present too much, too soon (recall that for Freud, the primal trauma was flooding). Sensitivity is taxed with more than it can bear and manage. We have to grow equipment to process what is too much for us. We have to become the kind of beings that catch up with our breakdowns, not so much to master them as to enable experiencing to develop.

Early parenting tries to compensate, as much as possible, for the infant's insufficient equipment. The mother does a great deal of processing of what the infant is going through for the infant. She holds the situation open until the infant has time and ability to accommodate its own experiencing capacity. She helps the infant over periods of breakdown. She helps her child develop a certain flexibility (not simply compliance) in face of incapacity and gives her child time to recover and grow.

The situation is complicated by the fact that the parent inevitably adds to the infant's burden (and vice versa). At any time, too much of the wrong thing or too little of the right thing may be present. The mother may inadvertently tax the equipment she means to ease and cause breakdowns which she tries to repair; her own equipment may be sorely taxed as well. What is crucial is that personal care survives breakdown. The mother's devotion comes through her own and the infant's incapacity. She is the kind of being one can forgive and link up with after the storm or blackout. The thread of personal being survives and may be strengthened by disruptions, as new areas of experiencing continue to open up.

Typical Winnicottian therapy addresses "the schizoid spot" that develops to compensate for persistent failure in personal care (Winnicott 1971b, p. 67). Where the link with one's most basic self and mother cannot survive disruption and breakdown, the individual "cures" himself not simply by use of repression or splitting but by means of serious dissociations from himself and others. Depersonalization/derealization not only signals breakdown but results from it. As Freud indicated, the building up of delusional compensations is an attempt to maintain or regain a sense of continuity, an attempt to continue or start again: self–other connectedness survives horrific devastation, especially devastations tied to vicissitudes of self–other connectedness/disconnectedness.

The sense of unreality acts not only as a protective cocoon or distancing operation. In the case of Winnicott's patients, it is also a goad, an irritant. They are appalled as their life passes by unlived. Whether they are withdrawn or are very active and keep up the appearance of living, they are compelled to bear witness that something crucial is missing in their sense of self. They are bothered by being dissociated from themselves and others. They are basically sensitive beings who are bothered by their success or failure in attempts to immunize themselves from their sensitivity (Eigen 1990).

Winnicott's therapy created an atmosphere in which two people could be alone together without all the time trying to make sense of what was or was not happening. Developing a capacity for play (transitional experiencing) went along with tolerating unintegration and madness.

> The person we are trying to help needs a new experience in a specialized setting. The experience is one of a non-purposive state, as one might say a sort of ticking over of the unintegrated personality. I referred to this as formlessness in the case description. (Winnicott 1971a, p. 55)

> In the relaxation that belongs to trust and to acceptance of the professional reliability of the therapeutic setting . . . there is room, for the idea of unrelated thought sequences which the analyst will do well to accept as such, not assuming the existence of a significant thread (Ibid.)

One does not have to irritably reach after facts or meaning or anything at all. One can just be and grow into and out of just being. One can be missing. The great secret of being missing, so taboo, can be experienced. One can relax into not being there and stop pretending. One can stop forcing oneself this way or that. The possibility of being truly alive—free—in the presence of another person emerges.

Winnicott always emphasized the importance of non-intrusiveness on the part of the analyst. He was all too conscious of the way analysts imposed their dogmas on patients, substituting one sort of straitjacket for another. Patients were prone to be compliant/rebellious, and too often, therapy provided ample opportunity to continue a reactive style in more subtle ways. In Winnicott's writings, nonintrusiveness is often linked with the analyst's silence and capacity to wait. He wanted to give individuals every chance to get beneath reactive styles, to unintegrate, to grow out of chaos or no-thing. He wanted to give them every chance to be free.

He wrote that when he was younger he was more prone to say clever things, but in time he learned the wisdom of silence so that the patient can find himself. Nevertheless, it is also clear that Winnicott talked, and could talk a lot, and could be directive (presumably as part of "holding" or "provision"). Winnicott indicated that he did not remain silent long if he felt the patient would be injured by too much silence. He might say something to let the person know he was there or become aware of limitations of Winnicott's understanding. Silence can foster a sense of omniscience which speaking dispels (Eigen 1989; 1986, Chapter 8).

Winnicott also indicated that a patient may benefit from displays of the analyst's hate and madness. There are instances when what is missing is the realness of hate (Winnicott 1949). Nothing may seem real or believable until hate is real and believable. At times what is missing is the realness of madness. Some of the best, most surprising, and usable things an analyst can say may at first seem crazy to the patient (and possibly the analyst), yet ultimately make the patient (and possibly the analyst) feel more real (Winnicott 1971b, pp. 73–74).

Winnicott wrote a lot about the craziness of secretly being the opposite sex (1971b, pp. 72–85; 1971c, pp. 119–137). We all have unconscious cross-sexual identifications which can lead to fear and confusion and feel like a kind of madness. But there are more unbearable and nameless agonies, more formless dreads (Winnicott 1974). The analyst who can live at the cutting edge of his own madness may enter into a creative and redeeming relationship with madness (Green 1975).

He may provide immunizing doses of madness in such a way that the patient begins to link up with the unnameably unbearable and develop a relationship with the horrifying holes that scare experiencing away.

The analyst's use of madness, if placed in the service of growth processes and not simply or mainly narcissistic masturbation, enables the patient to link up with what the latter supposed could not be tolerated. Experiencing can link up with itself across periods of breakdown, the more so insofar as one *owns* madness (Winnicott's transitional *owning*) and learns the art of enabling it to contribute to overall movement. As Milner emphasized, what seems mad (and perhaps *is* mad) can prove saving (1987; see also Eigen 1973, 1986). Without madness one cannot be free, although literal insanity is terrifyingly enslaving (Eigen 1984, 1986, 1990).

Writing about transitional experiencing was one step in Winnicott's growth toward being able to admit and use madness, to the point of feeling freer through it and becoming more radically helpful. to the overly operational or objective attitude, transitional experience must seem a bit mad. Similarly, the subjectively enclosed individual might idealize transitional experiencing but actually find it threatening and disorganizing. Both must let go of one-sided madness to tolerate the sort of paradoxical madness Winnicott treasured, the madness associated with creative living and the birth of culture. The letting go Winnicott described in object usage and unintegration is part of the mad growth that makes life worthwhile. Through it, our sense of the mystery of freedom deepens.

It is no accident that two of Winnicott's most mature sympathizers recently published books with madness in the title (Green 1986; Milner 1987). My own book, *The Psychotic Core* (1986), must be considered in this category. Late in life Winnicott wrote, "I was sane and through analysis and self-analysis I achieved some measure of insanity" (1964a, p. 450; quoted by Phillips 1988, p. 152). In the closing sentence of *Winnicott* (1988), Phillips remarks that "his measure of insanity is, I think, an inspiration."

## The Incommunicado Self

Winnicott's most well known and apparently valued contributions revolve around his emphasis on the infant–mother dyad: there is no such thing as an infant, but an infant–mother psychosomatic field. The quality of the surrounding and supporting milieu is the crucial medium for development of the psychosomatic life of the child. Throughout his career, Winnicott stressed the contribution of the ordinary good-enough mother and what can happen should the environmental provision be lacking. Elements of child care that foster personal growth were his persistent concern. It is natural for practitioners to pick up Winnicott's emphasis on the "holding environment" in clinical situations.

It is also natural for practitioners to do a double take when, in the midst of his interactive emphasis, they come upon passages which claim that the most precious core of self is noninteractive—permanently incommunicado. These are Winnicott's most passionate passages, almost pleas or prayers. They contain his most religious language.

> [E]ach individual is an isolate, permanently non-communicating, permanently unknown, in fact unfound (Winnicott 1963, p. 187)

> At the centre of each person is an incommunicado element, and this is sacred and most worthy of preservation. . . .Rape, and being eaten by cannibals, these are mere bagatelles as compared with the violation the self's core, the alteration of the self's central elements by communication seeping through the defences. For me this would be the sin against the self. (Ibid.)

*The* sin against self: communication with the core of cores, the self beyond reach, the self which is essentially private, one's psychic heartbeat. This is Winnicott's moral imperative: Do not reach what must be unreachable. Do not seep into the core of another person so as to steal him from himself.

Not many practitioners have taken this teaching of Winnicott to heart. Someone as close to Winnicott as Guntrip tried to brush it aside. Guntrip never accepted Winnicott's positive valuation of aggression (Guntrip 1975; Eigen 1981b, 1986), but he also rejected Winnicott's emphasis on the essential incommunicado self, a permanently noncommunicating core of cores (Guntrip 1969; Eigen 1973). A self that depends on an interpersonal matrix for its development—how can what is most precious about it be outside the range of human communication? A self that must not be found, that requires hiddenness—this did not sit well with the "neediness" Guntrip felt most basic. for Guntrip, Winnicott was not Winnicottian enough.

However, the problem was that Winnicott was all too Winnicottian. He fought everything else. He made use of everything else. It is hard to think of Winnicott as a fierce fighter because he was a gentle soul, so light of touch. His writing melts in one's mouth like butter. Yet he gave voice to his own brand of biblical reality in developmental terms, as uncompromising as a prophet.

The incommunicado self is the center of his work, the still, quiet center. Everything else revolves around it, grows out of it, guards it, extends it. Transitional experiencing, object usage, and unintegration link up with the unlinkable. They open a path of experience and expression for what is most true and real and free about oneself, a kind of vector of freedom, a thread of personal creativeness. Winnicott's language expresses, opens, and discovers waves of what is most precious and personal, the core that must not be betrayed. He finds a way to make people feel pulsations of the core in everyday life, in analytic sessions, in cultural work.

Guntrip was dismayed by Winnicott's insistence on an incommunicado core, in part because it reminded him of Freud's id, which was basically out of contact with the outside world. Indeed, Winnicott knowingly used Freudian locutions to paint a picture of a state of being prior to awareness of externality. Winnicott's insistence on a sacred, silent core was his version of the primordial beyond contact.

Freud had a passionately personal relationship to his concepts. But for the sake of formal presentation and scientific respectability, he followed acceptable epistemological guidelines. We never know the id and the rest of the repressed unconscious directly, only by inference and hypothesis. If it is a reality, the id is as out of reach as external things-in-themselves. By contrast, Winnicott's assertion of a core-out-of-contact self is meant as more than a bow to Kantian considerations, and is certainly not meant to appease canons of scientific respectability. It is an expression of personal faith, an attempt to preserve room for the most precious point of existence.

Winnicott described freedom partly as flexibility of defensive organization, and he recognized the usefulness of an adaptive false self. But he also wrote that for each person there must be a place of no compromise.

> I suppose that it would be true in a general way to say that although a compromise is usually possible in everyday life, there is no compromise for each individual in some area that is chosen for a special treatment. It may be science or religion or poetry or games. In the chosen area there is no room for compromise. (Winnicott 1964b, p. 70)

Winnicott (spontaneously, through creative struggle, over years—his "secret" continuity across chasms) built an expressive fence around the core of cores with his transitional area, true self/false self, use of object, unintegration, use of madness. For Winnicott these were not concepts cut off from experiencing but expressed what for him made life feel most real. May we not say that here is his chosen area where there is no room for compromise?

## More Than the Heart Can Bear

Winnicott does not underestimate the complexity of the situation in which we find ourselves. In order to use objects or madness and live creatively, we must have the equipment to do so. Psychophysical equipment may be damaged from birth or from something lacking in the environmental provision. It may suffer from immaturity which in some way remains chronic. Depth-psychology tries to enable growth of psychic equipment as much as possible and develop better compensations insofar as equipment is irreparable.

One does not help another individual find/grow equipment for creative living without sacrifice. Winnicott repeatedly speaks about the importance of the analyst growing the capacity to wait (responsive waiting, waiting-in-aliveness). The analyst "must" outgrow cleverness for his own satisfaction and cultivate the silence that lets the core of core do its work. At the same time, the analyst "must" act naturally, like the ordinary good-enough mother who (for a time) spontaneously molds herself along the infant's developmental lines. Such paradoxical demands permeate analytic work. The analyst must bear and enjoy the tension of paradoxical living, as paradoxical truths shift from stage to stage.

The ordinary good-enough parent bears a lot. Analyst and parent alike suppress themselves in order to help children and patients find their paths. To a very significant extent, the helper dampens himself and becomes compliant and uncreative in order to be a good-enough helper. Winnicott notes that this is partly offset by the satisfaction gotten for a job well done. Our identifications with the helped one and helping process partly compensate for temporary or long-term loss of self.

> Where we are bringing up children or starting babies off as creative individuals in a world of actual facts, we do have to be uncreative and compliant and adaptive; but, on the whole, we get round this and find it does not kill us because of our identification with these new people who need us if they too are to achieve creative living. (Winnicott 1970a, p. 54)

People who have undergone grave, deadening processes in order to survive cannot take too much life in the analyst. The analyst learns to keep stimulating aspects of the session within semitolerable bounds. If necessary, he becomes dead enough for the patient to feel safe enough to come alive more. As the patient is able to tolerate more aliveness, the analyst may allow his own personality more play. In therapy, analyst and patient must grow the equipment to bear and ultimately enrich each other.

Yet even if the analyst must sit on himself and make it look easy, muted aliveness remains. In some way the analyst finds ways of surviving the impact of deadening processes, even those self-imposed for therapeutic reasons. The core of cores remains unaltered, hallowed and hallowing. It resurfaces and continues being, quietly glowing beyond the necessary darkness. The inherent creativeness that makes life worth living for the analyst, suitably modulated, finds ways to let the patient discover and reach for his own openings.

Winnicott firmly believed that we need to attack goodness (1970b, pp. 262–268). He also believed that we deeply wish for the survival of the goodness we attack. We need to attack falseness, compliance, hypocrisy, and we hope there is enough to us and our lives that something really good and true wins out. Yet that goodness, too, must be tested. Can it truly endure? Is goodness indeed more basic than evil or is it one more phoney layer aching for exposure? Can the good take our hatred of it as well as our love?

The pressure the analyst is under is immense. An ultimate aim of the analysis is the real survival of goodness. This requires sacrifice of personality and natural inclinations. It also requires maintenance of basic aliveness and spontaneity. The analyst must rein himself in, yet survive his own discipline. The analyst must survive being an analyst. Paradox is all!

The fact that mutual adaptiveness, recognition, and appreciation characterize mother–infant relationships from earlier on than previously believed does not mitigate the fact that the mother modulates use of her equipment to work with the infant's capabilities. Devotion enables the mother to find ways of being spontaneously that are usable by the infant. The fact of the matter is that the mother cannot do with the infant what she can do with other adults. Yet there is something she can get from being with a baby that slips away from adult living. A loss, a gain.

The mother grows equipment she did not know she had by playing down well-used equipment. As her child grows, old equipment comes back ready for use in new ways. Every analysis that goes deep, long, and far combines these processes. The analyst must grow the equipment usable for the particular analysis at hand. Who knows what twists and turns of self this might take? Let us say it—who knows how he will have to twist himself out of shape for a particular person who could not bear to be with him otherwise? Still the analyst's ruthlessness and madness also will contribute to the patient's growth, if real creativeness is to survive destruction, if aliveness is to come through—if goodness is to stand the test of the analysis and survive the destructiveness of patient and analyst alike.

Similar considerations may operate in our relations with colleagues. Will our professional milieu survive us and we it if we make our fullest and truest offerings? To what extent do professional interchanges support transitional experiencing and object usage and contribute to real growth of personality and culture? We need each other to bounce off, fight with, communicate and noncommunicate with, interact with, gain real confirmation/disconfirmation. But how much exposure can we bear? How much do we dare or have the right to dare?

Winnicott's first major heart attack came shortly after his father died, and this was followed by a long-needed divorce. Apparently Winnicott's psyche-soma was unable to hold and process the affective impact at hand without explosive collapse. The timing of his coronary, linked as it was to a revolution of his life, appears to establish a somatic vulnerability tied in with Winnicott's exquisite sensitivity.

As a result of the crises, he resumed his life on better footing and made enormous strides on personal and professional fronts. *True Self* activity increased. It is no accident that he associated the True Self with heart and breathing:

> The True Self comes from the aliveness of the body tissues and the working of body functions, including the heart's action and breathing. (Winnicott 1960, p. 148)

In this quotation one might substitute "especially" for "including."

Near the end of his life, Winnicott was even more vulnerable somatically, partly because of a fragile, aging body, but also because of his need to be alive in experiencing, which at times left him too open. His sensitivity could be too much for his psyche-soma to bear.

When I saw him in the middle 1960's, he told me he was considering speaking in New York. He repeatedly asked how he would be received. Clearly he was worried about the New York psychoanalytic climate. It was as if he was afraid to believe that they could really receive what he had to say, that equipment to make use of his work grew out there. He had hopes, but he was aware of his vulnerability, although he had practice in his own world being odd man out. I was flattered by his anxious questions but I was only a graduate student. He treated me like an equal, like *someone*.

*I* would be receptive. *I* would love to hear him talk. I knew others in *my* boat who would, too. But what did I know about the particular world he addressed with his fears and hopes. At that moment, my own oddness in graduate school vanished. I saw his awkward intensity and thought, "He's like me. It's all right to be the kind of person I am." He moved around the room, found an edge of the couch and doubled over, reaching for a way of conveying something about the kind of work he did. He wanted it to be alive. He did not seem to care much if he looked "foolish"—he was digging into something, being true to an experience, a life work, an area of discovery. He was giving me permission to be myself, so much as I dared. Now I'm tempted to say that in his anxious state he was expressing a foreboding, a premonition.

He came to New York and gave his "use of object" paper in 1968. I am told he was attacked and did not defend himself; true to the mother-analyst's position in this paper, he did not counterattack or retaliate. He went to his hotel room and had a heart attack. The tension between hope and fear, between ruthlessness and waiting, must have mounted to a breaking point once again. He was lionized posthumously.

Winnicott continued working creatively three more years until his death. His prayer, "May I be alive when I die" (C. Winnicott 1978), pertains to more than physical death. It refers to his need for sensitive aliveness in the midst of nothingness, attack, catastrophe, madness, and a variety of agonies. Winnicott sometimes paid a high price for his need for aliveness, but it gave as well as perhaps took everything. (Winnicott's title for his autobiography was, *Not Less than Everything* (C. Winnicott 1978).)

We do not know to what extent or in what ways his vision of the self's attempt to burst shells and find real experiencing was fulfilled within his lifetime or after his passing. Clearly, he did not always survive the destruction that greeted him, his own or others. But his vision of survival is a legacy. In one of his last pieces, while speaking of the monarchy, Winnicott writes:

> The survival of the thing (here, monarchy) makes it valuable, and enables people of all kinds and ages to see that the will to destruction had nothing to do with anger—it had to do with love of a primitive kind, and the destruction occurs in the unconscious fantasy, or in the personal dream that belongs to being asleep. It is in the personal inner psychic reality that the thing is destroyed. In waking life, survival of the object, whatever it is, brings a sense of relief and a new sense of confidence. It is now clear that *because of their own properties* things can survive, in spite of our dream, in spite of the backcloth of destruction in our unconscious fantasy. The world now begins to exist as a place in its own right; a place to live in, not as a place to fear or to be

complied with or to be lost in, or to be dealt with only in day-dream or fantasy indulgence (1970b, pp. 263–264)

Here is the voice of a master, the ring of simple nobility. It comes from and touches the heart. The living of this vision—finding/creating its realness—involves risks which require equipment to support the latter. The achievement Winnicott depicts is made possible by evolution of psychosomatic equipment sufficient to support it, at least for moments, then across moments. One's equipment may fail and leave one stranded in aliveness too much for the heart to bear. What is alive in one's work may be passed on to others. Surely something of Winnicott's "area of no compromise" is growing for us today.

## References

Buber, M. 1958. *I and Thou*. New York: Charles Scribner's Sons.

Eigen, M. 1973. Abstinence and the schizoid ego. *International Journal of Psycho-Analysis* 54:493–497.

______. 1981a. The area of faith in Winnicott, Lacan and Bion. *International Journal of Psycho-Analysis* 62:413–433.

______. 1981b. Guntrip's analysis with Winnicott. *Contemporary Psychoanalysis* 17:103–117.

______. 1983a. A note on the structure of Freud's theory of creativity. *Psychoanalytic Review* 70:41–45.

______. 1983b. Dual union or undifferentiation? A critique of Marion Milner's view of the sense of psychic creativeness. *International Review of Psycho-Analysis* 10:415–428.

______. 1984. On demonized aspects of the self. In *Evil: Self and Culture*, M. C. Nelson and M. Eigen, eds. New York: Human Sciences Press (Plenum Press).

______. 1986. *The Psychotic Core*. New York: Jason Aronson.

______. 1989. Aspects of omniscience. In *The Facilitating Environment: Clinical Applications of Winnicott's Theory*, M. G. Fromm and B. L. Smith, eds. Madison, Conn.: International Universities Press.

______. 1990. *Coming Through the Whirlwind: The Sensitive Self and Rebirth Processes in Psychotherapy*. Unpublished manuscript.

Green, A. 1975. The analyst, symbolization and absence in the analytic setting (On changes in analytic practice and analytic experience). *International Journal of Psycho-Analysis* 56:1–22.

______. 1986. *On Private Madness*. London: Hogarth Press.

Guntrip, H. 1969. *Schizoid Phenomena, Object-Relations and the Self*. New York: International Universities Press.

______. 1975. My experience of analysis with Fairbairn and Winnicott. *International Review of Psycho-Analysis* 2:145–156.

Milner, M. 1987. *The Suppressed Madness of Sane Men*. London: Tavistock.

Phillips, A. 1988. *Winnicott*. Cambridge, Mass.: Harvard University Press.

Winnicott, C. 1978. D. W. Winnicott: a reflection. In *Between Reality and Fantasy*, S. Grolnick et al., eds. New York: Jason Aronson.

Winnicott, D. W. 1945. Primitive emotional development. *International Journal of Psycho-Analysis* 26. Reprinted in *D. W. Winnicott: Collected Papers* (New York: Basic Books, 1958).

———. 1949. Hate in the countertransference. *International Journal of Psycho-Analysis* 30. Reprinted in *D. W. Winnicott: Collected Papers* (New York: Basic Books, 1958).

———. 1952. Anxiety associated with insecurity. In *D. W. Winnicott: Collected Papers*. New York: Basic Books, 1958.

———. 1953. Transitional objects and transitional phenomena. *International Journal of Psycho-Analysis* 34:89–97. Reprinted in *Playing and Reality* (New York: Basic Books, 1971).

———. 1954. Mind and its relation to the psyche-soma. *British Journal of Medical Psychology* 27:201–209. Reprinted in *D. W. Winnicott: Collected Papers* (New York: Basic Books, 1958).

———. 1960. Ego distortion in terms of True and False Self. In *The Maturational Processes and the Facilitating Environment*. New York: International Universities Press, 1965.

———. 1963. Communicating and not communicating leading to a study of certain opposites. In *The Maturational Processes and the Facilitating Environment*. New York: International Universities Press, 1965.

———. 1964a. Book review: *Memories, Dreams, Reflections* by C. G. Jung. *International Journal of Psycho-Analysis* 45:450–455.

———. 1964b. The concept of the false self. In *Home Is Where We Start From*. New York: W. W. Norton, 1986.

———. 1969. The use of an object and relating through identifications. *International Journal of Psycho-Analysis* 50:711–716. Reprinted in *Playing and Reality* (New York: Basic Books, 1971).

———. 1970a. Living creatively. In *Home Is Where We Start From*. New York: W. W. Norton, 1986.

———. 1970b. The place of the monarchy. In *Home Is Where We Start From*. New York: W. W. Norton, 1986.

———. 1971a. Playing: creative activity and the search for self. In *Playing and Reality*. New York: Basic Books, 1971.

———. 1971b. Creativity and its origins. In *Playing and Reality*. New York: Basic Books, 1971.

———. 1971c. Interrelating apart from instinctual drives and in terms of cross-identifications. In *Playing and Reality*. New York: Basic Books, 1971.

———. 1974. Fear of breakdown. *International Review of Psycho-Analysis* 1:103–107.

# Transitional Phenomena in Clinical Practice: The Toad Is Always Real

Lena B. Ross

In "Poetry," Marianne Moore entertains the paradox of "imaginary gardens with real toads in them" (Bain, Beatty, and Hunter 1977, p. 583). This phrase elegantly captures the combination of the real and imaginal that poetry seeks to grasp. It is in the vision of the artist that the extraordinary can be seen in the ordinary. Through the vision, for example, of Ernest Hemingway or Diane Arbus, a river or café or a middle-class suburban home can be seen to contain terrors, depths, grotesqueries, apparent through the eye of the artist.

Similarly, patients in psychotherapy live with "real toads," the negative experiences they have had with others in their lives when they were small, around which grew "imaginary gardens" of complexes. In turn, these complexes often form a paralyzing context of behaviors and thinking toward both the internal and the external world. But what has grown in the imagination can change in the imagination: the task of the therapist becomes identification of the real toad at the center of this garden; then, the loosening up of the strictures imposed by the old

**Lena B. Ross**, Ph.D., is a psychotherapist in private practice in New York City, and a senior candidate at the C. G. Jung Institute of New York. She has published articles on the psychological study of fairy tales and is presently writing a book on the connection between written fairy tales and the growth of consciousness.

reality; and finally, mediating a new identity. The therapist, as Moore's "literalist of the imagination," can begin the disentanglement of the real toad from the garden of complexes grown to deal with it.

There is a passage on the way from the spell of the real toad through the imaginary garden to a new identity. Jacques Lacan describes the passage in this way: "There, where it was just now, there where it was for a while, between an extinction that is still glowing and a birth that is retarded, 'I' can come into being" (Lacan 1977, p. 300). The passage can be described as transitional—"the passage from one condition or action to another," as the *Oxford Dictionary of English Etymology* defines transitional. In some languages, such as Old English, the transitional case expresses motion toward. Transitional, then, would appear to have an implied function: to carry one over to a different state of being. Objects, or phenomena, would also be necessary to carry the perceptions and to allow the two worlds of the real and imaginal to combine and create something different.

**"Nick"**

I had been working with Nick, a man of about forty, for a year and a half; there was a frustrating, stasislike quality to the work. In the beginning, Nick spent most sessions talking about "Mary," a woman friend of the same age with whom he was obsessed and toward whom he had a projection of great strength and tenacity involving his view of her power, talent, and beauty. A dream from early in Nick's work was the following:

> Dream: *Two cobras are winding up my body, trying to enter my anus. I am able to keep them out but a woman who is my boss in the dream tells me not to be worried about the snakes, they won't hurt me. I am frozen with fear.*

The feelings of this dream reflected my experience of the therapy with Nick. He seemed frozen, with no sense of a separate self. By entering the therapy, he had consciously invited penetration, yet unconsciously was strongly defended against it. I sensed both how powerful I seemed to him and at the same time how threatening was any potential entry into his psychic space. I soon recognized that, to one degree or another, this characterized all of his relationships with women.

In that early dream there were two cobras, symbolic of an attempt on the part of the unconscious to manifest something new. In addition,

Nick was able to keep his anus closed. The entry of the snakes into his anus would have indicated an incestuous, unbroken cycling of energy, rather than an ability to keep the potential new manifestation flowing out toward consciousness. Whatever the dream indicated as new, however, was still very far from consciousness. The paralyzing fear in the dream, as well as the "lies" of the boss woman, felt far more present in our work.

Nick could only experience himself as alive through a woman. Information about him came very slowly in the beginning, interspersed around long, meandering tales of his interactions with Mary. He would tell me what she did, how she looked in great detail (he described her as though her beauty were goddesslike); she regaled him with detailed stories about the men in her life, despite his attempts to make her stop by telling her how much he loved her and how painful this was to hear.

In his life, Nick's energy had been captured by Mary, a woman whom he experienced as hypnotizing her prey, like a cobra. Nick had handed over to Mary a substantial amount of his inheritance. He did little day and night, except wait for her calls and the errands on which she would send him. I felt the need to act as an opposing pole in Nick's life, one which would not allow him to sink into oblivion as a slave in service to Mary.

Having worked before with men's obsessions toward women, I was familiar with the feelings that men ordinarily experienced. Nothing that I had previously encountered, however, prepared me for this level of total paralysis of life or unreality of perception. Most obsessional material of this sort usually involves goddesslike projections onto the mother, projections that are later replicated with other women. None had ever had this peculiarly paralyzing quality. The scale of the affect contained the kind of total negation of human life seen in ancient myths of a human encounter with a god (e.g., flood mythology, Niobe and her children). Mary and her human scale seemed too insignificant to promote this godlike affect. With this puzzle in mind, I began to explore with Nick the affects involved. He then began to tell me about feelings aroused in him by thoughts of his grandmother.

Nick associated her with feelings of repulsion and horror, not at all the typical memories of one's grandmother. He was not quite sure why he had these visceral reactions to her memory. He told me of being left with her from about age two through eleven, weekend after weekend. He had no clear idea why he was left but assumed his parents had gone away on trips. Then he told me that "I slept with her in her bed—I had to." Although he had no concrete memory of sexual abuse (in fact, no real memory at all of sleeping with her, only of the bare fact that he did), it was clear to me from the sweep of the affects related to grandmother as well as the amnesia regarding concrete events with her that sexual abuse may actually have taken place, that she may have petted and played with him in a sexually arousing way.

It was not difficult to get from these events and feelings to his current state of an unlived life, with his energy bound up in Mary. In the snake dream, the threat is the penetration and possession by the phallic mother, that aspect of the archetype that can penetrate and possess one's insides. In order to protect against it, Nick's energy must be concentrated on locking his anal muscles to prevent entry. Symbolically, this shows how his spontaneity was crippled by the phallic mother. His total domination in a psychological and physical way by the grandmother explained much more than such a relationship with the mother would have. The grandmother represents an image of the negative aspect of the archetype—an archaic and frightening piece of psyche. Old beyond imagining to a young boy, any instinctual physical responses to her in bed would seem repulsive to him and about him, as well.

In *The Virgin and the Gipsy*, D. H. Lawrence describes a grandmother like Nick's. In the novella, the grandmother's son is transfixed inside the son-lover relationship; Lawrence, who wrestled in his own life with a similar powerful relation to his mother, was well aware of this archetypal power which could hold a man in its grip. Here, Granny controlled the household with an iron grip, but with a pretense of weakness; her relationship to her son was psychically and emotionally incestuous. Lawrence describes her in this way: "The ancient, toad-like obscene *will* in the old woman, was fearful once you saw it: a toad-like self-will that was godless, and less than human! It belonged to the old, enduring race of toads . . . and it made one feel that Granny would never die" (Lawrence 1968, p. 96). Lawrence captures here the feeling of the larger and deeper scale of the archetype.

Nick's relationship with Mary had aspects reminiscent of the myth of Actaeon and Diana. In this Graeco-Roman myth, Actaeon is wandering aimlessly in the forest. He comes across the goddess Diana bathing in her sacred grove. Transfixed by the sight of the naked goddess, whom Ovid describes as standing "head and shoulders above all the rest" of her nymphs, Actaeon cannot bring himself to move. Diana then vengefully turns him into a stag as punishment for seeing her naked (it was forbidden for a mortal man to see any goddess naked except Aphrodite). She knows that his own dogs will hunt him down and tear him to pieces now that he is no longer human. Actaeon retains his human mind so that he may suffer more fully.

Nick's inability to resist "seeing" Mary in her "naked" state (emotionally and psychologically) led to his continual dismemberment by his own raging libidinal instincts, which had gone over in service to her. Nick had wandered into the force field of the archetype in an unmediated way. He suffered a deep sense of guilt, not from an oedipal/incest issue, but rather from the much more deeply rooted archetypal pattern in which he was engulfed, human trespass into the archetypal sphere.

The dogs in the myth were Actaeon's friends and hunting companions; they are seized by the power of the goddess and turned to her service to destroy Actaeon because he saw her naked. Nick's own instinctual life, meant to serve him, was seized by the power of the destructive aspect of the Great Goddess archetype as embodied and mediated to him by grandmother. Only in service to this archetype, then, replicated in his relationship with Mary, could he find punishment for the dual sin of seeing the archetype in this raw, unmediated way and of feeling both aroused and repulsed by it. In Mary, he found the ideal punisher: for all her outward beauty, she reminded Nick of his grandmother.

In reflecting on Nick's situation in this way, I began to see the fated aspect of his life. Actaeon wandered into the forest on that particular day and came across Diana bathing. This was not something he had planned; in Ovid's words, he wandered "through the unfamiliar woods with unsure footsteps and enter[ed] Diana's grove; for so fate would have it" (Ovid, *Metamorphoses*, III, 175–176). Once there, Actaeon was drawn to the sight of the naked goddess and, fascinated, could no more remove himself than could Nick, a small child in the bed of his grandmother.

Here is Ovid's description of Actaeon's plight after Diana turned him into a stag: " 'Oh, woe is me!' he tries to say; but no words come. He groans—the only speech he has—and tears course down his changeling cheeks. . . . What is he to do? Shall he go home . . . or shall he stay skulking in the woods? Shame blocks one course and fear the other" (Ovid, *Metamorphoses*, III, 201–205). These same affects left Nick a victim: like Actaeon, he was vulnerable to attack by his own "dogs." I wondered whether the fact of my seeing this and reflecting on it could in any way inductively alter that early, fated aspect. Perhaps by enabling the energies to constellate differently, Nick's fate might be returned to his own hands, rather than his remaining vulnerable to the self-destructive aspect of a fate dependent solely on the autonomy of the archetype.

It was not only Mary who had this effect on Nick: he experienced his mother, sister, *all* women as more powerful than he. Our early interactions were dominated by powerful and puzzling affects of paralysis and disgust. Nick had developed the ability to sniff out a woman's strength and then *lose* to it, sacrificing his own desires in service to fusing with her. This represented a perfect masochistic defense which masked deep, paralyzing, and unconscious rage. With Mary, it seemed to be her own grandiose valuation of her physical beauty that she needed to have reflected continuously. I found myself becoming caught countertransferentially around intellectual issues. I found that if I didn't stick with feeling, I could be seduced into displaying my "superior" knowledge and thus further act out the phallic mother. But when I caught the countertransference, which was a "satisfying" feeling of being "right" or "winning," I could begin to bring these feelings back to our sessions and reopen what our interaction had been, no matter how seemingly small the subject.

It was after a year and a half of this kind of work that the following dream came to Nick:

> Dream: *I am sitting at a lunch counter. There is a man to my left, an older friend, and there is a woman to my right. On the counter is a little golden-yellow frog. It is young and we are playing with it like a kitten or puppy, petting it.*
>
> *The man and I know a huge tree in a forest—6 or 8 feet in diameter—it has gnarly bark and hollows in it. We decide to take the frog there and put it in a hollow in this tree—there is water dripping in the hollows. The woman protests, she wants to keep it to play with but the man and I protect the frog and take it to the tree. The woman leaves. We put the frog in a safe place in the tree.*

The transitional phenomena demonstrated in the dream, which I shall discuss below, reached deep into the heart of Nick's process. It was this dream also which gave me faith that the individuation process was stronger than the negative mother in her worst aspect, which had captured this man's whole instinctual life. The two-ness motif, represented by the snakes in the earlier dream, was an attempt on the part of the psyche to offer some kind of threshold experience. The two snakes held out the promise that something new would emerge. This promise, however, was not to be fulfilled that early in the therapy.

The frog dream, however, was different. The setting is at a lunch counter, indicating the possibility of integrating transitional material (lunch is the midday meal). The counter recalls the etymology of "trans": the Latin *trans* is related to the Sanscrit *tiram*, brink and *tar*, to put across. So at the opening of the dream, Nick stands poised at a brink—but before that can be crossed, something needs to be taken care of. The little frog must be put somewhere safe to prevent it from being toyed with, where it can grow, protected. The tree symbolizes *the emergence of a transitional object while Nick was still in the grip of the negative mother*, a transitional object capable of containing and promoting the transmutation of the frog.

The frog itself constitutes a symbol of transition. An amphibian, it is a tadpole at birth, living in water; it transforms into a land-living frog. Folklore provides further transformation: frogs turn into men or women. The golden color of the frog in the dream raises the symbol to a different level, since gold or yellow implies the capability of transfiguration into the highest form.

Nick associated the woman in the dream to Mary. Mary toys with Nick, keeps him as a plaything; similarly, the woman in the dream wants to keep the frog on the counter for her pleasure, preventing its passage to a place where it could grow. This represents the negative feminine aspect that Nick took in from his grandmother, who wanted to "play" with him. Nick could be controlled by this unconscious negative feminine aspect, tortured by it. The woman's desire is to keep the frog restricted on a brink, to prevent its passing over to a place that would allow growth. This reflects the effect of the sexual abuse Nick most probably received from his grandmother: such abuse always blocks the constellation of transitional phenomena needed for more normative development.

R. D. Laing, in his *Politics of the Family*, speaks of a dreamlike state in which he feels almost all of us exist throughout our lives:

> I consider many adults (myself included) are or have been, more or less, in a hypnotic trance, induced in early infancy: we remain in this state, until—when we dead awaken, as Ibsen makes one of his characters say—we shall find that we have never lived. (Laing 1972, p. 82)

He goes on to say, "Anyone in this transitional state is likely to be confused" (ibid.). In the therapy, Nick began to wake from this hypnotic trance and indeed experienced confusion, just as Laing describes. The transitional state is not an easy passage.

Nick had no association to the older man in the dream, the only such figure to appear in his dreams. Nowhere in Nick's life had there been any meaningful masculine companionship. Nick's father had been a passive figure with a weak heart; the only "strength" he exhibited had been in putting Nick down when they were alone or preventing Nick from using his considerable intellect or musical gifts. In addition, the figure of the old man compensates for Nick's too youthful attitude, demonstrated in his naiveté with Mary, for example. The appearance of this figure was crucial in restarting Nick's blocked process. This kind of masculine "friend," nowhere to be found in Nick's personal history, had to be found on the archetypal level; once shaken loose, it provided a necessary masculine element to move Nick's retarded process.

With the woman in the dream gone, the older man and Nick go to the tree, the most extraordinary transitional phenomenon in the dream, as it represents the place through which transformation will occur. The shelter for Nick's growth would need to be older and deeper than the reality of grandmother. The ancient tree, connected to the positive aspect of the Great Mother, rooted solidly in the earth, provided the necessary counterbalancing force to the negative aspect mediated to Nick through his grandmother. Through the archetypal level, as embodied in the analytic process, the energy could become redirected.

By discerning the real toad—the possible sexual abuse in Nick's early life—in this imaginary garden of complexes, and seeing and holding that perception as a felt, living reality inside, Nick could begin to metamorphose a new self, never before known. Jung sees the tree as a symbol of the personality and of the self. He cites the tree as "the Guardian of the treasure," (Jung 1954, par. 407) and a symbol of the *chrysopeia* (gold-making) (ibid., par. 414) and underscores it especially "as the seat of transformation and renewal" with "a feminine and maternal significance" (ibid., par. 418). In Nick's dream, the ancient tree was a symbol for the archetype of the individuation process.

Such a symbol was indeed necessary for such a profound manifestation: an entirely new identity born out of preexisting genetic material (both somatic and psychic), pieces of *prima materia* that were prevented, through the early interactions with the grandmother, from cohering. As in Lacanian thinking, the therapist replaces "the mode of the voice and the ear with the image, becoming a 'pure unruffled mirror' . . . it is in the mirror that the ego is first born as an identity: the analytic mirror must displace—subduce—these archaic imagos" (McCannell 1986, p. 63). In circumstances such as Nick's, the analysis of a personal transference becomes decidedly secondary and of the archetypal transference, not really necessary. The transference is *always* present, but, as Nick's situation demonstrates, it cannot always be the primary focus of the therapy.

Lacan's mirror seems related to folklore, where mirrors have greater properties and can show much more than an outer reflection, perhaps the viewer's real, inner identity. Here the therapist becomes the magic mirror, where a patient can see his or her identity forming, via the agency of the therapist. In such a model, the analytic mirror constitutes a containing force, a transitional phenomenon capable of not merely reflecting in the Kohutian sense of vicarious introspection but of fostering and sheltering the patient's capacity for individuation. In Nick's process, it became clear that the drive toward individuation could survive the negative aspect of the archetype and prove, in the end, stronger.

The tree in the dream represents this Lacanian "magic" mirror, where on a level equal to, perhaps greater than, grandmother/Great Mother/personal mother/woman, Nick could experience himself held by the positive aspect of the Great Mother as embodied by the therapist. From this container, Nick was able to start seeing and labeling his grandmother the "evil grandmother." At this point, for the first time, I used the actual word "incest" in the therapy. Nick could now take this in and begin to experience profound physical sensations *in his body*, primitive shudders and moans.

Nick's spontaneity, which had been lost in the dynamic initiated with grandmother, returned. Laughter became possible for Nick—at me, at Mary, at himself. These changes were reflected in the enlivening of the atmosphere in our sessions, sessions with a marked difference from the early stage of the work, which had been characterized by the stasislike quality that had dogged Nick's life. His grandmother had mediated a negative aspect of the Great Mother; with its paralyzing grip loosened, transitional phenomena then became available to Nick, so that his retarded growth process could at last begin to move.

## References

Jung, C. G. 1954. The philosophical tree. In *Alchemical Studies, CW* 13:251–349. Princeton, N.J.: Princeton University Press, 1967.

Lacan, Jacques. 1977. *Écrits: A Selection*. New York: W. W. Norton and Company.

Laing, R. D. 1972. *The Politics of the Family and Other Essays*. New York: Vintage Books Edition. 1972.

Lawrence, D. H. 1968. *The Virgin and the Gipsy*. New York: Bantam Books.

McCannell, Juliet Flower. 1986. *Figuring Lacan*. Lincoln, Neb.: University of Nebraska Press.

Bain, Beatty, and Hunter, eds. 1977. *The Norton Introduction to Literature*, 2nd ed. New York: W. W. Norton and Company.

Ovid. *Metamorphoses*. Translated by Frank Justus Miller. Cambridge, Mass.: Harvard University Press, 1916.

# Active Imagination as Imaginal Play-Space

August J. Cwik

*For, to declare it once and for all, man plays only when he is in the full sense of the word a man, and he is only wholly man when he is playing.*
Schiller

*The debt we owe to the play of imagination is incalculable.*
C. G. Jung

Jung regards active fantasy as "one of the highest forms of psychic activity." He describes it as the "third element" in which the opposites merge and developed the technique of active imagination to elicit it (Jung 1921). This paper looks at active imagination as an attempt to create a transitional space, an imaginal play-space, within the individual. The technique of active imagination and its psychological goals will be compared to Winnicott's theories on the psychoanalytic understanding of play and the capacity to be alone.

---

**August Cwik** is a diploma candidate at the Analyst Training Program of the C. G. Jung Institute of Chicago. He is a clinical psychologist and hypnotherapist in private practice in Chicago and a member of the senior adjunct faculty at the Illinois School of Professional Psychology.

## Transitional Objects and Phenomena

Winnicott (1960, 1963a, 1971) describes the prototype of the optimal infant–mother relationship. In the beginning of life, he says, the good mother provides for the baby's needs just as they occur. Using an interesting vocabulary, Winnicott postulates that this unique matching of mother's satisfactions with the infant's needs creates an "illusion" in the infant that he or she and mother are one, a deeply affective "holding" of the child. This leads the infant to a healthy sense of omnipotence. As the child grows older, however, he or she must develop a sense of separateness from mother and become an independent, functioning human being. The mother must mete out frustrations that are appropriate to the child's ability to handle them. To the extent that she can accomplish this, he says, she is "good enough." This is the "disillusionment" stage in which the child realizes that mother is separate and cannot continue to gratify all his or her needs. The mother's acceptance of the infant's anger which naturally arises from these frustrations prevents the infant from excessively splitting off parts of the personality. Conversely, the child's integration of the mother who is both satisfying and frustrating, an ambivalent object, leads him or her to have more mature relationships with whole people rather than only with "all good" part objects.

Between the illusion and disillusionment phases, Winnicott (1951, 1971) posits a major accomplishment by the healthy child which is establishing a transitional object. In early childhood, a number of inanimate objects (i.e., dolls, blankets, toys) are placed before the developing child. Winnicott states that "it is well known that after a few months infants of either sex become fond of playing with dolls, and that most mothers *allow* their infants some special object and *expect* them to become, as it were, *addicted* to such objects" (1951, p. 229, emphasis added). Soothing qualities appear as the infant uses the object to help go to sleep or stay comfortable away from home. Often the child regresses back to using the object at emotionally overwhelming times. This first special "not me" object is the transitional object. Transitional phenomena, on the other hand, are not tangible objects. Rather, they are activities or products of activities (i.e., rocking, fantasies, and dreams) which function in a similar manner.

Winnicott's (1971) theories focus on the creative and imaginative aspects of play as they lead to invention and mastery. He views the establishment of the transitional object as the individual's first experience of play because the child "creates" a mental concept of an object which symbolizes both the self and mother—the "me" and the "not me." To this extent, his view coincides with Jung's description of a true symbol in that it involves an image that can unite opposites. Although experienced as an aspect of oneself, this object begins to carry the tension-regulating function previously provided by the mother or idealized object. This is the basis of its soothing and sedating qualities (Tolpin 1971). It helps to alleviate the normal developmental stress of separation-individuation. One should not ask whether the object exists before the child creates it—it exists in a nether world, between inner fantasy and outer reality.

A metaphor of an intermediate area or space describes this nether world in which the infant both creates and experiences illusions and is allowed to do so, in attempting to cope with separation (Barkin 1978). The "transitional" nature of the object not only relates to how the child uses it, but also describes the infant. The child is "in the transitional state of self- and object-representation differentiation, from symbiosis to separation and individuation, [and] from part to whole object relating" (Barkin 1978, p. 514).

The fate of the object is that it slowly looses meaning as transitional phenomena spread out over the child's whole cultural field. But the need for play remains throughout life to relieve the strain between the inner fantasy world and the outer real world. Winnicott says all of life consists of a transitional interplay between self and reality. Rose (1978) similarly describes how the transitional process—remnants of the original transitional phase—can be observed in the creativity of everyday life.

Winnicott states that psychotherapy itself has to do with two people playing together. And where this is not possible, the task of the therapist is to help the patient attain a state where he or she can once again play. Winnicott describes how the "holding function" of the therapist supplies the affective component in this process. He states that "holding . . . often takes the form of conveying in words at the appropriate moment something that shows that the analyst knows and understands the deepest anxiety that is being experienced, or that is waiting to be experienced (Winnicott 1963b, p. 240). Winnicott's goal in therapy is to help the patient engage in "creative or imaginative living." He states that "it is creative apperception more than anything else that makes the individual feel that life is worth living" (Winnicott 1971, p. 65). Greenbaum (1978) states that if therapy is indeed modeled on the early mother–child relationship, remnants or derivatives of transitional phenomena should appear as the patient relinquishes neurotic bonds to infantile dependence. Likewise, Grolnick (1978) describes how dreaming and dreams themselves could be used as transitional phenomena. He presents case material in which the original transitional object appeared in an individual's dream material during therapy.

Winnicott has attempted to trace the developmental line of *creative illusion* formation and to relate its function to the healthy adult. The next section explores the technique of active imagination in relation to these concepts of play.

## Active Imagination

Understanding the technique of active imagination through Jung's writings is not easy. He admits that although he talked about it extensively, he wrote very little about it. In the beginning, he wanted to keep the results of the method quiet to avoid suggesting what content should emerge from using it (Jung 1950). It developed from his confrontation with the unconscious after breaking from Freud around 1916 (Jung 1965). He first used the term "active imagination" during the Tavistock Lectures of 1935. The theory behind the use of the method grew concomitantly with Jung's view of the nature of the psyche.

Jung approached his unconscious by a number of different means. He began to engage in some childhood games to regain the freedom and openness of a child at play. He built buildings of stone in the sand. More importantly, he began to elaborate his fantasies by writing them out or painting them.

In this encounter, Jung eventually began to meet the "subpersonalities" that would influence him and his theories for the rest of his life. He encountered the wise old man and the anima and felt deeply impressed by their apparent autonomy. He began to understand that growth, or "individuation," resulted only after coming to terms with these internal contents. He states that

> the essential thing is to differentiate oneself from these contents by personifying them, and at the same time to bring them into relationship with consciousness. That is the technique for stripping them of their power. It is not too difficult to personify them, as they always possess a certain degree of autonomy, a separate identity of their own. Their autonomy is a most uncomfortable thing to reconcile oneself to, and yet the very fact that the unconscious presents itself in that way gives us the best means of handling it. (Jung 1965, p. 187)

In short, Jung's encounter became the paradigm of what he later called active imagination and the cornerstone for his understanding of the nature of the unconscious. His paper, "The Transcendent Function" (1916), outlined the procedure for practicing it, although he further elaborates it in other, later works (1935a, 1936a, 1936b, 1951, 1955).

The starting point of active imagination can be a mood, a dream image, or any spontaneous visual image. The participant *sinks down* into this mood *without reserve*, or attends to the image with focused concentration and observes any changes that occur. Here the subject willingly and consciously produces an *abaissement du niveau mental*, an altered state of consciousness, for therapeutic purposes. Jung notes in several places that all criticism must be suspended in this process and that the happenings observed should be noted with absolute objectivity.

The product of this work *must* be concretized in some form. That is, it can be written, drawn, sculpted, etc. Jung emphasized the importance of this step, because having actual ocular evidence effectively counteracts the ever-present tendency to self-deception and helps to prevent the contents from slipping back into the unconscious (1955). One of the more common forms of active imagination is an internal dialogue. It appears as a script written between two characters. One is the ego, that conscious part of the personality perceived as "I." The second is an "other," the autonomous complex of the personified inner figure. Later, as Jung expanded his theory of the unconscious to include the archetypes, he saw that the "other" could also represent personified archetypal images. The final result of active imagination is a product of both the conscious and the unconscious, which "embody[ies] the striving of the unconscious for the light and the striving of the conscious for substance" (Jung 1916, par. 168).

After making the image concrete, the individual begins consciously to confront these products of the unconscious. He or she must ask, "How does this affect me?" with openness and honesty. Jung states that no *a priori* answer exists about what to do with the material obtained by this process and suggests that it not be interpreted. He recognizes that the individual may deal with this material in mainly one of two ways: creative formulation or understanding. When creative formulation predominates, the material is worked and reworked to fit the individual's aesthetic or artistic sense. When the principle of understanding predominates, the individual struggles to comprehend the meaning of the unconscious product and has little interest in the aesthetic aspect. Both principles have inherent dangers and can lead the individual astray.

Creative formulation, first of all, can lead to an aesthetic problem which states that the products are "nothing but" art. An example of this is Jung's own confrontation with an anima figure while he was producing some paintings inspired by unconscious contents. In this case, the inner figure stated that the product was artistic, but Jung vehemently argued against this inner voice—it would just have seduced him into seeing himself as only a misunderstood artist. This attitude would necessarily have led him away from any attempt to understand the meaning of the material (Jung 1965).

On the other hand, if the principle of understanding predominates, the aesthetic form-valuing aspect may be lost and with it the possibility of losing the mysterious symbolic essence of the product. Here one imagines the thinker who intensively struggles for meaning and looses the sense of wonder of why just this image and not some other.

Jung states that "the ideal case would be if these two aspects could exist side by side or rhythmically succeed each other: that is, if there were an alternation of creation and understanding" (1916, par. 179). Again it is interesting to look at Jung himself as the prototype: he painted or sculpted his fantasies and, at the same time, amplified these emerging images intellectually through his understanding of myths and alchemy.

In the next step, the ego comes to terms with the unconscious, once it has shaped the content, and begins to understand the meaning of the formulation. While the unconscious has dominated up to this point, now the ego assumes the lead. Jung emphasizes the importance of the ego at this stage, saying, "The position of the ego must be maintained as being of equal value to the counter-position of the unconscious, and vice versa. . . . It is exactly as if a dialogue were taking place between two human beings with equal rights, each of whom gives the other credit for a valid argument and considers it worth while to modify the conflicting standpoints by means of thorough comparison and discussion or else to distinguish them clearly from one another" (1916, par. 183). Through this work, Jung began to formulate the idea that "health" or growth comes through a correct relationship between the conscious and the unconscious. he accentuates this point in his article, "The Relations Between the Ego and the Unconscious" (Jung 1935b). In it, he describes in detail a woman's work on a vision actively perceived by intense concentration on the background of her consciousness and the effect of this work on her psychological functioning.

Other writers have expanded on Jung's notion of active imagination. Von Franz (1983) emphasizes the ethical nature of the ego's confrontation with the unconscious. She warns that the individual must enter the fray with his or her own true ego, not with a fictitious one. In this step, the actual emotional state of the patient's ego should coincide with that in the imaginal story. That is, the ego in active imagination must behave the same as the everyday ego. She emphasizes that the patient must apply whatever is said, ordered, or asked for in the active imagination to daily life. This is a powerful way to bring the body into "play." Similarly, Johnson (1986) emphasizes the need to ritualize the understandings gained from the process in order to facilitate the integration of the experience into conscious, waking life. In other words, one must often perform some physical act to deepen the understandings into a body experience rather than simply allowing them to remain at an intellectual level. He states that "ritual is *symbolic behavior, consciously performed* (Johnson 1986, p. 102, author's italics).

Hannah (1953) defines active imagination as a "creative function" and a "scientific form of meditation," while Dallett (1982) compares it to a "dialogue with the gods." Casey describes active imagination as a kind of spontaneous amplification of the archetypes: "To imagine actively is to make archetypal patterns psychically real: actual and effectual in the psychic life of the imaginer" (1974, p. 5). In Humbert's words, "Active imagination leads to concrete contact with 'the one who knows.' This is neither the analyst, nor the intellect, but a function unique to each of us which expresses itself by a kind of inner inclination" (1971, p. 106).

Watkins (1976) places active imagination in the broader-based background of approaches accessing the imagination in general; she calls this level of imagination "waking dreams." She says they are "not just an experience of dreamlike character received while awake, but an experience of the imagination, undertaken with a certain quality or attitude of awareness" (Watkins 1976, p. 31). She believes that Jung's work reintroduced the importance of the imagination, especially its mythopoetic function—the fantasy-weaving part of the unconscious—to modern psychology.

Watkins (1986) describes how several developmental theories explain the emergence and fate of imaginal dialogues—here broadly understood as active imagination. The problem, as she sees it, is that most theories view imaginal dialogues as primitive and inferior processes, which individuals gradually overcome, and which disappear in favor of either direct communication to the external world or more abstract and logical thought. She argues in favor of the adult's need to continue developing imaginal dialogues. She states that

> imaginal dialogues do not merely reflect or distort reality, but create reality; that the real is not necessarily antithetical to the imaginal, but can be conceived of more broadly to include the imaginal; and that personifying is not an activity symptomatic of the primitivity of mind, but is expressive of its dramatic and poetic nature. (Watkins 1986, p. 58)

She proposes keeping several lines of development open, depending on what purpose is being sought from the dialogue.

All of these writers emphasize the "active" part of the method, whether in the ego's willingness to listen and focus, or the ego's activity in confronting and questioning the material that arises from the unconscious. Both Jung and Winnicott make distinctions on how individuals relate to fantasy material. Winnicott (1971) observes that patients can vary qualitatively in how they use various psychic phenomenon. He describes a case in which the patient's use of fantasy did not imaginatively enrich life but, rather, helped her to avoid living and relating. Her fantasies resembled obsessive phenomena or "wheel-spinning" which filled a void in her life. Winnicott felt that the patient first needed to come to a state where she could *play* with the material of her fantasies. This is similar to Jung's discrimination between true imagination, or active fantasy, and passive fantasy. Imagination is creative, synthetic, and active, while passive fantasy results from the dissociation of the psyche and is antithetical to consciousness (Jung 1921).

Active imagination can thus serve a practical application—as the foundation of the transcendent function. This function mediates opposites: real and imaginary, rational and irrational, and conscious and unconscious. Often expressed in the form of symbols, it helps to avoid the destructive tendency to be pulled into a one-sided view. Thus, "it facilitates a transition from one psychological attitude or condition to another" (Samuels, Shorter, and Plaut 1986, p. 150). In short, active imagination is tantamount to an actual expression of the relationship between the ego and the components of unconscious. It has the potential to produce the third between opposing attitudes most clearly seen in Jung's rhythmical oscillation between understanding and creative formulation. In this manner active imagination closely resembles Winnicott's notion of a transitional space where the "me" and "not me" are creatively brought into a conscious relationship. In this imaginal play-space the individual is "in the transitional state of self- and object-representation differentiation " (Barkin 1978, p. 514).

The imaginal play-space of active imagination parallels Khan's (1972) notion of the dream-space. The dream-space is the internal psychic equivalent of the transitional space that the child established to discover the self and external reality. Khan states that dreams which actualize in this inner space help the individual to personalize the dream experience and curtail acting out dreams in social space. The capacity to *use* dream mechanisms and the dream itself as psychic experience only results from having received phase-adequate environmental provisions—good-enough mothering. Similarly, the establishment of an imaginal play-space through active imagination allows an individual the opportunity to diminish the acting out of complexes by playing and relating to them in fantasy.

Fordham (1977) addresses the dynamic roots of the process to help understand its effectiveness. He believes that many people refer to the contents of active imaginings as archetypal forms and relate them to the imagery of myths. Yet, he says, how these manifestations emerge during the development of an individual remains obscure. He argues that the roots of active imagination may be found in the transitional process Winnicott describes. Fordham emphasizes that when the transitional object appears to loose its importance to a child, mental imagery begins to take its place. He states that, "instead of a specific object, a whole class of phenomena appears which are transitional phenomena; play expands, stories and creative phantasy emerge and dreams take on transitional features. All are essentially mental states expressed in imagery and, except for play, not in physical objects" (Fordham 1977, p. 318).

Fordham further demonstrates this connection between transitional phenomena and active imagination using Jung's own childhood experiences and his later encounter with the unconscious. He focuses on the early dream of finding an underground phallus and the carving of a manikin which Jung secretly kept hidden away. Jung thought of the manikin and would visit it when he was under stress from external and internal sources. Jung believed, he says, that the dream signified the unconscious beginnings of his intellectual life. Fordham further hypothesizes that these events occurred in Jung's life during times of emotional upheaval in his family life and when he felt alienated by his school experiences. Fordham, similar to Greenbaum's and Grolnick's observations noted above, argues that the dream functioned as a transitional phenomenon while the manikin served as a transitional object that helped Jung to cope with the emotional separations he experienced.

Moreover, Fordham points out, in Jung's confrontation with the unconscious, which later became the paradigm for active imagination, he recalls the forgotten dream of childhood as he built an altar in the sand. Thus, Fordham believes, active imagination originated with Jung's attempt to cope with separation: the original unresolved conflicts of childhood in which were hidden Jung's true self. His traumatic separation from Freud in adulthood later activated these anxieties.

Fordham's observations constitute an object-relational analysis of Jungian theory and the roots of active imagination: a personal, developmental side of active imagination that bridges separation anxieties. This view compensates the usual archetypal, numinous side of active imagination as a "dialogue with the gods." Fordham believes that the views of active imagination usually presented in the literature (e.g., Dieckmann 1971 and the comments following that article, and Weaver 1973) are rarely those which patients actually use. He states that "not all persons having problems of becoming conscious of their true selves have such vivid cultural interests as Jung, nor do they have his imaginative capacities" (Fordham 1977, p. 327). Perhaps, he suggests, it would be more important for therapists to become aware of when transitional data, *other than creative imagination*, become manifest in a session in order to focus on holding rather than interpreting. Regarding interpretation, he states, "it is not so much whether a therapist interprets or not, as whether he interferes with (impinges on) the establishment of a play-illusion which the patient needs as part of differentiating further between reality and his subject ego" (ibid., p. 328). In this explanation, he uses Winnicott's concept of subject ego to cover all the experiences classified as "me and my inner world," in contrast to the "real" object.

Fordham emphasizes how Jung worked to assimilate his "secret experiences." He describes how Jung "sought out from books others who could share his illusions and likewise believed them to be real and true—they were especially the alchemists with whom he shared so much and through whom he came to share with others. *This is like finding a mother who would agree that his experiences were both real and true*" (Fordham 1977, p. 323, emphasis added). The importance of finding a mother who can validate inner experience is accentuated in a paper by Winnicott. The next section explores the qualities of this facilitating mother.

## The Capacity to Be Alone

Winnicott identifies the individual's need for a good object in his or her inner psychic reality in order to be comfortably alone. "Good-enough mothering" allows a child a chance to believe in a benign environment. In the paper, "The Capacity to Be Alone" (1958), Winnicott describes what it might mean "to be by oneself" from a object-relational, psychoanalytic viewpoint. He points out the positive aspects of the ability to enjoy solitude, as contrasted with withdrawn states that imply expectations of persecution or enforced states of solitary confinement. The paradoxical nature of this state is that it entails being with someone. He explains that "although many types of experiences go to the establishment of the capacity to be alone, there is one that is basic, and without a sufficiency of it the capacity to be alone does not come about; *this experience is that of being alone, as an infant and small child, in the presence of mother*" (Winnicott 1958, p. 30, author's italics). To signify the special type of relationship between the child or infant who is alone with the mother or mother-substitute who is *reliably* present, Winnicott suggests the term "ego-relatedness."

Within this framework of secure ego-relatedness, Winnicott poignantly says, "It is only when alone (that is to say, in the presence of someone) that the infant can discover his own personal life" (1958, p. 34). He believes that pathology exists in a false life, a self built purely on a reactive stance to external stimuli. The developing child needs to be alone in order to truly discover him- or herself. Only then can he or she feel the sensations and impulses emerging from the unconscious as real.

Storr expands Winnicott's concept, stating that, "*the capacity to be alone thus becomes linked with self-discovery and self-realization; with becoming aware of one's deepest needs, feelings, and impulses*" (1988, p. 21, author's italics). He argues that the field of psychology has developed a one-sided bias in its sole emphasis on relationship as the most important factor in the growth of the personality. His entire book, *Solitude*, serves as a much-needed compensation to this lopsided situation by pointing out many of the creative aspects of being alone.

This ability to be alone would seem to be an important prerequisite in order to perform active imagination. As Fordham clearly states, "To tolerate being alone is an essential condition for active imagination to occur" (1967, p. 62). More specifically, he states, the ability to imagine actively indicates a "capacity to be alone, in a positive and creative sense, without isolation and without retreat from the outer world or absorption in a world of fantasy, or without otherwise being cut off from outer relatedness" (Fordham 1958, p. 73). The implication is that "being alone" means being *receptive* to the unconscious: Winnicott's child, being alone and present to the impulses, becomes conscious; the adult, engaged in active imagination, becomes familiar once more with his or her impulses as expressed through imagery and dialogue.

But Fordham (1956) also expresses the need to clearly discriminate active imagination proper from imaginative activity in general. He believes that imaginative activity—such as children's play and artistic activity—leads to growth of the ego, while active imagination—the ego's confrontation with the unconscious—leads to consciousness of the Self.

In active imagination the autonomy of "the other" is always emphasized. Watkins (1986) believes that allowing the imaginal others to *remain autonomous* rather than insisting on their dissolution and integration into a broader "ego" or "self" can be instructive. Relating to a multiplicity of personified others does not necessarily strengthen the ego as much as it enhances the possibility for greater awareness. This process *relativizes the ego* rather than making it stronger. If imaginal dialogues continue over a period of time, the ego becomes only one of many voices and a detached awareness or "observing ego" begins to develop which can view situations from a variety of different perspectives.

Perhaps, in the end, Winnicott's ego-relatedness provides the necessary foundation for eventual Self-relatedness: the establishment of the ego-Self axis. Then active imagination designates one of the most mature forms of the capacity to be alone in its highly conscious and concentrated focus on being present to, and in active encounter with, the unconscious.

## On the Ability to Actively Imagine

It is clear that Jung saw active imagination as an activity performed alone and usually only toward the end of, and after the termination of, analysis. He claims that the technique is not for everyone and that the biggest danger in the approach is that the activation of unconscious contents might overpower the conscious mind and take possession of the personality (Jung 1916). Yet, Jung's high regard for active imagination and what it might accomplish can be heard in his statement that

> the transcendent function [or "active imagination"] not only forms a valuable addition to psychotherapeutic treatment, but gives the patient the inestimable advantage of assisting the analyst on his own resources, and of breaking a dependence which is often felt as humiliating. It is a way of attaining liberation by one's own efforts and of finding the courage to be oneself. (1916, par. 193)

Jung's writings imply that the energy and emotion which the patient first projects onto the figure of the analyst eventually transfers within the imaginal work onto an inner symbolic "one who knows." Each person thus freely finds his or her own individual way instead of following the dictates of an all-knowing analyst. It may be interesting to hypothesize on how this transfer from analyst to patient might occur in actual clinical practice.

Davidson (1966) suggests that the transference carries aspects similar to active imagination: it can serve as an "imaginary" dialogue between the patient and a figure from the individual's inner world appearing in the form of the analyst. In analysis, the analyst functions for the patient, as the patient's ego functions in active imagination: to *allow* the unconscious material of the patient to emerge without criticisms and judgments. In this manner, the aware analyst *holds* the patient's affective projections in a way that allows an image to "incarnate." Only then can explanations and interpretations be of use to the patient. Thus the transference-countertransference matrix compares to active imagination.

Powell draws similar conclusions in "A Bridge to Understanding: The Transcendent Function in the Analyst." She states that "we may say that the symbolic attitude is mediated through the analyst until the patient is able to allow the unconscious contents of the psyche to enter consciousness freely and the ego is strong enough to tolerate the tensions of psychic suffering when the opposites are encountered" (Powell 1985, p. 31).

These approaches suggest that, in the analytic container, the therapist becomes like Winnicott's mother—a figure who is *reliably present* and allows the individual the space "to be alone" in order to find him- or herself. It may be argued that the internalization of this figure is what eventually allows the analysand to be truely alone during the more formal practice of active imagination. And if active imagination is, in fact, a realistic and desirable goal in therapy as Jung suggests, then perhaps more direct imaginal work within analytic sessions might facilitate this internalization process. With this inner figure in place, the establishment of an imaginal play-space becomes possible.

Watkins (1976) points out that many clinicians have explored using fantasy as a method of doing therapy. Hypnotherapy and guided affective imagery are but a few of the approaches that embrace working with imagery more directly. Bosnak (1988) describes some excellent techniques for imaginal work with individuals and groups. Hall (1989) elaborates the use of hypnosis in a distinctly Jungian framework. He states, "The best situation, in my experience, is for the therapeutic approach to consist of a combination of dream interpretation, active imagination, and hypnoanalysis" (Hall 1989, p. 103). And more recently, Middelkoop (1989) describes casework in which he uses active imagination as the primary form of treatment.

In conclusion, active imagination can be a powerful technique which embodies the transcendent function and leads to the establishment of an imaginal play-space. But its shadow should also be appreciated. Fordham (1967) discusses the possible pathology of active imagination. He argues that patients can use it defensively as a shield to hide their infantile affects in need of attention. At the same time, he acknowledges that the technique can be useful for controlling pathological disorders and not only for individuation. The developmental approach reminds us that images arising out of the play-space harken back to an individual's earliest transitional experience. In this realization the therapist may be better able to *hold* the affective experience of the patient as he or she attempts to navigate separation anxieties. This would be the reductive side to active imagination. The constructive, synthetic approach—which focuses on the continuous symbolic processes of the psyche—informs us of the continued need for *play* in the human condition. This calls out for a creative and imaginative approach to living. Fordham reminds us that both methods are important in a thorough analysis and that reductive as well as synthetic analysis can lead to individuation.

## References

Barkin, L. 1978. The concept of the transitional object. Between Reality and Fantasy: Transitional Objects and Phenomena, S. Grolnick, L. Barkin, and W. Muensterberger, eds. New York: Jason Aronson.

Bosnak, R. 1988. A Little Course in Dreams. Boston: Shambhala.

Casey, E. 1974. Toward an archetypal imagination. *Spring* 1–32.

Dallett, J. 1982. Active imagination in practice. *Jungian Analysis*, M. Stein, ed. La Salle, Ill.: Open Court.

Davidson, D. 1966. Transference as a form of active imagination. *Technique in Jungian analysis*, M. Fordham, ed. London: Heinemann, 1974.

Dieckmann, H. 1971. Symbols of active imagination. *Journal of Analytical Psychology* 16(1): 127–148.
Fordham, M. 1956. Active imagination and imaginative activity. *Journal of Analytical Psychology* 1(2): 207–208.
______. 1958. *Objective Psyche*. London: Routledge and Kegan Paul.
______. 1967. Active imagination—deintegration or disintegration? *Journal of Analytical Psychology* 12(1): 51–65.
______. 1977. A possible root of active imagination. *Journal of Analytical Psychology* 22(4): 317–330.
Greenbaum, T. 1978. The "analysing instrument" and the transitional object. *Between Reality and Fantasy: Transitional Objects and Phenomena*. S. Grolnick, L. Barkin, and W. Muensterberger, eds. New York: Jason Aronson.
Grolnick, S. 1978. Dreams and dreaming as transitional phenomena. *Between Reality and Fantasy: Transitional Objects and Phenomena*. S. Grolnick, L. Barkin, and W. Muensterberger, eds. New York: Jason Aronson.
Hall, J. 1989. *Hypnosis: A Jungian Perspective*. New York: Guilford Press.
Hannah, B. 1953. Some remarks on active imagination. *Spring* 38–58.
Humbert, E. 1971. Active imagination: Theory and practice. *Spring* 101–114.
Johnson, R. 1986. *Innerwork*. San Francisco: Harper and Row.
Jung, C. G. 1916. The transcendent function. In *Collected Works*, vol. 8. Princeton, N.J.: Princeton University Press, 1981.
______. 1921. Psychological types. In vol. 6. Princeton, N.J.: Princeton University Press, 1971.
______. 1935a. The Tavistock lectures. In vol. 18. Princeton, N.J.: Princeton University Press, 1980.
______. 1935b. The relations between the ego and the unconscious. In vol. 7. Princeton, N.J.: Princeton University Press, 1953.
______. 1936a. Yoga and the West. In vol. 11. Princeton, N.J.: Princeton University Press, 1977.
______. 1936b. The concept of the collective unconscious. In vol. 9i. Princeton, N.J.: Princeton University Press, 1977.
______. 1950. A study in the process of individuation. In vol. 9i. Princeton, N.J.: Princeton University Press, 1959.
______. 1951. The psychological aspects of the Kore. In vol. 9i. Princeton, N.J.: Princeton University Press, 1977.
______. 1955. Mysterium coniunctionis. In vol. 14. Princeton, N.J.: Princeton University Press, 1976.
______. 1965. *Memories, Dream, Reflections*. New York: Vintage Books.
Khan, M. 1972. The use and abuse of dream in psychic experience. In *The Privacy of the Self*. London: Hogarth Press, 1974.
Middelkoop, P. 1989. *The Wise Old Man: Healing Through Inner Images*. Boston: Shambhala.
Powell, S. 1985. A bridge to understanding: the transcendent function in the analyst. *Journal of Analytical Psychology* 30: 29–45.
Rose, G. 1978. The creativity of everyday life. *Between Reality and Fantasy: Transitional Objects and Phenomena*, S. Grolnick, L. Barkin, and W. Muensterberger, eds. New York: Jason Aronson.
Samuels, A., Shorter, B., and Plaut, F. 1986. *A Critical Dictionary of Jungian Analysis*. New York: Routledge and Kegan Paul.
Storr, A. 1988. *Solitude: A Return to the Self*. New York: Free Press.
Tolpin, M. 1971. On the beginnings of a cohesive self. *Psychoanalytic Study of the Child* 26: 316–352.
von Franz, M.-L. 1983. On active imagination. Supplement in M. Keyes, *Inward Journey: Art as Therapy*. La Salle, Ill.: Open Court, pp. 125–133.

Watkins, M. 1976. *Waking Dreams*. New York: Harper Colophon.

______. 1986. *Invisible Guests: The Development of Imaginal Dialogues*. New Jersey: Analytic Press.

Weaver, R. 1973. *The Old Wise Woman: A Study of Active Imagination*. New York: G. P. Putnam's Sons.

Winnicott, D. W. 1951. Transitional objects and transitional phenomena. In *Through Paediatrics to Psychoanalysis*. New York: Basic Books, 1975.

______. 1958. The capacity to be alone. In *The Maturational Processes and the Facilitating Environment*. New York: International Universities Press, 1965.

______. 1960. The theory of the parent-infant relationship. In *The Maturational Processes and the Facilitating Environment*. New York: International Universities Press, 1965.

______. 1963a. From dependence towards independence in the development of the individual. In *The Maturational Processes and the Facilitating Environment*. New York: International Universities Press, 1965.

______. 1963b. Psychiatric disorder in terms of infantile maturational processes. In *The Maturational Processes and the Facilitating Environment*. New York: International Universities Press, 1965.

______. 1971. *Playing and Reality*. New York: Basic Books.

# On the Threshold of Change: Synchronistic Events and Their Liminal Context in Analysis

Robert H. Hopcke

*Incident 1*

A patient in his early forties, during a long struggle in analysis with his emotional neediness, had projected upon his analyst the image of his mother, a dominating, narcissistically disturbed woman. He saw his analyst as withholding information from him which he needed to know, preventing him from becoming independent and powerful because of the analyst's own wish for power. Coinciding with the gradual climax of this struggle was a large tropical storm which knocked out electrical power in the area five minutes before the beginning of this patient's analytical hour. The session went on, somewhat dimly by the light of the small window of the analyst's office. Forty minutes into the session, the patient finally began to recognize that his image of the analyst was more his own projection than reality. At the moment that the analyst

**Robert H. Hopcke** is a licensed marriage family child counselor in private practice in Berkeley, Calif., and is on the adjunct faculty of California Institute of Integral Studies in San Francisco. He is author of three books, including *Jung, Jungians and Homosexuality*, as well as numerous articles and reviews.

commented on how important it was for the patient to have the analyst accept the patient's decisions, the electrical power went back on.

*Incident 2*

A patient in his mid-thirties who tended to follow every analytic gain with some form of self-punishment or self-inflicted physical injury had begun slowly to experience the anger that lay beneath his masochism, anger at being denied independence and respect in his rigid, conflictually enmeshed family of origin. However, long-standing cultural proscriptions against feeling and expressing anger were a large part of the patient's self-image, which led to a prolonged period of emotional emptiness and seeming lack of progress in the analysis. During one particularly empty session, the patient began to complain about the uselessness of the analysis, how strange and distant the work was from his "real" life, and how little change it seemed to be effecting in his outside, "important" relationships. The analyst commented on how the patient seemed to be looking at life outside the sessions as "real" and "important," whereas analysis seemed to be "unreal" and "insignificant." At that moment, the session was interrupted by a knock on the door, one of the analyst's neighbors. Although the analyst explained to her that he was in a session, the neighbor insisted on waiting outside the office, thus ensuring that the patient and she crossed paths on the patient's way out. The following session, the patient reported that the interruption had had a profound effect on him emotionally and that he had begun to understand what the analyst had meant by his interpretation around the "unreality" of his experience of the analytic work.

## Synchronicity and Liminality as Aspects of Analysis

These two incidents, from work with two men in mid-life, are both examples of one of Jung's more controversial ideas, synchronicity. The title of Jung's work on the subject, *Synchronicity: An Acausal Connecting Principle*, provides the term's definition: synchronicity is a principle that links events acausally, that is, in terms of the subjective meaningfulness of the coincidence, rather than by cause and effect. The numinous quality of synchronistic events showed Jung that "the emotional factor plays an important role" in these occurrences and that "meaningful coincidences—which are to be distinguished from meaningless chance groupings—therefore seem to rest on an archetypal foundation" (Jung 1952, par. 846).

As meaningful coincidences occurring in conjunction with emotional and archetypal factors, synchronistic occurrences not surprisingly can play an important role in analysis. In bringing to awareness psychic contents hitherto unconscious, analysis is by its nature involved in an archetypal and, therefore, highly charged level of existence; a lack of synchronistic occurrences during the course of this process would be perhaps more a cause for wonder.

Although it is necessary to insist on the fundamental acausality of such events, many analysts have come to see that synchronistic occurrences occur in a particular kind of analytic context to which the term "liminal" has come to be applied. The concept of liminality comes to clinical psychology by way of anthropology, specifically, by way of van Gennep's and, subsequently, Turner's research on *rites de passage* (van Gennep 1960; Turner 1969, 1974). As used in these writings, liminality denotes the middle state of initiation rituals, the "betwixt-and-between" condition of the initiate, removed from previously held social roles or positions but not yet conducted ritually into the new social status which is the end of the initiation process.

The application of the concept of liminality to the analytic process of change and transformation is obvious. Moreover, it is felicitously consonant with Jung's own idea of the nature of analysis and human growth. Jung rejected the idea of analysis as a series of technically teachable, mechanical psychic manipulations on the part of the analyst, feeling certain that psychic phenomena are purposive and serve the ends of human growth according to a fundamental teleological principle within the human soul. Thus, analysis was simply to provide a space, a *temenos*, a magic circle, a vessel, in which the transformation inherent in the patient's condition would be allowed to take place.

Liminality, therefore, might even be called the very essence of effective analytic work, the goal of which is change and transformation. The derivation of the term is instructive in this regard, from the Latin *limen* or "threshold." Just as change always involves a threshold experience of "moving from" and "moving to," which can be disorienting, exhilarating, or sometimes both at once, analytic work must provide and even at times create a place where, for a prolonged period of time, the patient can allow previous self-conceptions, persona masks, and ego directives to dissolve. Here the Greek origin of the word *analusein*, meaning to break apart or dissolve, is to be given its proper due. Analysis, if it is to effect change, must be a place where psychic unmooring is tolerated, even suffered (hence the term "patient") so that the deeper ground of the archetypal field can be seen, experienced, and allowed to flower.

At such liminal points in analysis, one would expect the archetype of the Self to be active in pointing the way forward. As Bolen points out in her brief book on synchronicity, *The Tao of Psychology: Synchronicity and the Self* (1979), one can nearly always discern the archetype of wholeness behind synchronistic events, and so, in analytic work, synchronistic events can hardly be separated from their liminal context. Synchronicity and liminality are partners, so to speak, in the process of archetypal transformation.

The two incidents above, therefore, bear examination. As synchronistic events, both were effective in moving the two patients toward a wholeness in themselves and in their relationships. Highly charged, indeed, numinous, both events showed the archetypal processes at work writ large. Thus, to examine the deeper, symbolic nature of these two events is to serve a clinical purpose, that is, to indicate how one might go about understanding and using such important and unusual occurrences in analysis.

Further, these two events in particular reveal the nature and function of the liminality of the analytic context, as two especially apt symbols of that betwixt-and-between state so necessary for human growth. They merit a closer look for an equally significant clinical purpose, namely, a clearer vision of what creates and maintains the therapeutic liminal space, the threshold to change.

## The Power Failure and Its Restoration: Incident 1

When "Paul" had begun analysis some two-and-a-half years before the occurrence of the synchronistic event reported here, he had begun it with the intention of resolving a set of symptoms that were themselves related to that well-known period of liminality, mid-life. Thirty-eight years old, Paul was dissatisfied with his marriage and dissatisfied with being underemployed at a trade job that paid well but held no intellectual stimulation or challenge: his *lieben und arbeiten* were not what he had wanted or expected. A certain agitated restlessness had therefore set in, a thirst for more from life which Paul had thought to slake by undertaking a series of extramarital affairs, at times sequentially, at times simultaneously, even seeing as many as five women at one point. When these liaisons began to have the same taste as his marriage and job, growing into responsibilities and commitments which, of course, seriously compromised their allure, Paul would then drift away, sometimes into another affair, sometimes inward, into himself. At one point of inward-turning, he came for therapy.

Exploration of this almost classic mid-life symptomatology revealed a number of factors that had hampered Paul's own resolution of the transition from youth to age, in particular and most prominently, a pernicious and long-standing negative mother complex. In order to appreciate the character and effect of this complex, however, one must first understand that Paul presented himself as an extreme thinking type, prizing logic and intellectual analysis above all. Seeking to base all his decisions on a careful consideration of the various elements of any given situation in order then to follow the most sensible course, Paul had found his methodology workable throughout the first half of his adult life. Indeed, in light of his relative lack of formal education, he was enormously bright, well read, familiar with a number of languages. His demeanor was composed, and he was rational literally to a fault. In attempting to say anything, his prodigious intellect found it necessary to qualify all his statements with whatever further insights he would have at the moment about the subject of his statements, insights which, given his native intelligence, were considerable but which accordingly turned his communications into a process of endless digression and self-qualification.

In connection with his hypertrophied thinking function, Paul's experience of his mother had made such a wholesale "flight into logic" his only sane alternative and functioned as the determinative factor in making Paul's relationships with women his psychological stress point. His description of Mother conformed to a textbook description of narcissicism. Physically large, she nevertheless was easily wounded, emotionally and literally, always complaining with much drama about slights, insults, illnesses, or aches. Despite her claim that "she needed to be needed," she tended to be demanding and domineering, at times using her physical size to intimidate her husband and her only son Paul through frankly histrionic scenes in public and private, at times preferring more emotionally manipulative methods to hold the reins of the family.

That this experience of Mother had formed a complex which rested on an archetypal foundation became clear in the stark contrast between Paul's usual self-presentation and the manner in which he spoke about Mother. In describing various childhood incidents, as well as other more recent examples of how Mother, now advanced in years, was handling her declining health, Paul's descriptions lost their measured, analytic, self-reflective quality. His images of Mother became large, larger than life at times, exaggerated into near monstrousness, and Paul's descriptions of the incidents were told and retold in a way that lent them a kind of mythic, ritual importance. Sometimes, one found it difficult to tell where Mother stopped and Paul began. He reported that a characteristic way in which she asked for things was to say, "You would like to get Mother a drink of water, wouldn't you, Paul?" and it was precisely this kind of psychological infiltration that made it difficult for Paul to tell the difference between himself, his experience of his Mother, his mother as she actually was, and the deeper constellation of an archetypal Mother, phallic in her self-centeredness and yet all-encompassing in her strength and passion.

Power, Paul's own power over his life, was immediately the central issue of the analysis, and accordingly, the analyst became the screen upon which the all-powerful Mother of his personal and archetypal experience was projected. At first, the projection seemed reasonable, lifelike, almost benevolent: the analyst was the "doctor" to whom Paul had come for cure, a trained professional who would "know what to do" and on whom he could "count for help." Much important work was accomplished in the environment of this "power projection." A relationship of mutual trust and an atmosphere that permitted and indeed honored Paul's long-neglected feelings came to be established. Such a relationship widened Paul's circle of self-awareness, and this growing closeness to his emotional life complemented Paul's already potent capacity for understanding. Thus, his relationship to his wife grew more honest and direct, if not any closer emotionally. His interest in extramarital adventures waned. He felt confident enough to switch professional fields and take on a job that demanded much personal initiative and interpersonal interaction.

However, the considerably less benign, more complex factors that lay beneath the benevolent but highly transferential image of the analyst soon began to poke through the screen. As the analyst maintained a neutral stance and began to explore Paul's feelings about the analytic situation and their relationship, the sessions grew tense. The proximate cause within the sessions for much of this exploration was Paul's requests for information from the analyst, sometimes inappropriately personal information, sometimes appropriately professional advice. These requests, moreover, were framed in such a way as to preclude any answers from the analyst other than a simple "yes" or "no."

The long-hidden dark side of Paul's experience of the analyst began thus to emerge. If the analyst did not answer the questions in the prescribed "yes" or "no" format, he was unsympathetic, uncaring, unwilling to share or be real. Moreover, it seemed to Paul, to fail to give him the information he requested was a way in which the analyst intended to maintain control over him by denying him what he needed and wanted. How could he make decisions about what he wanted if the analyst was withholding what Paul needed to decide? How could he trust the analyst if the analyst was so tied to his own need to control him? The analyst consistently attempted to interpret Paul's experience for him, to point out Paul's own need to control, to explore the assumption that the analyst held what Paul needed to grow, to note aloud the similarity that this image of the analyst had to Paul's own emotional experience of Mother. With his own rigorously honest intellectual gifts, Paul could both see and accept these interpretations as objectively true. However, the emotional integration of such a projection seemed at times a nearly impossible task. Paul's subjective recognition that the ambivalent power of the analyst to harm or help was really grounded in Paul's own conflictual relationship to his own autonomy, which in turn was tied to an equally ambivalent archetypal Mother that had so strongly colored his own personal experience.

After one particularly pitched session of recrimination from Paul and interpretation from the analyst, the synchronistic event described above occurred. If the character of these occurrences is, indeed, "like a waking dream," as Bolen puts it (1979, p. 37), then the synchronistic power failure and its restoration in the context of this highly charged emotional situation merit considerable reflection, as a symbol of the archetypal forces at work in Paul's process of change and as a symbol of the transition space of this change.

The dreamlike quality of this power failure and the moment of its restoration is based on the almost incredible complementarity between the form of the event and its meaning within this particular analytical situation of conflict. Electricity with all its various properties is clearly the central symbol of the event, and no better symbol could have been found to represent the many aspects of that particular analytic moment. Describing emotional states with a terminology of electricity drawn largely from physics is practically a psychological convention. One speaks of "charged situations," the "shock" of recognition, feeling "plugged in" or "disconnected." Moreover, electricity, itself describable only as an ineffable "something" midway between a "process" and a "thing," is an altogether apt image for one's emotions, which are never so finite that they can be pinned down fully and yet never so formless as to permit a denial of their existence. For the electricity to fail before a session, and particularly due to, of all things, a tropical storm, is an obvious allusion to the emotional blockage that Paul and the analyst were experiencing, perhaps largely due to the rather intellectual, interpretive way that they had been going about understanding the heated conflict, the "tropical storm," between them.

The aptness of using electricity as an image for emotion, one can see, is based on the equation of "electricity" with "power." Such a semantic equation functions symbolically to indicate both the experience of power inherent in any deeply felt emotion as well as the empowering result of deep emotional experiences. Just as modern life is inconceivable without the generation of electricity, a meaningful existence, a life with texture, substance, and worth, is just as inconceivable without the successful generation and channeling of one's inner emotional power. Indeed, this power of feeling and this feeling of emotion's power is the very fuel of analysis and human growth.

Going further, however, one sees that the psychological metaphor of electricity as "emotion" and as "power" rests largely on electricity's inherent physical character as a phenomenon of transmission. Its charge and utility is proportionate to the quantity conducted from generation to use. Even so-called static electricity is only in evidence and experience when the two conductors (such as an index finger and a door knob) are close enough to permit discharge. The psychological parallel, namely that the power of emotional experience is a phenomenon of interrelationship, is equally germane to the symbolism of the synchronistic event under examination.

Thus, the literal electrical outage that created the physical context for Paul's analytical session was synchronistic precisely because of the multiple figurative meanings it held for him and his analyst. It clearly had meaning for the analytical relationship as a symbolic depiction of Paul's inner experience. Powerless before the analyst as before his mother, deprived of functionality from within by a storm of feeling, Paul found himself in the midst of his own power failure. Moreover, this inner power failure served to highlight the analyst's own sense of frustration and lack of movement: interpretations and strict adherence to analytic neutrality were not enough to resolve the conflict, and thus, his power, too, had failed him. Together, therefore, the relationship had failed: its charge, its force, and its nature as an interrelationship all had seemingly come to naught.

One looks, for this reason, with great interest at the equally important moment at which power was restored, specifically, the point at which the analyst commented on how important it was for Paul to have the analyst respect Paul's own decisions about his needs and desires. Here, it is of paramount importance to understand the nature and function of Paul's transference.

His early experience of emotional powerlessness, severe and consistent enough in his childhood to have been tinged with collective images, led him to an archetypal transference experience of the analyst. However, this transference experience remained split between the all-good Benevolent Mother, constellated as a way to compensate his feelings of deprivation and lack of nourishment, and the phallic Destructive Mother, the archetypal image at the base of the complex that evolved from his interaction with his own disturbed personal mother. In his analysis as in his childhood and his life, to get what he needed for himself emotionally became a highly conflicted proposition. Unable to imagine providing for his own emotional needs, since Mother never did, he could only look to others—his wife, his mistresses, his analyst—to take care of him. If they did so, the situation stabilized for a while and the positive pole of the archetypal transference held beneficent sway. However, if the situation was otherwise, as with his analyst who was more interested in exploring and understanding than in providing, the negative pole of the transference became constellated, in which being deprived emotionally was felt as identical to destruction at the hands of the Terrible Mother.

Obviously, such an intense, split transference experience, with its attendant experience of powerlessness regardless of which valence of the archetype was dominant, rendered the analytical relationship dysfunctional, hence the potent synchronistic symbolism of the power failure. That the analyst's comment on Paul's desire for respect was underlined dramatically by the literal restoration of power to the building indicates the depth of archetypal transformation which such an understanding brought about. Having worked so extensively with his negative transferential image of the analyst, Paul was ripe to see that the analyst's refusal to answer "yes" or "no" questions did not necessarily indicate any lack of empathy or respect for Paul's experiences or decisions. Indeed, the analyst's insight into what Paul wanted on a deeper level, that is, true respect for his autonomy, and the analyst's verbalization of this insight proved to Paul that the analyst's refusal to answer did not come out of a lack of empathy or desire to control and destroy. The analyst's refusal came rather from a much more profound desire to respect Paul's complete autonomy, from his trust that Paul, and only Paul, could and would find his own inner source of strength. Within this experience of respect, inner autonomy, and understanding, the charge, the power, and the connection of the analytical relationship could resume: power had been generated to useful ends.

With regard to the analytic process, however, one sees that Paul's movement from dependence to independence came about only through an intense and sometimes frightening experience of liminality within the analytical relationship. Intended to heal Paul's difficulties in negotiating his mid-life transition, the analysis itself quickly turned into a situation of liminality, in which Paul's previous self-conceptions were challenged as he grew to use more of himself, as he found himself changing. The analyst, moreover, in permitting the development and exploration of the negative-mother transference, permitted an even deeper sort of liminality to come about, in which Paul was plunged not only into uncertainty as to his own motivations and experience but into an equally (perhaps even more) excruciating experience of uncertainty as to who the analyst was. Was the analyst a real person or simply an unfeeling analytical role-player? Had the analyst actually become Paul's abusive mother, or was he an archetypal figure of beneficent healing with an awful, savage shadow?

Thus, the power failure, in its symbolic use of light and darkness, served as a helpful image of this liminal uncertainty. Not only had electricity failed in this critical liminal breach but so had the light: consciousness, awareness, discrimination, growth. The session went on dimly, in the faint morning light of the small window, in a gray zone between seeing and not seeing, knowing and not knowing, feeling and not feeling. In tolerating this grayness between Paul's conception of himself as dependent and another conception of himself as independent and strong, in sitting with the transference-induced uncertainty and permitting a conception of others to move from seeing them as mere objects of controlling providence to the possibility that others might care for and respect him on a level beyond need, in peering with the analyst through gray liminal light of the present at what he had been and what he could become, in seeking to understand this liminal symbol of a session lit dimly, Paul crossed over the threshold of change. The light returned.

Clearly, the essential synchronicity of the incident, its meaning for analyst and patient, is to be found on both the level of liminal process as well as on the level of analytic content. One might ask if all examples of in-session synchronicity comment upon both the nature of the archetypal transformation engaged at the moment of occurrence and the liminality of the analytic context. The second incident to be examined provides evidence in support of this hypothesis.

## The Encounter in the Doorway

"Mark" had sought out psychotherapy to resolve recurrent and debilitating depressions and to make a decision about whether or not to leave his high-pressured and unsatisfying job. Now in his mid-thirties, he had attended a good school, had worked hard, and had both the diligence and presentation of someone who would make a success of himself in his field. Thus, to his analyst as well as to himself, the recurrent depressions were inexplicable and intensely frustrating, interfering with his ability to work productively or with confidence. Indeed, much of the job pressure had come about because his depressed mood and concomitant listlessness, alternating with periods of agitation and insomnia, had affected his productivity to the extent that his supervisors had noticed.

Unlike Paul, Mark's feeling function was not overshadowed by his thinking, despite the highly analytical nature of his professional field. However, due in part to cultural proscriptions against the expression of emotion and in part to a natural introversion, Mark's tendency to internalize his emotional life seemed to stand behind his chronic low-grade depressions and a long-standing, painful series of psychosomatic symptoms, including asthma, various "accidental" injuries, and a whole gamut of stress-related colds and flu.

The most debilitating part of his difficulties in emotional expression was the interpersonal barrenness of his life. His family of origin tended to play helpless, calling upon Mark constantly to resolve one or another various crises and, although they were more draining than enriching, family activities constituted most of his social life. Closeness with them, as conflicted and enmeshed as it was, nevertheless was the only closeness consistently available to him. Outside of the family, his life was a whirl of places and people, one-night stands, and brief affairs. He suffered from what the analyst came to call "geography," that is, from the mistaken notion that a change of place would effect a change of life. Mark traveled constantly, almost compulsively, never settling down enough to really get to know anyone very deeply, staying in one place only long enough for some fleeting sexual contact before moving on to another place and another face. In large part, his "geographic" tendencies protected him from the vulnerability of emotional expression, but the resultant shallowness of his life and relationships had cast a pall over his professional career, successful and productive though it was.

Analysis was undertaken largely with the goal of aiding Mark in understanding and expressing his inner life. However, as might be expected, progress was slow. The cultural proscriptions with which he had grown up against "losing face" had endowed him with a carefully prepared, almost seamless persona of politeness and compliance. Moreover, his tendency to take vacations at regular intervals ensured that analysis, at least initially, was more a series of interruptions than a series of meetings. Since his conflicts with his "helpless" family and the role they had given him to play were especially sore points for him, much initial exploration concentrated on how he felt when with his family and how he might wish to change his behavior toward them in response to their demands. Nevertheless, the sessions had an air of unreality about them: Mark was bright and compliant enough to know that he was supposed to talk about his feelings, but actually to experience these feelings with the analyst in the sessions was still a great distance away.

Dream work, however, successfully injected a touch of real inner experience to the sessions. Mark's difficulty in sleeping meant, ironically, that he had access to many of his dreams. Further, his highly developed visual sense made the dream images fascinating to him, and some of the understandings he gained through exploration of his dreams succeeded in convincing him that analysis could help resolve his inhibitions, dissatisfactions, and conflicts. Yet, even with this working alliance and the aid of unconscious imagery, the sessions retained their distant emotional quality, lacking any truly spontaneous expression of self.

As the dream work eventually began to give him more and more access to the inner world of his feelings, a state of conflict began to form in the sessions. Although his emotional life grew strong and vivid, all his barriers against emotional expression and fears of vulnerability still stood firm. The situation began to resemble a pot with a tightly placed lid being fired up slowly from below. Something had to give.

As this conflict between inner emotional experience and inexperience in sharing his feelings with others grew hotter and hotter, Mark began to re-experience many of the old symptoms that had fallen by the wayside, especially the insomnia and agitated depressions. Unintentional self-injuries, sprained ankles and twisted knees, even a broken bone, followed any deep experience or communication of feelings with the analyst or with others, and thus, to Mark, the analysis seemed useless, hopeless, inadequate to change him. He soon began to express directly the frustration he felt with the slowness of the change, the distance that the discussions seemed to have from the rest of his life, the absurdity of the mutual roles, the emotional emptiness of the sessions.

Feeling that frustration, anger, and irritation were perhaps the most important emotions for this inhibited, compliant patient to express directly, the analyst encouraged Mark to bring forth all his discontents. The sessions grew still more heated. Mark's persona began to show signs of wear and tear. He would begin to speak more loudly, begin to cry, find himself gesticulating. Then, he would catch himself, calming himself down, retreating into his "good client" pose of composure and self-effacement, mumbling, avoiding the analyst's eyes, only to resume his complaints about the ineffectiveness of the analysis in changing his "real" life.

After one such sequence of Mark sallying forth with anger and retreating again into a thicket of complaints, the analyst pointed out that Mark seemed to be making a distinction between "real life" and "analysis." He further wondered out loud if such a view of "analysis" as something divorced from "real" experience might be standing in Mark's way of truly enjoying or using the emotional freedom he had begun to find with the analyst in the sessions. At that moment, "real life" intruded as described above, "real life" in the form of the knock on the door and a neighbor who insisted on waiting outside.

The symbolic character of the event at that particular moment, its synchronistic meaning, is based on its relationship to three discrete aspects of the analytic situation: first, the inner transformation of the patient taking place; second, the liminality of the analytic situation at that point in time; and third, the resolution of this analytic liminality. Each of these aspects and their corresponding symbols within the occurrence are to be examined, for in these lies the significance of the event for Mark and for greater knowledge of the analytic process.

On the level of Mark's inner transformation, the event's character as an interruption of the analytic hour and an intrusion into the relationship between analyst and patient seems to make a powerful, symbolic comment on the artificial unconscious distinction Mark had made between analysis, which he experienced as "unreal," and life outside the analytic session, experienced as "real life." In the course of keeping the lid on the boiling pot of his feelings, Mark had clamped a tight lid on the analytic vessel, too, such that only a dramatic "break-in" could bring home to him the falseness and potential harm in this distinction. This provident intervention of the Self to reveal the way forward at such a critical moment makes this synchronistic incident seem once again "like a waking dream."

However, the solution to the insolubility of Mark's conflict was not only awareness of the strict emotional compartments into which he had placed his various experiences and relationships. The healing power of the incident, its symbolic nucleus, was the very intrusiveness of the event, which bridged Mark's emotional compartments, broke down the invalid distinctions between his experiences, and injected "reality" into the analytic "unreality." The event did more than simply make a point, i.e., that Mark needed to remove the lid from his feelings and from the analytic relationship, or that he needed to let the analytic reality of his inner life seep more and more into his previously distant outer relationships. As an interruption, intrusion, and intervention, the event itself acted purposively, in fact, actually to remove this lid for Mark and to let in real life and real relationship.

The second aspect of the event's synchronistic meaning is tied to the liminality of the analytic situation then at hand. This aspect of the event is centered upon the symbol of the threshold, so prominent figuratively and literally in the story of the occurrence. Inexorably drawn out of a persona-ruled existence of inhibitions and compliance and slowly initiated into a vivid world of sensation and feeling, Mark found himself inextricably, painfully, betwixt and between. Unable to go backward and put his emotions back into the box he and his analyst had opened through dream work and their relationship of mutual trust, Mark still remained too frightened to go forward and admit into existence the person he was becoming, a person with deep feelings, a person capable of sharing. He thus found himself in a liminal situation, on the threshold of change. This threshold, the literal, physical *limen* of Mark's analysis, stands as a dramatic symbol of the transitional experience that analysis had led Mark into, standing between two worlds, his past and his future, his weakness and his strength, his introversion and his extraversion, his isolation and his community.

The incident here, though, seems to go farther than a mere marking of liminality's presence, for the neighbor's obstinacy forced Mark to pass by her on the threshold and not merely to remain there, undecided and uncommitted to movement. This third symbol, this "neighborly encounter," clearly comments on the necessity of going past a liminal experience and onto resolution and acceptance. In Mark's case, such resolution meant beginning to share some of his inner wealth with others, taking the analysis "out of the room," so to speak, and into his relationships with others, thereby realizing—making real as well as acknowledging—the potential for growth that analysis had helped him find.

A danger lurks in having found in the term "liminality" such an excellent and etymologically well-grounded description of that essential condition for analytic transformation. By focusing on liminality's importance in analysis as a core condition, one may be tempted to confuse the means of liminality with the true end of analysis, inner and outer transformation. Mark's neighborly encounter points out the importance of moving off the threshold experience and onward to the change such an experience engenders.

As the midwife of the analytic relationship, liminality is also the midwife of the transformation which is the larger goal of analytic work. At the point of ripeness, the lights must go on, and the liminal grayness must be left behind. At the propitious moment, one must step off the threshold of change into the change itself, into a more integral sense of self and others.

## Clinical Considerations

Both these synchronistic events within analysis serve as symbols for the liminal analytic context and the changes that such a context affords. Thus, one must examine what elements of these two relationships worked to establish the liminal experience in which the Self, through synchronistic events, made itself apparent.

In both cases, the analyst refrained as much as possible from cutting off any negative experience of the analysis that might have developed. In Paul's case, such restraint meant permitting a full-blown and painful negative-mother complex to be projected onto the analyst for an extended period of time. In Mark's case, such restraint meant permitting all of the patient's irritability and anger to develop slowly and in a focused way around the seeming uselessness of the analytic work. Far from the somewhat derogatory stereotype of a silent, Freudian attitude which permits and even encourages such "negative transferences" to develop out of misguided cynicism about human nature, this analytic attitude of restraint and acceptance of negative attitudes is based on a number of factors: first, the abiding conviction that wholeness can only come if *all*, good *and* bad, is experienced within analysis; second, the Jungian conviction that even seemingly "pathological" phenomena serve a purpose which may not always be immediately evident; and third, an attitude of trust that, if the patient's process is allowed the widest berth, resolution will occur. The events described here support such beliefs and such trust by showing, within the synchronistic phenomena, archetypal wholeness at work on both the physical and figurative levels of everyday life.

Clinically, such neutrality means not rushing to point out the "positive" factors at work in any given situation or set of feelings. "Positive" often simply means "that which feels good," and a "negative" experience, although painful, might well be as potentially "positive" as any or even most situations of "feeling good." The two examples above make this point eloquently.

Such neutrality also means not rushing to interpret or comment about archetypal movements or events. Not only does the collective unconscious seem not to have needed mortal intervention over the millennia in order to find its way forward, but, as the highly dramatic quality of the synchronistic events reported here indicates, contact with such archetypal images and feelings require a sagacious and respectful attitude toward them, a sacred sense of their untouchability. Their power is great, and the proper container is required.

Thus, in Paul's case, the analyst made no comment regarding the possible synchronistic character of the blackout, even though the analyst was obviously quite aware of the symbolic parallels. In the analyst's judgment, Paul's emotional state and his capacity for overintellectual analysis of symbolic material made an emotional experience of powerlessness within the analysis more important for Paul than any potentially distracting analysis of the synchronistic symbolism of the power failure. Indeed, worse than distracting, to point out such synchronicity might actually have been frightening, given the intense liminality and Paul's concomitant psychic disorientation. Unable to disentangle himself and the analyst from the personal and archetypal projections in the room, Paul lacked the firm ground required to meet such archetypal events on their own terms.

In contrast to Paul's situation, Mark's extensive involvement with his dreams and the home he had thereby created for his symbolic inner life provided him with the container he needed to examine the meanings which lay behind the fortuitous event. Far from frightening or distracting, the analyst's wondering aloud about what the interruption and intrusion might have intended to highlight for the two of them allowed Mark to begin to do precisely what the symbolism of the event seemed to move him toward, that is, to begin to stitch together the wholeness of his life from the scattered, unrelated pieces of his experiences and relationships. The analyst's questions over a series of weeks and their joint examination of the incident brought home to Mark in a decisive, concrete way both the cause and the effect of his artificial distinctions between "real" and "unreal" and thus enlarged his awareness of his life within and without.

Clinical work, particularly when such deep sources of archetypal transformation have been engaged through the establishment of a liminal state, also seems to require the analyst to "expect the unexpected" and to have a sharp eye out for the symbolism of everyday life. As Stein and others, in their work on liminality, have pointed out, synchronistic phenomena occur in conjunction with liminal contexts: liminality renders the unusual usual (Stein 1983). The numinous quality and surprising nature of synchronistic events are precisely what endow these occurrences with their meaning and power to change. Usually too dramatic to ignore, especially when occurring within the analytic sessions such as the ones discussed here, synchronistic events in a liminal context recast and unseat previous ways, our previous categories and self-conceptions. Yet, how easy it would have been simply to put the power outage down to an inefficient utility company or to curse the neighbor for her obtuseness, and go no farther in thinking about these strange happenings or their analytic context. Or worse still, how much easier to ignore the possible synchronistic significance of other events, for example, those that occur outside the analytic hour or in the dream life of individual analysts or patients.

In *The Unbearable Lightness of Being*, a novel in which chance meetings and symbolic events play a major part, Czech author Milan Kundera writes:

> Our day-to-day life is bombarded with fortuities, or to be more precise, with the accidental meetings of people and events we call coincidences. "Coincidence" means that two events unexpectedly happen at the same time, they meet. . . . Early in the novel that Tereza clutched under her arm when she went to visit Tomas, Anna meets Vronsky in curious circumstances: they are at the railway station when someone is run over by a train. At the end of the novel, Anna throws herself under a train. This symmetrical composition—the same motif appears at the beginning and the end—may seem quite "novelistic" to you and I am willing to agree, but only on the condition that you refrain from reading such notions as "fictive," "fabricated," and "untrue to life" into the word "novelistic." Because human lives are composed in precisely such a fashion.
>
> They are composed like music. Guided by his sense of beauty, an individual transforms a fortuitous occurrence (Beethoven's music, death under a train) into a motif, which then assumes a permanent place in the composition of the individual's life. . . . It is wrong, then, to chide the novel for being fascinated by mysterious coincidences . . . but it is right to chide man for being blind to such coincidences in his daily life. For he thereby deprives his life of a dimension of beauty. (1984, pp. 51–52)

Synchronistic occurrences and their liminal context, therefore, offer analyst and patient just this sort of beauty and wholeness. In bringing us to the threshold of change, they can help us step beyond this all-important threshold and into a new, changed world.

## References

Bolen, Jean Shinoda. 1979. *The Tao of Psychology: Synchronicity and the Self*. San Francisco: Harper and Row.

Hopcke, Robert H. 1988. Synchronicity in analysis: various types and their various roles for patient and analyst. *Quadrant* 21:55–64.

Hopcke, Robert H. In press. The barker: a synchronistic event in analysis. *Journal of Analytical Psychology*.

Jung, C. G. 1952. Synchronicity: An acausal connecting principle. In *Collected Works* 8:419–531. Princeton, N.J.: Princeton University Press, 1969.

Kundera, Milan. 1984. *The Unbearable Lightness of Being*. New York: Harper and Row.

Stein, Murray. 1983. *In Midlife*. Dallas: Spring Publications.

Turner, Victor. 1969. *The Ritual Process*. Chicago: Aldine.

______. 1974. *Dramas, Field and Metaphors: Symbolic Action in Human Society*. Ithaca, N.Y.: Cornell University Press.

van Gennep, A. 1960. *The Rites of Passage*. Chicago: University of Chicago Press.

# The Interactive Field in Analysis: Agreements and Disagreements

J. Marvin Spiegelman

The following (a shortened version of lectures given to the Chicago Society of Jungian Analysts and to the Independent Group in London in the spring and summer of 1989) is a discussion of four areas each of agreement and disagreement among analysts, particularly Jungians, regarding our common understanding of the transference. I include, as a special consideration, the issue of self-disclosure and, therefore, I make use of personal examples.

## Areas of Agreement

### *Therapeutic Situation as a Field*

We Jungians often refer to the therapeutic situation as an analytic "field," without realizing, perhaps, that this term has some history to it in physics, mathematics, and even in academic psychology. For our

---

**J. Marvin Spiegelman**, Ph.D., has a private practice in Studio City, Calif. He is author of three books in psycho-mythology, most recently *Jungian Psychology and the Passions of the Soul*, co-author and editor of five books on Jungian psychology and religion (in press, *Sufism, Islam, and Jungian Psychology*) and *Jungian Analysts: Their Visions and Vulnerabilities*, in addition to many articles.

present purposes, however, I want to focus on the pragmatics and experience of this field in our daily work.

For example, I very often get "symptoms" when a patient begins a session, or after some moments of work. These are usually body reactions of various kinds, such as headaches, stomach aches, heartaches, shortness of breath, sphincter tension, fatigue, etc. They do not usually have a direct connection with what is being said, but whenever I reveal these reactions, I almost always discover that the patient is having, or had in the recent past, the same symptom or one related to it. Most of the time, an underlying symbolic parallel is associated to the psychological content being discussed. When this occurs, I am relieved and take it as a fact that the "therapeutic field" is now operating; there has been a constellation of complexes and an energy exchange so that both the patient and myself are embedded in that field. The work of awareness, interpretation, and integration of content can now proceed in a harmonious, therapeutically useful fashion. It is my task, now, to be alert to what is happening in myself and in the patient, as always, but to share that awareness and understand what it means. This generally results in a clearing up of the symptom.

My second kind of apparently unconnected reaction has to do with feelings. After a session begins, I may become quite sad or dreamy, so that my energy level seems to be depressed, as well as my mood. When I mention this condition, particularly sadness, to the patient, a similar awareness usually emerges, or they seem to fall into that condition and some repressed content emerges.

The loss of energy is more complicated. There I may mention the fact that I feel listless or energyless or even bored, am drawn into the unconscious, and wonder what is happening to my therapeutic partner. When a parallel condition is reported, I suggest that we both "drop" into the unconscious at that point, into fantasy or aloneness for a few moments, and then return to share the content. This, too, has useful consequences and confirms that not only is there a therapeutic field in which we are embedded, but there is a concrete movement of psychic energy that also takes place.

These kinds of experience, I think, are not uncommon among psychotherapists, although my way of revealing these reactions is not likely to be typical. Some analysts, particularly Freudians, suggest that this loss of energy, for example, is because the patient is sucking our vitality out of us, or because, via projective identification, a content is being thrust into us. I cannot fully agree with the interpretation that the patient is doing such things to us, consciously or unconsciously, although at times this is certainly the case. The patient often experiences us as doing something to him or her which we do not think we are doing at all, we need to remember, and we are likely to chalk this up to projection. What makes our judgment of who is doing what to whom so certain?

I think it is more useful to suggest that a field is set up, whereby some content of the patient, usually, sets off something in us, consciously or unconsciously, and the interchange takes place. Reactions of both patient and therapist are connected with the archetypal forms in the background, and the admixture of psyches includes the personal and transpersonal on both sides. The analyst's advantage is that he or she is more experienced in dealing with these unconscious invasions or reactions, has tools of understanding, and is committed to helping the partner.

Even if one agrees with the foregoing understanding, there remains the question, why are the analyst's responses just those of sensations or feelings? Is this typical or typological? My answer is that it is both. I happen to be an introverted intuitive/thinking type, so when the unconscious is mobilized in the work, the content that emerges will understandably have a lot of feeling and sensation in it. I would imagine that sensation and feeling types would get the reactions of intuitions and thoughts. But, since so many Jungian analysts tend to be intuitives, I would not be surprised that reactions of many colleagues are often similar to mine. The sensations and feelings, arising from our unconsciously evoked third and fourth functions, can then be combined with our differentiated intuition and thinking to produce useful interpretations or comments. In any case, the unconscious first strikes us with emotion, so we would all encounter that first.

But we must not pass too quickly over this experience of real energy exchange going on in the analytic process. Few of us have the sensitivity or skill to read auras or energy fields but it is precisely in this area that we are treading. We think that our interpretations of behavior or dreams or fantasies is what has effect, but it is obvious to many of us that the energy exchange going on in the room is profound and is just as healing—or disturbing—as the exchange of words. Indeed, it has long been apparent to me that many of my dream interpretations get their power and significance from the fact that I am in tune with the patient and thus all my knowledge and experience comes to use in the service of that connection. I shall later give an example of the attunement in connection with body symptoms.

*Openness to the Patient*

All therapists are agreed that we are open and receptive to each patient or analysand who comes into our office and psyches, attentive to what they say and, very soon, also to their impact upon us. The field eventually created is dependent, first of all, upon what they are and what they bring. This is as it should be, since the purpose of the relationship is healing and enlightenment of the paying customer, after all, and whatever benefit the therapist gets from this process is merely included as a fringe benefit. Yet, in reality, things are more complicated: the patient reacts, too, to the office and the person of the therapist. He or she selects and responds to all of that, consciously or unconsciously, and we all know that to think of ourselves as a blank screen for our analysands is inaccurate and even merely defensive. But we do need to protect ourselves from patients, also, do we not? From the abuse and passing on of toxic conditions, even poisons? Yet we also know that our capacity to contain and transform these noxious processes is crucial to the healing process.

We recall that the original meaning of the German word for transference, *übertragung*, referred to the ancient Teutonic practice of applying a bandage to a wounded are of a person and then putting this same bandage on a healthy tree. The idea, of course, is that the healthy tree could absorb this "transferring" of the wound to itself and thereby cure. Psychologically, we might see this as an act whereby the analyst is open to the poisons of the patient—as a consequence of wounds—and allows these to enter into himself or herself and be absorbed by one's own "tree," the Self, as manifested in this relationship, accomplishing healing thereby. Or, rather, it is the Self that does the healing, evoked by the patient, carried by the therapist, and experienced jointly in the process: damaged Self evokes healthy Self, followed by awakening of healthy Self in the process and in the patient.

The foregoing is, perhaps, a bit idealized, since we often do various things to avoid such exposure, even unconsciously. One can make a case, for example, that the traditional analyst's stance of objectivity and interpretative "throwing back" of the projections is, in truth, a defensive maneuvering to ward off impact. Yet, as Jung told us repeatedly in his therapeutic papers, our effect on patients is proportional to their effect upon us, and to ward off the impact is to reduce the possibility of healing. Once more, we are brought to the concept of the "field."

I am reminded of C. A. Meier's (1959) paper, in which he discusses the "totalistic" character of the analytical situation and concludes that not a few analysts "go under," so to speak, as a consequence. The high suicide rate among therapists, plus the folk fantasy that they do not possess a lot of mental health are hints at the partial validity of this point (Spiegelman 1988).

An example that graphically illuminates the foregoing is unusual in that it is not from a traditional analytical situation, but from a kind of marriage counseling, one that had been going on for three years at the time of the illustrative event. I hasten to add that this is a unique situation for me; I have often worked with couples for some sessions or months, finding it a valuable task in the holding of opposites and enhancing the capacity to empathize with divergent positions, but this case expanded into years, since both the love and the difficulties went deep, indeed. Briefly, the couple, well into middle age, foundered on the belief of the wife that her husband, a retired executive, was unfaithful and even had attempted to poison her. This—to him, false—accusation drove him to both rage and despair. The unravelling of the relationship and the antecedents in youth and childhood took a lot of time, including work with dreams. At the time in question, the man had been suffering from extreme depression for some months, reactivated from years past. His dreams were positive, reminding of a happy time in his youth, but he was split and bitter. My own attempts were to attend to him, connect with him as best I could. At the time in question, I had done so and found that I was ineffective, failing and sinking back into despair myself. After I said this, the man reported that he was feeling much better, uplifted. It was noteworthy that the dark mood, transferred to me, allowed his positive condition in the unconscious to emerge. This process repeated itself, but then we shifted to the fact of the wife's suspicion and our hopelessness in convincing her that this was not a concrete fact, but a psychological one (his rage, during the earlier years of their marriage, and her fears had "poisoned" her).

At that moment, I experienced a sharp pain in the stomach and nausea, as if I had been literally poisoned. When I reported this experience to the woman, she was astonished and said that this was exactly what was happening to her at that moment. This simultaneous, field-connected link-up with both spouses provided a kind of turning point in the process, permitting a more rapid transformation of the toxic conditions damaging to both of them. Analysis, interpretation of dreams, work on the relationship, all had been insufficient to this point and the depth of the disturbance required not only the openness to the unconscious on my part, but a concrete participation. Thus we experience not only a *participation mystique* that Jung so often spoke of, but one that includes a consciousness of that mutual immersion. This leads us to the third area of agreement, that of the analyst being touched by the process.

*Analyst Effected by the Process*

My previous example, that of the depressed husband and suspicious wife, is unusual only in the sense that it is couple's therapy and therefore includes more in the analytic field, triangularity particularly. We are immediately reminded of Jung's use of the alchemical metaphor of the Royal Couple and their transformation. The famous "axiom of Maria Prophetissa," of the sequence of stages in the transformation process from one to two to three, with the fourth arising out of the third, is mentioned frequently by him. Both he and others have illustrated that the interplay of analyst and patient implies at least a foursome: analyst and his or her anima or animus, patient and his or her anima or animus. Freud always felt that at least three people were present, psychologically, in the sexual act—referring to the presence in the psyches of the couple of the primal scene and the oedipus complex—and Jung was at his most profound in referring to the alchemical imagery arising in the transference. For us inheritors of the pioneering efforts of our founders, it has been important to convince ourselves of these facts by experience. Advance in understanding has been more uncertain.

My own experience has been that the unconscious usually appears and effects me as a "third," between analysand and analyst, rather than as a fourth. For example, a shadow figure or content is projected onto me, which evokes a shadowy reaction. The patient dreams of me as licentious or money-grubbing. My feelings are hurt at this projection, like it or not, even if I am aware of the projective character and the fact that I provide hooks for this, both consciously and unconsciously. The feeling of being "misunderstood," for example, arises when I have contributed to this projection by reporting a sexual fantasy. I know that I have done so, but I also know that my motive is that of honesty, or making conscious, and it hurts to be adversely labelled, even by the patient's unconscious. My shadow is apparent, but the hurt is that I am only partially seen and judged. But the hurt induces the archetype of the "wounded healer," leading to further awareness and healing.

The "fourth," in such conditions, usually emerges only later on. I am thinking now of a patient I had seen for over a year who dreamed of being married to an "older man," with certain characteristics similar to me, but she also had a lover in this dream. The "older man" had a "housekeeper" with whom he had had a previous liaison who did not like the new marriage. This dream came after a session wherein I had gone over the hour; boundaries were transgressed, so to speak, and the deeper transference, in the alchemical sense, was finally achieved. A foursome resulted.

But these foursomes are not always what Jung reported. I recall a very early case I had, only a couple of years after becoming an analyst, in which the patient dreamed that she and I were at the seashore observing two strange fish. One was a "harem-fish" and the other was a "cat-fish." The harem-fish entered into her vagina while the cat-fish suckled my penis. Both fish then went into the ocean and united with each other. I thought immediately of the famous anima/animus foursome of alchemy, but my patient said that the harem-fish was female and the cat-fish male, so we were in for long shadow-integration work, rather than anima/animus sharing that I had anticipated.

In any case, the analyst is ultimately touched in his own soul by any work which goes beyond superficial counseling, and this demands increased consciousness on his or her part. We continually get affected and infected and thus have to work on ourselves, as well as with the patient. This is supposed to be good for us, and I suppose it is in the long run, since it helps us to realize our myth as healers: we continually are re-wounded and have to be healed in deeper fashion. In our being affected, however, there arises the issue of whether one communicates this effect or contains it, the "reveal versus conceal" dilemma I referred to in an earlier paper (1988). Since this brings up an area of disagreement, I shall defer its discussion, and briefly speak of the final agreement, in Jungian circles, about the transference, that of the archetypal dimension.

### *Archetypal Basis*

Jungians agree that the ultimate basis of psychic functioning is archetypal in nature and that the complexes evoked and treated in the work have such a root foundation. It is this foundation that both provides the similarity between analyst and analysand and also serves as the healing source. Whether this archetypal basis is dealt with on a conscious level or not depends, of course, on the necessities of the patient, but normally these occur with increasing frequency as the work progresses, in time and depth. Where disagreement occurs, it has to do with the nature and importance of the myths that arise and how to handle these.

## Disagreements

### *Mutual Process versus Asymmetry*

Ever since the early 1960s, I have been arguing in favor of the approach to analysis and the transference as one in which a "mutual process" takes place, ultimately, if not from the very outset (Spiegelman 1965, 1972, 1980). The interplay of psyches, the evocation of the analyst's complexes, leads to the archetypal level of connection and the two parties are then embroiled in an alchemical stew. This requires the analyst to leave his perch of authority and defensive objectivity and relate to the unconscious as a participant in that process. In various papers, I have spelled this out and have invoked Jung as one who shares my conviction (Jung 1946). Interest leads to involvement, which leads to being affected, which leads to embroilment, which results in a mutual process and equality.

The opposition to this view has said that my mutual process idea is exaggerated, that the very nature of the relationship is unequal: the patient comes to the therapist, pays for sessions, relies on the knowledge and control of the analyst, holds us as ultimately responsible. The analytical relationship, therefore, is asymmetrical rather than symmetrical.

I have responded that the process indeed begins in this asymmetrical fashion, but as the unconscious enters into the relationship, the two parties are so affected that now the connection is symmetrical. The analyst, I have said, has to give up his or her claim to authority and, using one's knowledge and greater experience with the unconscious, apply oneself to the discovery and service of the authority of the Self as it manifests in both patient and therapist. Both are equal, I have claimed, in the sense of the American Declaration of Independence: we are equal under God. To translate that into psychological terms, patient and analyst are equal under the authority of the Self which emerges in an alchemical transformation to which both are submitting.

To prove that the money exchanged is not the crucial issue, I have worked with a number of people where there was no fee and the process was not so terribly different. Furthermore, I have been in what might be called "mutual process" with friends, at various periods and for varying lengths of time, in which my therapeutic responsibility was abdicated and these, too, were not terribly different.

More recently, however, I have come to see that my "proofs" were far from adequate. In those cases where no money was exchanged, there was either an implied "gift" on my part, as one does in a free-clinic situation, or the partner was a former patient. With friends, furthermore, I found that mutual process work was usually only for brief periods, in which something particular was accomplished, rather than a long-term alchemical seeking of the gold of the Self. I have been fortunate to have friends where my psychological experience has been of use in the relationship, such as supervision or sharing of life, and who have been, in turn, equally benefiting of me in various ways, so that I have not been "the authority." Yet these experiences have not proved that mutual process, in the sense of equality, does exist characteristically. I have to admit, therefore, that I was wrong.

Inequality does pertain in the analytic relationship, as my critics have maintained, not only with money, seeking for service, and expertise, but in the difference in psychological consciousness. We are equal under God, of course, but not in the world, including the world of therapy. It is obvious that we are all created unequal in abilities, station in life, etc. Our equality occurs only in the belief that we are all fragments of the divine, and no fragment is less divine than another. The sharing of divinity does not presume equality, however, and I was mistaken.

Where I am right, I believe, is in the fact that one can face this inequality and make an *individual* relationship to it, decided *mutually*, which, paradoxically, increases the *equality*! This joint decision, repeated at different times in the process, enhances the Self of each partner. In this process, inequality (on both sides!) is accepted, but the fundamental and equal meeting of Self with Self is acknowledged. I can think of several examples of this, but the ones that come to mind all entail some violation of social custom or general expectation of therapists which I am loathe to report, both because of my respect for these customs and my fear of opprobrium. But I shall mention two anyway, since I feel obliged to give evidence for my view.

The first example is that of a clergyman with whom I worked in analysis for the first time more than twenty years ago. We worked for several years, off and on, and then completed an analytic process in an intense two-year period. Some time after termination, we became friends, in another context, and participated together in an on-going study group of therapists and clergy on the problems of psychology and religion. Periodically, he returned to work with me for a time, and we needed to discuss this changing relationship and mixing-up of roles. We decided to continue. Later on, there were more connections of friendship between us, in a variety of ways, and still later, he came to me for supervision for therapy work he did himself. At times, I also was his pupil in both other areas of therapy, in which he was expert, and in friendship exchanges of a religious character. This relationship has continued; its flourishing has depended, I believe, on the consciousness of both parties and making ourselves aware of the risks and values of the individualizing of our relationship. This relationship, although unique, is not the only one where analysis has shifted to friendship and to other ways of connection.

A second example that comes to mind is that of a friend since my early teens, one with whom I went to school, served in the Merchant Marine, and shared deeply in life. Some time ago, some marital counseling was needed by him and his wife, and the situation was such that they did not trust anyone else. After discussing this with them at length, I agreed to attempt the counseling, noting the confusion of roles, the possibility of my being prejudiced in favor of my friend over his wife, etc. I also noted the possible threat to our friendship. We tried it, anyway, with my friend giving me works of his art in exchange for my time and effort. The result was quite positive; I am particularly proud of the fact that the wife found me to be as supportive and understanding of her as of him. Surprisingly, the friendship itself proved to be of particular value, since I was compelled to be honest about my personal reactions and values in their relationship. When it became possible for them to make use of another therapist, for a time, I was pleased that this was accomplished easily and effectively. They were not dependent upon me in a destructive way. The friendship has not only continued, but has deepened and developed with both parties.

I could give other examples of this nature, as well. In so doing, however, I in no way want to imply that the general ethic warning against such confusion of roles on the part of therapists is erroneous. On the contrary. I think that, in general, modalities of ethics are the result of collective experience and values and should be regarded highly. Their abrogation should take place with prudence and circumspection and only in connection with the value equal and opposite to collective truths, namely individuation. Individuation and the collective are worthy opposites and need each other. It is this very struggle that is involved in analytic work, is it not?

An awareness of this antinomy can assist us in understanding the successful outcomes of the above two relationships. If I ask myself why these thrived in spite of the ethical dangers involved, I can readily see that they did so because my friends had their own Self well in hand; it was not—or no longer—projected onto me. They were either religious persons who had their higher authority from the outset, or had discovered it in the course of their development, with me or with others. I conclude, therefore, that I was both wrong and right about "mutual process" and equality. It really only is achieved when both parties have their inner authority, have an independent Self that can be and is effected by the other, but remains solidly within. This, in the end, is what we seek generally in analytic work. We help each person, we hope, to come to and unite with his or her own inner authority, the Self. On the way, we rely on our own connection with the Self to enhance this possibility. As the process continues, furthermore, this Self-to-Self relationship becomes more conscious. Equality, therefore, is a *result*, more than a given.

My opponents are right and I, too, am right. To resolve this paradox, I suggest that we are dealing here with both an archetypal potential and an actualization. Equality "under God" (read Self) is there, archetypally, at the outset of the analysis, but it has to be made conscious and, therefore, is achieved.

### *Analyze versus Connect*

A second area of disagreement about analytical work has to do with the nature of the analyst's response to the patient, rather than the nature of the work itself. Should one analyze the communications of the patient, including behavior, questions, comments, etc., or connect with him or her? Sometimes this is expressed as a conflict between the work conceived as that in which the discovery of the roots of complexes and symptoms is at issue versus the patient's need of "re-parenting" as required for healing. Every analyst engages in both activities, of course, but the conflict as to which attitude should be the primary one is great enough to suggest that the difference between analysis and psychotherapy rests on this distinction. I recently heard a psychoanalyst, for example, admit that she made a grave error with a patient when she responded to a compliment of his by saying "thank you" instead of analyzing it. I imagine that one could just as well say "thank you," if one felt like that, and only afterwards raise the question as to whether the patient had some motive in mind in making such a compliment. If the warm, appreciative comment is not accepted, then what might be the chap's nice overture toward a healing eros is unnecessarily turned into a problem to be dissected. We are all familiar with the fun made of our profession's question, "What did he mean by that?"

Extremes certainly exist in this field, with the psychoanalysts usually occupying one end of the continuum and "re-parenting" psychotherapists occupying the other end. Michael Fordham once said, after reading my contribution to *Jungian Analysts* (Spiegelman 1988), that I did "confrontation therapy" rather than analysis. I responded that I analyze dreams and the relationship rather than the person. "Analyzing" everything can prove to be merely a defense against the natural embroilment in the process; pure "responsiveness" can turn the situation into a chat fest or friendly exchange rather than analysis. Probably, one needs to "connect" as deeply as possible in order to make meaningful analytic interpretations, whether of content or person. Equally, one needs to interpret what is taking place in the relationship in order to bring about consciousness. Healing need both.

The foregoing analysis of the situation seems rather obvious, so we might do better by asking ourselves why there needs to be a conflict between two necessary components of the analyst's activity, response and analysis. Is it a typological difference, say, between thinking and feeling? Or a fundamental difference as to what really heals, consciousness or empathy? I think both are true. My own typology, which is introverted intuitive/thinking with extraverted feeling, finds the Freudian extraverted thinking analysis of the person as both distancing and existentially inaccurate. Philosophically, I can only know how I experience the other person, not how he or she really is. I therefore can speak of what I feel, think, observe, intuit, etc., rather than say that Mr. A is doing such and such because of a particular motivation. Both the Freudians and I can agree to interpret dreams (objective evidence), but the accuracy of our interpretation, from a scientific point of view, is subject to the agreement or disagreement of the patient. The impactful effect is what really matters. Differences in analytic viewpoint arise, for example, when we choose to focus on behavior or experience. When I say that the interpretation of the person is a presumption and unscientific, they might say that I am derelict in not analyzing behavior and thus missing the point of the work. So, it is a typological matter.

Yet it is also an even more fundamental one, when we think of the therapeutic relation as a field of psyches interacting, as most analysts agree. I can recall discussions with a classical Freudian colleague in London, during my study years in Zurich, in which we both agreed that the central aim of analysis was to "make the unconscious conscious," allowing maximum freedom of choice for the patient, and not to attempt to "heal" at all! In this, a classical Freudian and a classical Jungian were more attuned than either one was with the "neo" variants based on healing rather than awareness. For Jungians, generally, however, the crucial difference, I think, is that of the archetypal basis of the psyche. I will address this issue later on. Here, we need to acknowledge that both modes of response, analyzing and connecting, are necessary, depending on the particular needs of the analytical relationship at the moment.

*Self-Disclosure versus "Use" of the Transference*

This same pair of opposites continues to polarize when we consider the role of self-disclosure versus the "use" of the transference for one's own therapeutic aim. For some classical Freudians, even the idea of self-disclosure of the analyst is a bizarre one: the point is to keep one's self as much of a blank screen as possible in order to facilitate projections and the working through of these for the sake of increased consciousness. Who can fault this lofty aim?

Yet the reality of the field condition of the process and the requirements of scientific veracity (mentioned earlier), suggest to me that I should report to the analysand what is happening with me, for comparison's sake, rather than merely attribute my reaction to what the latter is "doing" to me. The use of the transference, on the other hand, smacks of manipulation, and this is something clearly to be avoided, as both classical Freudians and Jungians are strongly agreed.

But even if one assents to self-disclosure by the analyst in the therapeutic process, what is it that should be disclosed? Facts about one's life or experiences are usually unnecessary or even evasions, although judicious presentation of such facts can provide a humanizing effect on the work, or else add to the "re-parenting" effect sometimes needed. What needs to be disclosed, I think, is one's apprehension of the unconscious impact of what is happening, without there being a sense of blame.

As I mentioned earlier, I often report body symptoms of the patient, such as sleepiness or impulses, carefully stating them as possibly meaningful contents connecting with the patient, rather than attributing these to the latter. I invite the patient to report the same, or tell me the impact of my reportage on them. We are both thereby attuned to the unconscious field between us and ready to work jointly on the conscious understanding of what is happening. This applies even more so to the reporting of fantasies, for now there is the possibility of embroiling the patient in one's now countertransference or even one's own complexes, without the constellation of a field at all! Yet the mistake is also useful, in that the therapist is seen as humanly in error and ready to abandon preconceived ideas or clinging to authority. As we all know, sometimes these fantasies are indeed accurate, so to speak, but premature.

I am reminded of a woman with whom I worked; early on, I had the strong fantasy of being a kind of Prince Charming who was going to "awaken" her, even though she was middle-aged, happily married, and mother of two! Although this was smilingly disparaged at the time, two years later it proved to be the compelling myth of the analytic work! So, it behooves us to attend to our fantasies, although we may be "out of time." Yet that is just what is expected of us, as Jungians: if we are attuned to the collective unconscious, we will be touched by its timelessness and will often be archetypally linked rather than immediately or superficially so.

The disadvantage of self-disclosure is that an opportunity is lost for the patient to experience these things in himself or herself first. If I "hold" my sexual fantasy for a time, even months or years, the theory is that the corresponding content will ultimately appear in the patient and will have a more compelling effect. When to hold and when not, when to reveal and when to conceal, these are a pair of opposites which are ever in our minds. There is no compelling rule of thumb as to how to choose, but my own guideline is to try to ascertain when the field is clearly activated in the two parties, such as by the presence of synchronistic or parapsychological events.

An example that occurs to me is not one in therapy, but at a Jungian meeting. I had presented a paper on self-disclosure, among other things, to a large group and a discussant was disagreeing with my views and presenting an alternative approach to dealing with transference. While she was speaking, I was increasingly aware of a need to urinate and recalled that this theme, urination, had popped up repeatedly during the previous hours among different speakers. When my discussant unexpectedly used an expression involving urination also, I spoke up and told the large assembled group what was going on. It seemed to me that we, the discussant and myself, if not the entire group, were embedded in a field in which the need to relieve one's self and even to express one's self (the interpretation of this instinctive activity by von Franz) was a key issue. Should one express or hold, risk being wrong or even humiliated by such revelation or expression? The group as a whole very much responded to what I said and got a clear understanding of both "mutual process" and what I meant when I suggested self-disclosure. My discussant, however, remained outside this sharing, although I was convinced that there was a heavy transference condition between us. I was able to confirm it later that night, when we were dancing at a post-conference celebration.

Another clue as to when to reveal rather than conceal is when the symptom or impulse or fantasy is so strong that it demands attention. The pressure is such that one cannot fully attend to what the patient is saying or doing. The conflict engendered between staying connected and being pressed by one's own inner content can only be resolved, as I see it, by reporting the content and saying that it has been forcing itself. Does the analysand connect with it or not?

So, keep aware of reactions is my counsel and be prepared to share these with analysands. Even if these reactions are "wrong" or out of sync, it is likely—because of the field conditions—that they have some link with truth or with healing. In any case, it generally proves to be valuable, particularly if one is not identified with or attached to these reactions as "truth," but sees them as useful indicators of possible connecting stories or myths.

As I have reported elsewhere (Spiegelman 1988), my own stance is to be present in the analytic work with both a "left hand" and a "right hand": one hand is connected with the unconscious, its taboos, impulses, imagery, while the other is related to the care-taking, responsible, connecting, parenting energies which "mind the store." I do not identify with either, but try to sit in the middle, going both left and right until wholeness is achieved.

### *Roots in Childhood or in Myth*

This leads us to the final area of disagreement I wish to address in the present discussion: whether the practical basis of the patient's difficulties lie in the wounds of infancy and childhood, or whether one's personal myth, its discovery and enhancement, is the focus of our work. At first blush, this sounds like a difference of opinion which would arise between Freudians and Jungians, but there have been enough newcomers to Jungian psychology, over the last generation or so, to indicate that at least the developmentalist branch of the latter is as focused upon the events of infancy and childhood and how these are played out in the transference as is any psychoanalyst (Samuels 1985). The impact of Klein upon our London colleagues has been immense; so much so that now there is a large group of Jungians, both in England and elsewhere, who are very much at home with this viewpoint.

The archetypalists and the classical Jungians, however, to continue with Samuels's differentiation, are rather of a different mind. Jung's psychology is archetypal, after all, they would say, and what the preoccupation with childhood is about is likely to be a fixation, with the myth of the divine child in the background.

Now we might ask, is this conflict in Jungian circles part of a general attempt at a reintegration among analytic schools, split endlessly since those of Freud and Adler and Jung? It might seem so, since people such as Kohut among the Freudians speak about "self psychology" in almost archetypal terms. Yet the differences, primarily connected with the religious attitude toward the psyche on the part of Jungians, remain profound.

Is this, then, typology once more, or school-centered conflict? I don't know, but it seems rather obvious that such differences are based on what one actually experiences in analysis, one's own or with patients. All of us know that most patients are much involved with their childhood, but we do not know if this is partially culturally conditioned, what one is expected to deal with in analysis, or is the "real thing." And, even if it is the real thing, we do not know if this is founded on the myth of childhood, which lies behind all these real experiences, the time when the archetypes were first unleashed in all power, or if the reported woundings were indeed the product of parent–child interactions. Surely, both are true, as well as the importance of one's own experience.

As a classical Jungian, one whose first analysis as a young man had much focus on childhood, and whose second training analysis in Zurich proved to be much more archetypal and myth-discovering, I can say yea to both. Furthermore, as a Jungian highly disposed to working with archetypal depths with patients, I have been compelled, by their need, to spend lots of time on their childhood. As a matter of fact, it is only the rare person, in my experience, who goes through the entire process described by Jung in "The Relations Between the Ego and the Unconscious" (1928) wherein the archetypal figures of anima/animus, old wise man/woman, mana personality, and Self are confronted and internalized, and the ego is relativized to the point where an ongoing ego–Self axis is arrived at and maintained. Yet parts of this process, even including an experience of and connection with the Self, are undergone by almost every patient. How to resolve this seeming paradox?

It is apparent to me, and to us all, I presume, that the structure of the psyche is archetypal, and that one or more myths underlie each of our dramas of existence. The myths of our patients and ourselves may be discovered, played out, and dealt with, particularly in our highly extraverted American society, in ways different from those investigated deeply by Jung. But it is also the same psyche, we must assume, and it is probably like that famous Indian elephant who was grasped by several wise men at various places and thus understood differently by each of them as consisting of trunk or tail, phallous or rump, depending upon which part was touched. The psyche is verily like a Freudian or Adlerian or Reichian or Jungian, indeed!

For Jungians, therefore, it is probably best for us to undergo the kind of deep process that he described, so that we can be helpful in this matter for those who need this from us (Jung 1946). It is also important, I think, to realize that those who are convinced that their particular handle on the psyche is the "true one" are probably basing this on their own experience. It is much like the general condition in the world today: we are faced with fundamentalists of all sorts, some of whom are even fanatic. Others are more pluralistically inclined.

It is a sad paradox, in the general psychotherapeutic field, that the most-committed analysts are likely to get best results, whereas the bland relativists are less likely to be effective. Ideally, it would be nice to be committed and connected with our own experience of the Self, like the fundamentalists, and flexibly open to other understandings, like the relativists. According to the great thirteenth-century Sufi mystic of Islam, Ibn Arabi, it is incumbent upon us to discover our own Rabb (or Lord), yet realize that the Lord of All (Allah) includes all of these particular lords, yet transcends them all also, even the god revealed in each of the great faiths. The more we can experience and comprehend the varying manifestations of the divine in all of these forms, the more we can approach the God who transcends us all.

To translate this task for our ordinary therapeutic work: the more we can help our patients to find their own myth, their own selves, the more we, too, can comprehend and relate to the greater Self which both includes and transcends us all. In this work, then, we are indeed doing a valuable thing: repairing the world (to use a Jewish mystical expression) by helping the soul and the sparks of the divine to reunite with the godhead. Maybe that is why our endless preoccupation with transference seems strange to others, yet so important to us.

## References


Jung, C. G. 1928. The relations between the ego and the unconscious. *CW* 7:121–241. Princeton, N.J.: Princeton University Press, 1953.

———. 1946. The psychology of the transference. *CW* 16:163–323. Princeton, N.J.: Princeton University Press, 1954.

Meier, C. A. 1959. Projection, transference and the subject-object relation in psychology. *Journal of Analytical Psychology* 4:21–34.

Samuels, Andrew. 1985. *Jung and the Post-Jungians*. London: Routledge and Kegan Paul.

Spiegelman, J. Marvin. 1965. Some implications of the transference. In *Spectrum Psychologiae: Festscrift fur C. A. Meier*, C. T. Frey, ed. Zurich: Rascher Verlag.

———. 1972. Transference, individuation and mutual process. A talk for the San Diego Jungian group, privately printed.

———. 1980. The image of the Jungian analyst and the problem of authority. *Spring* (1980):101–116.

———. 1988. The impact of suffering and self-disclosure on the life of the analyst. In *Jungian Analysts: Their Visions and Vulnerabilities*. Phoenix: Falcon Press.

# Playing with the Opposites: Symbolization and Transitional Space*

Ellen Y. Siegelman

*"Images that are true symbols . . . are the best possible expressions for something unknown—bridges thrown out towards an unseen shore."*
C. G. Jung, "The Relation of Analytical Psychology to Poetry"

*"Yes, always the opposites, always ready to stand on one's head for the glory of God. Not 'either-or' but both, always both. One needs two legs to walk with."*
Marion Milner, *Eternity's Sunrise*

In this paper I will explore the nature of the symbol-making capacity as a transitional phenomenon that mediates between opposites without destroying the tension that comes from experiencing them *as opposites*.

Psychological disorders can be viewed not only as interpersonal difficulties but as intrapsychic impairments in the symbolizing capac-

---

**Ellen Y. Siegelman**, Ph.D., is an advanced candidate at the C. G. Jung Institute of San Francisco and has a private practice in Berkeley and San Francisco. A clinical professor of medical psychology at the University of California, SF, she is the author of a number of professional articles and a recent book, *Metaphor and Meaning in Psychotherapy*.



*A portion of this material has appeared, in revised form, in Siegelman (1990), *Meaning and Metaphor in Psychotherapy*, New York, Guilford Press.

ity. Conversely, psychological health requires the capacity to play. In adults this is more specifically the capacity to fantasize and to imagine—to play with the products of one's own psyche.

Jung talks of symbols as "bridges" between domains, emphasizing in this way their transitional or mediating function. Those suffering from pathologies of symbol making are stuck in a bridgeless world: those who are stuck at the blurring of the "as-if" are lost in the symbolic with no connection to the mainland; those who are stuck at the inability to see the "as-if" are confined to a mainland with no possibility of a sojourn in the richer domain of the unknown shore opposite them.

In *Aion* (1959) Jung writes about these two kinds of symbolizing difficulties as pathologies in the relation of the ego to the Self. If the ego is absorbed by the Self, reality perception is severely disturbed. (This happens in a smaller, more fleeting way whenever the ego comes under the influence of an autonomous complex that seems to "possess" one temporarily owing to the power of its archetypal core.) If the Self is absorbed by the ego, the resulting inflation leads to excessive insistence on one's own control and the omnipotence of one's own will. In neither case is oscillation or temporary fusion possible: the person is unable to make untethered fantasy become true imagination by being linked with the pole of reality. And in neither case is the tension of opposites experienced or acknowledged. Without that tension of the opposites, as Jung repeatedly points out, there is no energy flow, for "every process is a phenomenon of energy, and . . . all energy can only proceed from the tension of opposites" (1943, par. 34). Jung introduces the electrical metaphor of the "spark of opposites" that permits psychic currents to flow (1943, par. 78).

I have observed repeatedly in my work with patients that the "as-if" or symbolizing experience requires that fantasy and reality not be split but that the two poles and, in fact, two contradictory positions must be held in tension. Thus, as I pointed out in my review (Siegelman 1989) of the important work of Thomas Ogden (1986) in explicating Winnicott's notion of potential space, when a little girl is playing house, ideally her self-experience would be *both* "I am the mother" *and* "I am the little girl."

## Clinical Examples of Failures to Maintain the Opposites

I will now look more closely at some clinical examples of the failure of the opposites that represent difficulties in the capacity to symbolize. These pathologies can be reframed as identification with the archetype versus identification with the ego.

### *Identification with the Archetype*

In a total identification with the symbolic, the ego is absorbed into the unconscious. The most extreme forms of such identification occur in psychotic or borderline states where the ego gets lost in or swamped by unconscious contents. But such identification can exist in more encapsulated ways in better-functioning patients. I take an example from Rosemary Gordon (1978), who describes a middle-aged patient as producing abundant material in her dreams and associations and in the transference revealing her unconscious identification with the Great Mother. The patient was so identified with this archetype that she acted out the Great Mother with her adolescent daughter by trying to give to her and to control her in a superhuman way. The daughter complied by becoming psychosomatically ill, bedridden and helpless. The process of disidentifying with unconscious contents requires that the ego must be helped to disengage, to step aside and note what is happening as an "as-if" rather than being immersed in or possessed by the complex.

Gordon describes the analytic work on this complex:

> Only when, as a result of analysis, a disidentification with this archetypal image had occurred, could the patient herself begin to develop, could a person emerge with an individual identity; only then could she begin to tolerate some change, some growth, some separateness, acknowledge the different needs of different persons, and become aware that children at different states of their development need a different type of mothering. Then could she also begin to relate herself to the helpless and hurt and frightened child inside her. This then broke up, at last, the matriarchal pattern that had gripped her family for three generations. (1978, p. 112)

### *Identification with the Ego*

We can also identify an opposite problem: a hypertrophied ego development arising from the failure of the child's early environment to provide the opportunity for "absentmindedness" or reverie. These are the patients who say, "A thing either is or it isn't." These literalists have typically experienced the excessive early impingement of controlling or disturbed parents as their own disturbance. To prevent this fusion with a disturbed parent, the child constructs boundaries rigidly and prematurely, leading to a precocious flattened "realism." Ego mastery introduced too early is associated with the belief in omnipotent control that we see in so many superfactual, rational, skeptical, "nothing-but" patients.

Marion Milner gives a case example of just such a patient in her classic paper, "Aspects of Symbolization in Comprehension of the Not-Self" (1952). Milner describes her work with an 11-year-old boy who had suffered early losses including the absence of his father at war just at the time his brother was born, the loss of his sense of safety during the bombing of London, and the more recent loss of a favorite toy—a soft rabbit that had been his beloved transitional object. All these impingements as well as a very unsatisfactory early feeding schedule forced him to take a stance of fortitude and self-control: he became the little man of the family. But the strain began to show, and difficulties at school led to his being seen in analysis.

Milner notes that for some time the child took a quasi-sadistic, hectoring tone toward her and treated her peremptorily:

> He so often treated me as totally his own to do what he liked with, as though I were dirt, his dirt, or as a tool, an extension of his own hand . . . it certainly did seem that for a very long time he did need to have the illusion that I was part of himself. (Milner 1952, p. 187)

Perhaps he needed to oscillate between the opposites: the perception that he and she were two and the illusion that they were one.

It was Milner's allowing him to use her as an object or extension of himself that eventually helped him transform his play. This play initially consisted of setting fire to toy villages. In its later elaborations, as he gained trust in the analyst, the play took on an almost religious quality: he would repeatedly light tiers of candles in play rituals reminiscent of ancient sacrificial rites or alchemical practices:

> It was in fact play with light and fire. He would close the shutters of the room and insist that it be lit only by candle light. . . . And then he would make what he called furnaces, with a very careful choice of what ingredients should make the fire, including dried leaves from special plants in my garden; and sometimes all the ingredients had to be put in a metal cup on the electric fire and stirred continuously, all this carried out in the half darkness of candle light. And often there had to be a sacrifice, a lead soldier had to be added to the fire, and this figure was spoken of either as the victim or the sacrifice. In fact, all this type of play had a dramatic ritual quality comparable to the fertility rites described by Frazer in primitive societies. And this effect was the more striking because this boy's conscious interests were entirely conventional

> for his age, he was absorbed in Meccano and model railways. (Milner 1952, p. 188)

This symbolic play had to do in its content with redeeming damaged objects. But in its process it had to do with the boy's withdrawing cathexis from the outer world and transcending his excessively realistic ego to make a new whole. This requires a temporary giving up of the sense of oneself as separate, of the reality ego that judges and discriminates. In this "aesthetic moment" of being merged with the object of creation or contemplation we recapture the original illusion of fusion.

Again, discussing the frame and the symbolic, Milner talks about the ability to allow illusion (neither to be compelled by it nor to exclude it, but to *allow* it), to feel "within the enclosed space-time of the drama or the picture or the story or the analytic hour, a transcending of that common sense perception which would see a picture as only an attempt at photography or the analyst as only a present day person" (1952, p. 190).

Milner could have chosen to see her young patient's early attempts to control her and treat her as part of himself solely as the regressive enactment of a destructive fantasy. Instead, she chose to see it as a necessary regression that was, in fact, forward looking. Ecstatic moments of fusion with the mother are essential if the world is to be anything other than static, gray, or literal. If the child becomes aware of his separateness too early and too continually, the result may be on the one hand chaos, or on the other, as in this case, a premature cathexis of a meager "reality."

In seeing the restitutive and even "artistic" quality of her young patient's symbolization, Milner recognized the health-promoting possibilities of primary process in the context of a holding environment. Indeed, she notes that the turning point in the analysis came when she in effect departed from the classical Fenichel-Jones view of symbolism as defensive and regressive. When she began to know in her bones that her young patient's use of her was not only defensive regression but an "essential recurrent phase in the development of a creative relation to the world, then the whole character of the analysis changed" and the boy became able to tolerate her as a separate object (Milner 1952, p. 194).

In reflecting on this case years later, in a memorial volume to Winnicott, Milner (1978) connects her young patient's heightened experience of the visitation of the gods with what Winnicott calls "creative apperception," that capacity for symbolic realization that adds depth and resonance to experience even in the presence of adversity and instinctual deprivation.

## The Emphasis on Play in Jung and Winnicott

At the beginning of their treatment, the two patients I have just described represented opposite difficulties in relating to the symbolic. The woman who was so unconsciously committed to embodying the Great Mother could not detach from her identification with the archetypal pole. And the little boy who had been forced to become prematurely responsible could not, at the outset, attach to symbols. Both these difficulties in symbolization represent a difficulty in sustaining the opposites that is required in all forms of play, from the baby's first peek-a-boo games (she's gone, she's here) to the highly sophisticated play that we call art.

Among depth-psychologists, Winnicott has most strongly and persistently sounded the note of play in his work, culminating in the essays in *Playing and Reality* (1971). But it is important to recognize that Jung anticipated him by a number of years, not only in his 1916 work on the transcendent function and his writing on active imagination but in a specific passage in "The Aims of Psychotherapy," delivered as a lecture in 1929. In that paper he says:

> All the works of man have their origin in creative imagination. . . . The creative activity of imagination frees man from his bondage to the "nothing but" and raises him to the status of one who plays. As Schiller says, man is completely human only when he is at play. (1931b, par. 98)

Winnicott himself abundantly knew how to play—to play music (he was a dedicated pianist), to play with children in endless versions of his squiggle game (young patient and doctor continue elaborating a scribbled doodle in cooperative "to-ing and fro-ing," as Winnicott called such mutual play). He also played, more seriously, with adult patients, insisting on maintaining the tension of the opposites. For example, in an analysis of a male patient (described in *Holding and Interpretation* [1987]), Winnicott responded to the patient's wish that he (Winnicott) would hold him by telling him that if he did that, the patient would be painfully aware of the awkwardness of the situation—one grown man holding another. Indeed, the literalness of the encounter would blot out the infantile experience that the patient was reliving. What was required was, indeed, holding, but of a symbolic nature, and *that* was provided by the couch. The patient was then able to make the symbolic connection and to tell him, "You are the couch." The couch had become a transitional object, and the patient was able to see that such objects can "stand for" something else in a less limited or encumbering way.

Winnicott not only helped his patients play but he also wrote playfully about play: he exulted in the paradoxical assertion of opposites, and he saw in play a vital energy—the sphere of art, culture, and religion—"the ability to create the world" (1986, p. 40). It was this belief that caused him to write so fully about symbolic phenomena and symbolic space—the space of creating as well as finding.

Winnicott confirms the centrality of play in his work by telling us that for many years he was haunted by a phrase of the Indian poet Tagore before he used it as the epigraph of his essay, "On the Location of Cultural Experience" (1971). The phrase is: "On the seashore of endless worlds/Children play." The quotation is worth deconstructing because it quintessentially embodies the Winnicottian stance. First, the seashore. What better description of a liminal or transitional space? Is it land or is it sea? Or is it the opposites interpenetrating—land about to become sea, a paradoxical sea/land. Next, "endless worlds." This has the same resonance for me as Jung's "bridges thrown out towards an unseen shore"—another image that uses the shoreline and opens out into uncharted, mysterious, and unknowable domains. And finally, "Children play" speaks to Winnicott's lifelong concerns, first as a pediatrician, then as an analyst of children and adults.

But I want to emphasize that the form of the quotation is as important as its content. It is the *music* of the phrase with its inversion that makes it live. If Tagore had written "Children play on the seashores of endless worlds," the sense would be the same but the *feel* would be different. And, I believe, it is just such attunement to the music—the artful, affective element of discourse, that marks not only the poet but the skilled analyst as well. I have written elsewhere (Siegelman [1990]) about musical metaphors for therapy. I am reminded of Richard Strauss's last opera, *Capriccio*, in which he articulates the theme that haunted him all his life: in opera, which is more important, the words or the music? His heroine, Madeleine, is forced to choose between the composer, Flamand, and the poet, Olivier. Unable to choose (for "in choosing one you must lose the other"), she leaves us with the unanswered question. The implied answer seems to be not either/or but both. When we preserve the tension of opposites, then the logical and the psychological, denotation and connotation, thought and feeling, the words and the music of discourse are held in a marvelous and delicate balance.

In his seminal paper on the transcendent function, Jung clearly had this play of opposites in mind. The transcendence he noted was not mystical but simply descriptive: a third thing that transcends two domains as a product of the dialogue between them; and the "third thing," while different from each of the others, also partakes of some of their qualities. The notion of a mediating third thing that bridges domains through imagination anticipates, although Winnicott did not apparently know it, the Winnicottian notion of transitional phenomena. When Jung talks of a third thing, it is often in the context of a specific application of the transcendent function—the process of "active imagination" in which a person loosens his conscious focus, puts himself in a state of reverie, and allows psychological contents from the unconscious, such as a dream image, to emerge and to become elaborated. This embellished product of the unconscious then becomes a partner in a dialogue with the ego in which neither dominates. What results is a symbolic product (using the written word or paint or clay) that contains elements of both.

So far Jung seems to have described what is very much the process of artistic creation. But he goes a step further and indicates that stopping with the merely aesthetic is not enough; in the work of active imagination the product thus created must be subjected to moral scrutiny and evaluation.

I have no quarrel with Jung's exposition of the process nor with its usefulness. But I myself do not deliberately use active imagination in my work, and according to Bradway and Wheelwright (1978), rather few Jungians do. This may be because they don't feel sufficiently trained or equipped or because they have been all too impressed with Jung's warning about the potential danger of the method and his recommendation that it be used late in an analysis as a groundwork for what the analysand can later do on his or her own.

My own problem about using the technique is that, in general, I eschew introducing material that does not come directly from the patient or our interchange. (There are, of course, small exceptions to this: I'm not above inquiring in a sterile period about what the patient's dream life has been like lately, or even suggesting, as I did recently with a patient who had a particularly powerful hypnagogic image of a wise jester, that he might want to draw or sculpt it. I do not supply art materials, but I would certainly be interested in looking at such products when a patient brings them in and in using them as a basis for the patient's associations.) My own style is to use a largely verbal medium of exchange in the consulting room and not to initiate activity myself.

Here I follow more closely on Winnicott, who believed that when the holding environment was sufficiently protective, the patient would be enabled to engage in symbolic activity on his or her own. What would then emerge would not necessarily be a separate and distinct third thing. Instead, by not questioning the opposites or separating them out from their strange union in the transitional space between analyst and analysand, we would generate a paradoxical containment that preserves these opposites. André Green has called this "the meeting in no man's land of what has been separated" (1987, p. 124). The "new thing" for Winnicott is not a tangible product so much as the acceptance of an unchallenged contradiction, such as: "You and I are one/You and I are two," or, in the case of a child with a transitional object like a blanket (which a friend of mine's child called his "loving thing"), "I made this/It existed all along for me to find."

Paradox does not resolve or dissolve the opposites: it maintains them in all their tension. Thus the potential space that "exists but cannot be allowed to exist" between mother and infant both joins and separates them. Winnicott has described a case of a boy who played obsessively with string: the string was what both joined him to and separated him from his mother. In *Playing and Reality*, he makes his most definitive statement on paradox:

> I am drawing attention to the *paradox* involved in the use by the infant of . . . the transitional object. My contribution is to ask for a paradox to be accepted and tolerated and respected, and for it not to be resolved. By flight to split-off intellectual functioning, it is possible to resolve the paradox but *the price of this is the loss of the value of the paradox itself.* (Winnicott 1971, xii, italics mine)

I gravitate toward Winnicott's paradoxes because they seem to me to represent accurately the instability of any resolution of the opposites. As Jung well knew, the opposites are always tending to pull apart, so any resolution *must* be temporary. Jung even spoke of the emergence of Self-symbols in dreams and active imagination as precursors of a unity that is hard-won and probably never fully attained: "the united personality will never quite lose the painful sense of innate discord" (1946, par. 400). The temporary resolutions that do occur arise not only because of what comes up in the patient's unconscious but through the analytic interchange itself.

## Analysis as Helping Patients Play

How can the highly defended, or fearful, or enraged, or regressed patient be helped to play? If we accept the judgment of Plaut (1966) that in order to play the patient must be able to trust the therapist, then we can reframe the question: What is it that will foster the patient's trust? Because the damage to the capacity to play often occurs at a preverbal developmental stage, it needs to be repaired at a preverbal level, that is, not simply at the level of interpretation. What we strive to supply is an atmosphere or environment, a space in which the patient can count on our steadiness, dependability, caring, benign lack of judgment, and our predictable "thereness," the Winnicottian "going-on-being" that has typically been so disrupted in the patient's infancy. It is this holding environment that eventually permits patients who are too frightened or constricted or too awash in their unconscious to play. "Awash in the unconscious" reminds me of Jung's wonderful comment when James Joyce brought his schizophrenic daughter, Lucia, to Jung for a consultation. In an interview with Joyce's biographer, Richard Ellmann, Jung later said that the father and daughter "were like two people going to the bottom of a river, one falling and the other diving" (Ellmann 1952). How can we help our patients swim in the unconscious rather than drowning in it or standing on the shore looking longingly at the water but afraid to take the plunge?

Examples of work with patients caught at the pole of the unconscious abound in the work of Winnicott, Margaret Little, Masud Khan, and Harold Searles, among others. Less has been written about working with people caught at the pole of the ego. In my own experience, this requires allowing the patient to proceed at his or her own speed, within the context of the transference/countertransference, and being alert to the presence of certain symbols occurring in the patient's "real life," so that occasionally the dreamlike properties of everyday life become highlighted. Two examples from my own practice may illustrate.

### *Allowing the Patient's Own Pace and Style of Symbolic Play: Case Example*

A patient I will call Howard K. was a 42-year-old systems analyst who came to see me because he "wasn't getting much out of life." Highly trained in a number of related technical fields, he was working at a technical job he hated. He was also feeling very lonely after having several years earlier ended an unrewarding seven-year marriage.

Howard rarely remembered his dreams and produced few fantasies. About six months into the work, he first approached the symbolic through a metaphor about himself. He told me he was fed up with himself and his life, tried of always living "on the periphery." He wished he were different—he wished his life was more like—he paused and groped for the image—"like a jar of jellybeans." In the gray sky of his abstract language, this image stood out like a rainbow. My abiding interest in metaphor (Siegelman 1990) prompted me to ask him to tell me more. Howard complied desultorily. I could have interpreted this denial of ownership of his image, but I chose not to.

Several sessions later, when he again wistfully expressed the desire for some excitement and play in his life, I recalled the "jar of jelly-beans" metaphor and asked him again to tell me what that had made him think of. His reply was dutiful and compliant, like a student being asked to respond in a class in which he feels ill-prepared and not much interested. "Well," he said, "I don't know. I guess jellybeans are colorful. And though they're all the same shape, they'd give you a sense of variety if you saw them all together." "Yes," I responded, "and they're usually connected with children." He agreed halfheartedly, and I suddenly realized that I had been playing a fruitless game of Twenty Questions.

Patients eventually teach you what you need to know about them, and at this point, I realized that expanding this metaphor was *my* agenda, and that that was why it wasn't working. So I shifted to talking about the process—about his dutiful but grudging desire to please me in something that seemed like my plan, not his. He agreed that this desire to please had characterized most of his dealings with authority figures, toward whom he would be outwardly compliant but inwardly resentful. I was then able to interpret that I had become just such a figure for him.

We did some useful work on this issue, and I was reminded of Plaut's injunction about the allure of what he calls "impact by image therapy" and how futile it is if not firmly ensconced in the field of interaction itself. It reminded me that I must not assume simply because a metaphor is produced that the patient and I are operating in what Jung would conceptualize as a "secured symbolizing field" (Goodheart 1980).

Some time later in the analysis, when this patient's trust of me was sufficiently solid, he did produce images of himself that arose spontaneously, not primarily as offerings to me, and were invested with his own affect. In an interesting progression, the first image was of his life as a flow-chart—an endless paper trail stretching in a linear way, flat and devoid of resonance. Some time later he told me that he had had another image that "just came to him"—it was of being surrounded by a dome, a huge white dome. (A dome is half a circle, and it seemed to me that whatever else it connoted, this was already a more rounded, full, and potentially fruitful image of his psyche than the flow-chart.) I asked him to help me see the dome by describing it. Well, he wasn't sure what it was made of—maybe opaque glass. It became clear that, on the one hand, the dome protected him from outside intrusion, but on the other, it shut him off from outside support. I understood that the dome was a particularly apt image for his isolating and intellectualizing defenses, showing at one and the same time what it protects against and what it forecloses. (This is, indeed, the paradox of defenses, those sanctuary/prisons that protect while confining, as Roy Shafer (1983) has brilliantly illuminated.) I did not need to make this understanding explicit because the image conveyed it to Howard experientially.

Over the next few months, he proceeded to sustain and embellish the image of the dome without any encouragement from me. It now seemed to be made of books (his intellectualizing defenses?), but these were more permeable than glass, and, indeed, I had been experiencing him as more "permeable" during the sessions.

In succeeding hours Howard wondered about the possibilities of escaping, of soaring through this dome. His desire to soar coincided happily with a real-life occurrence that, together with his therapy, helped him break through the dome: he fell in love with a woman who appeared to be a mature and resonant person, very different from his ex-wife. He also began to redefine his work life and to realize that he had been emphasizing the wrong aspects of himself: he was not interested in products or information but in working with people more intuitively to hear and translate the work of one set of experts to another. "It's as though I'm finally outside the dome and I can use it as a bridge," he said, and I was thrilled to witness a metaphor of isolation becoming transformed into a metaphor of connection.

Some time later, approaching termination, Howard produced another image of himself: "When I look at my life now, I don't see myself so much fixed in one spot, shifting from foot to foot with the old 'Yes, buts' and 'shoulds.' Instead I see atoms in motion." Surprised and delighted by this turn of figure, I asked him to tell me about it. "Well," he said a bit sheepishly. "Atoms move in what's called Brownian movement—it's kind of a zigzag as the atoms collide. It seems really random, but there's an order to it overall." He smiled, a little embarrassed at his flight of fancy. (Was this the kind of soaring he had hoped would enable him to break out of the dome?) "Well, see, it makes me kind of—kind of happy to think of myself that way."

The idea behind this metaphoric image—that both order and freedom could be combined—suggested an inner synthesis in which aspects of the self had been reconfigured. Motion and dynamism were paramount, while the underlying order was implicit rather than controlling. Howard had come to see that the external show of order—the flow-charts, the agendas—were no longer so necessary. In gradually trusting me and through our work on the products of his own unconscious, he had approached an elementary ordering principle in his own psyche.

### *Finding the Symbolic Toad in the Real Garden: Case Example*

Jung's crucial work on the symbolic attitude reflects his view that "it all depends on how we look at things, and not how they are in themselves" (1931b, par. 96). In one of his most explicit definitions of the symbolic attitude, he wrote:

> Every psychic product, if it is the best possible expression at the moment for a fact as yet unknown or only relatively known, may be regarded as a symbol, provided that we accept the expression as standing for something that is only divined and not yet clearly conscious. (Jung 1921, par. 817)

He emphasizes that whether or not something is a symbol depends on the *"attitude of the observing consciousness"* (ibid., par. 819). This is for me a very sympathetic way of relativizing the symbolic and escaping from the classical Freudian position (out of Ernest Jones) that symbols are fixed in number, generally sexual in content, and point to a specific meaning. The symbolic attitude asks embracingly, "What larger meaning can be seen at work here? What is this besides what it appears to be?" Marianne Moore wrote in one of her poems that the job of the poet was to help us see the "real toads" in "imaginary gardens." The job of an analyst may be to help patients see the imaginary or symbolic toads in the real gardens.

Let me give an almost literal example. A patient, Carla G., told me that she and her sons were building a pond in their yard. Suddenly, a huge tortoise appeared. It could not be contained in the pond. It moved according to its own antediluvian pace. When they tried to lure it out from under a bush, it wouldn't budge. When they least expected to see it, it was there. It lumbered and was noiseless.

The tortoise was, of course, a very real creature. It was not a dream image, a daydream image, or a hallucination. In fact, its very palpability was what made its mysterious presence so commanding. For me, and gradually for Carla, the tortoise began to operate as a natural symbol or metaphor to play with.

Of what it was a living symbol, my patient and I never clearly knew. I did know that no matter how we worked on this tortoise—work that felt more like play—we would not exhaust its meanings.

In the two years during which I had seen her, Carla had talked repetitively of her very active life as a hematologist. For most of her 39 years, she had been preoccupied with doing and making. Indeed, the pond was one such making: it was a project that, newly divorced, she could work on with her two young sons. But something mysterious and surprising had come out of the pond, just as she had found herself in the course of the therapy changing in ways she couldn't account for, ways that had been almost effortless and undeliberate—very opposite from the willful engagement she had heretofore had with life. She still wanted to know how this had happened and pressed me for some formulation that would allow her to duplicate the changes consciously. In our work to this point, she had for some time been impatient with the discouraging slowness of the process, although she acknowledged that from time to time she found herself doing things differently—allowing herself more "off-time" just to watch the leaves moving as she lay in her hammock. The change could be felt in the therapeutic process too; she was beginning to have fewer agendas and to relax more often into reverie. Whatever the tortoise might be as a natural symbol, both of us felt that it had presented itself to her as an exemplar of another way of being, another principle at work in the psyche—slow, patient, obedient to its own inner law, not to be coerced.

But more important than anything we could say about the tortoise was her feeling response to it as a mysterious visitant that compelled her attention and even her awe. It is this paradoxical union of opposites that we find in the infant's protosymbol, the transitional object. Thus the infant's paradoxical "I found this blanket/I created it" becomes, in later life, "I found this symbol/I created this symbol." This reconciliation of opposites is both paradoxical and psychologically true. She found the tortoise, but together we created it as a symbolic experience. And this kind of *coniunctio*, whether between patient and therapist, between inner world and outer world, or between various aspects of the patient's psyche, typically generates wonder and gratitude. Experiencing the tortoise as at one and the same time a real creature and an archetypal symbol greatly deepened Carla's sense of the richness and possibility of her life and of the reality of the psyche.

### How the Analyst Models the Play of Opposites

In writing of active imagination, Jung (1916) talks of the "third thing"—typically a product in words, paint, clay, or movement, that comes out of a dialogue between the conscious and the unconscious, partaking of both but different from either. I contend that a subtle kind of active imagination occurs repeatedly and without deliberate evocation in the work of analysis. This kind of movement between conscious and unconscious may occur not only because of what comes up in the patient to be elaborated and wondered about, but through the analytic process itself. Let me clarify this.

I propose two principles:

1) Among the unspoken, implicit forces for healing in the analytic process, a central one is the analyst's modeling of a way of attending that itself embodies the transcendent function.
2) Part of what a patient learns in an analysis is to approximate in him- or herself this more flexible subtle way of attending that mirrors the oscillating between opposites. The patient learns—not didactically but through observation and active participating in the "to-ing and fro-ing"—that the analyst can tolerate the tension of opposites and need not settle on only one pole or require only one kind of product (e.g., only dreams, only infantile experience, only transference material, only what is painful and shadowy, only the depths). The patient learns that the analyst doesn't repudiate the outer world in favor of the inner one, the personal in favor of the transpersonal or vice versa.

Those of us who hold such a nonreductivist view of the analytic process do this kind of modeling intuitively and out of our own natures, not as a ploy or as a deliberate heuristic. This stance may not produce a true union of opposites; that happens rarely. More often what occurs is an oscillation or suspension between the opposites that honors both poles.

These opposites include the opposites of attention. I have mentioned the analyst's attention as being flexible and receptive. That flexibility includes at times the capacity to be focused and active. Freud recommended a state of freely floating or hovering attention that is the counterpart to the patient's free association. This is a state of reverie, itself hovering somewhere between conscious and unconscious. As the analyst listens in this permissive way, bits of his/her own associations, images, and memories surface, as well as almost subliminal perceptions of the patient's nonverbal behavior: how he or she is sitting or lying or gesturing or yawning. This is an attentional process that feels meditative and receptive. It reminds me most of what Keats spoke of as the quality of the poet: a "negative capability"—the ability to tolerate "uncertainties, mysteries, doubts, without any irritable reaching after fact and reason" (Keats 1935, Letter 32).

At other times, however, the analyst is more actively looking, more direct and focused in what is seen and what is interpreted. The shift is rather like stopping down a shutter opening on a camera to get a narrow, more precise focus. This oscillation between reverie and focus, if it happens smoothly enough, does offer a model. I find that my hours with patients have a rhythm of attention: During the first half of the hour I generally make very few comments, just listening in the state of resonance I described above. This stance is not willed or deliberate; it just happens. I suppose I am waiting for the themes of the hour to work on me and my patient. Some time later, typically, I will say more and occasionally make an attempt at focus. Often as the hour progresses, the process deepens in some mysterious way, and a third state may supervene. In this "third state" I am often aware of how much more absorbed the patient is in his or her own process, while I function as an attuned observer. Or, to use Balint's phrase, some kind of "harmonious interpenetrating mixup" occurs between me and the patient so that we are moving together in a dancelike way.

I realize that this account is both schematic and somewhat idealized. What actually takes place at a more microscopic level are minute shifts that occur from moment to moment. For attention cannot truly hover for long. It seeks some kind of resting place, even if temporarily. But in modeling a stance that combines the yin of receptive waiting, mirroring, and listening and the yang of occasional active interpretation or structuring, we do not cast our lot with either pole. If a patient can learn from observing us an attentional flexibility that operates without too many preconceptions and without judgment, he or she will have learned a great deal.

That tolerance for the "both/and" of lived experience (rather than the "either/or" or "nothing but" reductions of that experience) enhances one's sense of meaning and depth. It is rather like a stereopticon, which tries to simulate the binocular vision of our own eyes.

Looked at in isolation, either of the two steropticon pictures is flat. Looked at together, the two images fuse, and the result is the perception of depth. This occurs whenever we can hold and preserve the opposites. By looking in this complex way, our experience of them changes. As Jung, in defense of the symbolic attitude wrote, "For it all depends on how we look at things, and not on how they are in themselves. The least of things with a meaning is always worth more in life than the greatest of things without it" (1931b, par. 96).

That ultimately is what the symbolic attitude does for us and for our patients: it allows us to expand our sphere of meaning. By hewing to a multivalent, richly ambiguous view rather than settling on something misleadingly simple, certain, and flat, we honor the tension of the opposites. And at rare moments, the symbolic attitude enables us to combine and thus transcend them.

## References

Bradway, K., and Wheelwright, J. 1978. The psychological type of the analyst and its relation to analytical practice. *Journal of Analytical Psychology* 23:211–225.

Ellmann, R. 1952. *James Joyce*. New York: Oxford University Press, rev. ed., 1982.

Goodheart, W. B. 1980. Theory of analytic interaction. *San Francisco Jung Institute Library Journal* 1:4,2–39.

Gordon, R. 1978. *Dying and Creating: A Search for Meaning*. Library of Analytical Psychology, vol. 4. London: Society of Analytical Psychology.

Green, André. 1987. Interview in *Winnicott and Paradox: From Birth to Creation*, A. Clancier and J. Kalmanovitch, eds. London: Tavistock Publications.

Jung, C. G. 1916. The transcendent function. In 8:67–91. Princeton, N.J.: Princeton University Press, 1960.

______. 1921. *Psychological Types*. vol. 6. Princeton, N.J.: Princeton University Press, 1971.

______. 1931a. On the relation of analytical psychology to poetry. 15:65–83. Princeton, N.J.: Princeton University Press, 1966.

______. 1931b. The aims of psychotherapy. 16:36–53. Princeton, N.J.: Princeton University Press, 1954.

______. 1943. On the psychology of the unconscious. *Two Essays on Analytical Psychology*, 7:1–119. Princeton, N.J.: Princeton University Press, 1953.

______. 1946. The psychology of the transference. 16:163–323. Princeton, N.J.: Princeton University Press, 1954.

______. 1951. *Aion: Researches into the Phenomenology of the Self*. vol. 9ii. Princeton, N.J.: Princeton University Press, 1959.

Keats, J. 1935. *Letters*. M. B. Forman, ed. New York: Oxford University Press.

Milner, M. 1952. Aspects of symbolism in comprehension of the not-self. *International Journal of Psychoanalysis* 33:181–195.

______. 1978. D. W. Winnicott and the two-way journey. In *Between Fantasy and Reality: Transitional Objects and Phenomena*, S. A. Grolnick and L. Barkin, eds. New York: Jason Aronson, pp. 35–42.

______. 1987. *Eternity's Sunrise: A Way of Keeping a Diary*. London: Virago Press.

Ogden, T. H. 1986. *The Matrix of the Mind: Object Relations and the Psychoanalytic Dialogue*. Northvale, N.J.: Jason Aronson, Inc.

Plaut, A. 1966. Reflections about not being able to imagine. *Journal of Analytical Psychology* 11:112–133.

Schafer, R. 1983. *The Analytic Attitude*. New York: Basic Books.

Siegelman, E. 1989. To-ing and fro-ing among the object-relations theorists. Review of Thomas Ogden's *The Matrix of the Mind. San Francisco Jung Institute Library Journal* 31:7–20.

Siegelman, E. 1990. *Metaphor and Meaning in Psychotherapy*. New York: Guilford Press.

Winnicott, D. W. 1971. *Playing and Reality*. London: Tavistock Publications.

______. 1986. *Home Is Where We Start From: Essays by a Psychoanalyst*. New York: W. W. Norton.

______. 1987. *Holding and Interpretation: Fragment of an Analysis*. Fred Pine, ed. New York: Grove.

# "The Shipwrecked Sailor": A Middle Kingdom Parable of Liminality and Transformation

James Wyly and Susan Grandy

"The Shipwrecked Sailor," a tale preserved in a Middle Kingdom papyrus dating from 1800 B.C., is an exceptional example of an ancient story with psychological meaning. Although modern Egyptology recognizes the psychological content of this story,[1] the analysis of this and other Egyptian tales from a modern point of view is a new arena for exploration. Moreover, this exploration takes place in a vast culture whose literature and religion indicate a high level of psychological awareness. Many elements from the cultural heritage of the ancient Egyptians, already established in the predynastic and Old Kingdom periods, have been used to compose this tale and to give it meaning on many levels.

Concepts taken from the oldest Egyptian wisdom literature encourage the development of good character and appeal to cultural

---

**James Wyly** is a clinical psychologist with a private practice in Chicago, a graduate of the Illinois School of Professional Psychology, and a member of the C. G. Jung Institute of Chicago. He is author of *The Phallic Quest: Priapus and Masculine Inflation*.

**Susan Grandy**, a graduate student in Egyptology at the University of Chicago's Oriental Institute, is a consultant in ancient art.

ideals concerning human conduct. The terms *wisdom literature* and *instructional literature* are used by Egyptologists to classify the written works of a number of learned and powerful men in ancient Egypt containing maxims, advice concerning social situations, and material describing the relationship between humans and gods. But what is often most characteristic of Egyptian wisdom literature is its attention to social etiquette, especially that pertaining to correct speech. The practice of speaking effectively and eloquently was considered to be the window of opportunity not only to a life of peace and quiet inner strength, but also to the means of acquiring material wealth, position, and favored status with those ranking above one. It will become evident as we study "The Shipwrecked Sailor" that a relationship to autonomous psychological material was cultivated in order to achieve these ends.

According to the maxims of the 5th dynasty sage and nobleman Ptah-hotep, which were widely copied and disseminated throughout dynastic history, this maintenance of self-control when speaking was the primary characteristic of the ideal man of society:

> Suppress your desires, control your mouth; so your counsel will be heard among the magistrates . . . be patient when you speak and you will say eloquent things; then the magistrates who hear will say, "how good is his utterance." (Simpson 1972, p. 175)

From the Middle Kingdom era's *Teaching for Merikare*:

> Be skillful in speech, that you may be strong . . . words are braver than all fighting, none can circumvent the clever man on the mat; a wise man is an example for the magistrates, and those who are aware of his knowledge do not attack him. (Ibid., pp. 181–182)

From Ptah-hotep:

> Hearing is good for a son who hears, when hearing enters the hearer, for he who hears will become a judge [literally "hearer"]. Hearing is good, and speaking is good, but he who hears will become a possessor of benefits. (Ibid., p. 173)

From the New Kingdom's *Instructions for Amenemope*:

> and take care of speaking thoughtlessly. When a man's heart is upset, words travel faster than wind and rain.
>
> He is ruined and created by his tongue. (Ibid., p. 251)

The literature can be read as recommending the removal of ego-determined desires from the immediate situation in order to raise consciousness to a higher, meditative level. As will be seen in the story itself, the shipwrecked sailor finds inner resources with which to do this and then is rewarded in both psychological and material ways.

"The Shipwrecked Sailor," believed to have been written during the 11th Dynasty, takes the form of a story within a story, a literary device common in ancient as well as modern literature. Other literary devices, however, are used to make the tale entertaining and appealing. Depictions of adventurous expeditions to foreign lands, the lengthy descriptions of costly and luxurious items acquired, and even the listing of various food items favored by the Egyptians attempt to make the listener's mouth water. Expeditions of this type are well documented in ancient history and were often depicted on the walls of temples and tombs along with detailed pictorial lists of the fabulous items brought from faraway and mysterious lands. The proceeds from these journeys may have fired the imagination of the ancients in much the same way the discovery of materially wealthy civilizations enlivened Europe during the Age of Exploration. As such, the stories that accompanied these journeys must have been sources of endless wonderment for the populace. These kinds of events, which rest on the plane of material reality, are established in the tale as a background for psychological messages.

Our new translation of "The Shipwrecked Sailor" that appears below attempts to convey as accurately as possible the psychological import of the text, which is elaborated in the succeeding discussion (DeBuck 1948). The tale begins with the return of a quarrying, mining, or military expedition. As we shall see, the commander of the expedition is despondent upon his arrival in Egypt. His attendant tells the story:

> The wise attendant spoke: "May your wish be satisfied, commander! See! We have reached home. The mallet has been taken, the mooring post driven in, and the prow rope set upon the ground. Praise has been given, God has been thanked, and every man embraces his companions. Our crew has returned safe without any loss to our troops. Now that we have reached the limits of Nubia and have passed the island of Senmut, we have returned in peace, and we have attained our land.
>
> "Listen to me commander! I am not exaggerating! Wash yourself! Pour water over your hands and compose yourself! Then you will be able to reply when you are being questioned and speak to the king with presence of mind. [This way] you will be able to answer without stammering. For the speech of a man can save him, and his words gain indulgence. All right, don't take my advice! Act according to your own judgment. Speaking to you in this way is so tiresome.
>
> "Let me tell you of a similar thing which happened to me when I went to the mining country for the sovereign. I went down to the Red Sea in a boat 200 feet long and 68 wide. One hundred sailors from among the best of Egypt

were in it. Whether they looked at the sky or the land, their hearts were fiercer than lions. They could foretell a storm before it came or a downpour before it happened.

"A storm broke out while we were at sea, before we had touched land. The wind relented for a moment, but then returned with a wave 14 feet high. A plank torn from the ship struck the wave for me [to hold onto]. And then the boat died. And of those who were in it not a single one survived.

"I was able to float to an island by the surf of the sea. I spent three days there alone, with my heart as my only companion. I slept under a wooden shelter, I clung to the shade. Then I got up and stretched my legs to discover what I might put in my mouth. I found figs and dates, and all kinds of excellent vegetables. Sycamore figs and notched sycamore figs and cucumbers as if they were cultivated. Fish and birds were there. In fact, there was not anything that was not there. Then I ate to my satisfaction, and put some down on the ground because there was more than I could easily carry. I cut a fire drill, lit a fire, and made a burnt offering to the gods.

"Then I heard a thunderclap and thought it the surf of the sea. Trees were shaking, the ground quaking. When I uncovered my face, I discovered that it was a serpent coming along. He was 50 feet long, his beard was 3 feet long, and his body plated in gold. His two eyebrows were lapis lazuli, and he was coiled up in front.

"He opened his mouth to me while I was lying in front of him and he said to me, 'Who is it who has brought you! Who is it who has brought you to this island, I will turn you to ashes, and make it as though you never existed.'

"Although he was speaking to me, I did not hear it; when I was in his presence, I did not know myself. He took me in his mouth and carried me to his resting place. He set me down without hurting me. I was intact, and nothing was taken from me.

"He opened his mouth to speak to me while I trembled before him. And he said to me: 'Who is it who has brought you, little one. Who is it who has brought you to this island of the sea, the two sides of which are in waves?' And I answered him, my arms bent in his presence, telling him all that I had experienced, of the ship and the crew and the storm, and of my survival alone, and he said to me: 'Don't be afraid little one. Don't be afraid! Don't be so pale! You have reached me—indeed, God has allowed you to live. He has brought you to the island of the Ka within which there is not anything which does not exist. It is full of all good things.

" 'You will spend month after month until you complete four months within this island. A boat will then come back from home with sailors in it whom you know. You will go home with them and you will die in your village.

" 'How joyful is the one who relates what he has tasted after painful affairs have passed. Let me tell you about something similar which took place on this island when I was on it with my brothers and sisters and the children among them. We were seventy-five serpents in all, not mentioning a little daughter whom I had obtained through prayer.

" 'One day, a star fell, and because of it they all went up in flames. It happened completely. Yet I did not burn, for I was not among them. But I could have died for them when I found them in a single heap of corpses.

" 'If you would be brave, regulate your heart. Then you will fill your embrace with your children, you will kiss your wife, and you will see your house again, for this is better than anything. You will reach the home where you were in the midst of your brothers and sisters.'

"As I was stretched out on my belly, touching the ground in his presence, I said to him: 'I shall relate your prowess to the sovereign, and I shall inform him of your greatness. I shall have brought to you laudanum, fine oils, cassia root, and incense for the temples with which to satisfy every god. I shall indeed relate what has happened to me through what I have seen of your prowess. You will be thanked in my town in the presence of the magistrates of the entire land. I shall sacrifice to you oxen as a burnt offering, and I shall wring the necks of birds for you. I shall have brought to you transport ships loaded with all the specialities of Egypt, as should be done for a god who loves the Egyptians in a distant land which the Egyptians do not know.'

"Then he laughed at me because of these things which I had said, out of the cleverness of his heart. And he said to me: 'Myrrh is not abundant with you, although you have become a possessor of incense. Indeed, I am the Prince of Punt; myrrh belongs to me. That oil of which you spoke, why, it is the main product of this island. Now it will come to pass that you will separate yourself from this place, and you will never see this island again, since it will become as water.'

"Then that boat came, as he had foretold. I went and set myself in a high tree, and I recognized those who were in it. I went to tell him, but he already knew. And he said to me: 'Farewell, farewell, little one, to your home. You will see your children. Place my good name in your town, that is all I ask of you.'

"I placed myself on my belly, my arms bent in his presence. And he gave me a cargo consisting of myrrh, oil, cassia, black eye paint, giraffe tails, large cakes of incense, elephant tusks, hounds, apes, baboons, and every kind of precious thing. I then loaded them onto this boat. It then came to pass that I placed myself upon the ground to thank him, and he said to me: 'You will arrive home within two months. You will fill your embrace with your children. You will become young again at home, and you will be properly buried.'

"I went down to the shore in the vicinity of this ship, and I called out to the troops who were in the ship. I gave praise upon the shore to the lord of the island, and those who were in the ship did likewise.

"We sailed northward to the residence city of the king, and we arrived at the residence in two months, according to everything that he had said. Then I entered before the sovereign, and I presented to him this produce which I had brought back from this island. I was appointed a lieutenant, and I was assigned two hundred persons as my servants and followers. Look at me, now that I have returned, after having seen what I experienced. Listen to me. It is good for men to listen."

The commander said, "Do not act the part of the wise man, friend. What is the good of giving water to a goose just before it is to be slaughtered?"

It has come from its beginning to its end, as it has been found in writing, in the writing of the scribe excellent of fingers, Ameny's son Amen-aa, life, prosperity, health!

Superficially, "The Shipwrecked Sailor" is tremendously distant from us. A piece of Egyptian wisdom literature nearly 4,000 years old speaks to us, after all, from a psychological past so remote as to seem almost totally inaccessible. In Homer's time, it was already older than the *Canterbury Tales* are now! What a shock of recognition we feel, of communication over millenia, when we recognize in it a form with which we are still familiar; for essentially it is a hero story, not unlike many which are current today.

The essential elements of the hero story are present: there is a hero; he goes on a perilous journey to a completely foreign place; in the process he loses all his old identification, props, companions, and possessions; there is a terrifying event or struggle which he perceives as life-threatening; he is given a transforming gift of great value; and he returns to his homeland to tell the tale. *Gilgamesh, Sinbad*, the *Odyssey*, and *Jack and the Beanstalk* all share their form as well as their basic psychological point with our incredibly ancient tale.

Psychologically speaking, the hero's journey is the story of ego's journey inward to the frontier of the unconscious, and of the encounter with the unknown that takes place there. There, all the ego-created props of position, possessions, etc., are meaningless; when they fall away, what remains—pure ego—encounters the unknown. The threat of ego being annihilated by what it meets is real. But if ego withstands it, ego is given a gift—which makes return to ordinary life possible and living in the world worthwhile. It justifies life and facilitates a serene death.

This we are told in the great manifestations of the heroic myth, such as the *Odyssey* or Dante's *Divine Comedy*. Compared to these monuments, "The Shipwrecked Sailor" seems almost microscopic. Yet its genius is that it carries a miniature yet complete statement about the process of finding this gift that is more sophisticated than many more elaborate renditions of the hero story.

Our hero, the sailor, journeys to an island which the serpent tells us is the island of the *Ka*. This unequivocally indicates the psychological nature of the story. We know it is not a real, physical island, for the serpent says that when the sailor leaves it, he "will never see this island again, since it will become as water."

In fact, the *Ka* is one of the nonphysical parts of a human being mentioned in many Egyptian texts. In other words, for the Egyptians, as for Freud and Jung, the ego was "relative" to the whole of the psyche, and its awareness did not encompass the human totality. For Freud, the whole human consisted of a body, an ego, an id, and a superego; for Jung, a body, an ego, and an "unconscious" within which could be discriminated such things as "complexes" and "archetypes." But for the Egyptians, the whole human consisted of nine entities, the names of which we know but some of whose meanings remain obscure: *Khat* (physical body), *Sahu* (spirit body), *Ab* (heart), *Ka* (double), *Ba* (heart-soul), *Khaibit* (shadow), *Khu* (spirit-soul), *Sekhem* (vital power), and *Ren* (name). "All these were . . . bound together inseparably, and the welfare of any single one of them concerned the welfare of all" (Budge 1895, pp. lviii–lxix).

Although the individual concepts represented by these names are sometimes vague to us, it can be seen that they are arranged in an intentional sequence from material to highly spiritual. The first part to have no implied physical component at all is the fourth in the series, the "double," or the *Ka*. We are being informed, then, about a journey to a nonphysical part of the human, which must be a psychological journey; for one can only go to nonphysical realms within.

The *Ka* has been described as an

> abstract individuality of personality, endowed with all [one's] characteristic attributes . . . [it] had an absolutely independent existence [and] could move freely from place to place, separating itself from, or uniting itself to the body at will, and also enjoying life with the gods in heaven. (Ibid., pp. lxi–lxii)

While its hieroglyph is a pair of uplifted hands, it is often portrayed in Egyptian art as the mirror image of the individual, sometimes shown as identical but with a black face, whereas the body is always shown in white. A noncorporeal manifestation of the personality might be an appropriate way to summarize the *Ka*.

Now the journey to the *Ka* involves meeting a new mystery—the serpent—who says, "Let me tell you about something similar . . ." and then tells an utterly mystifying story about the violent deaths of seventy-five relatives, a falling star, and "a little daughter whom I had obtained through prayer." It is mystifying to us, but it has an effect on the sailor, which must mean that from the point of view possible in the *Ka*, things can be comprehended that the everyday point of view cannot assimilate logically; the implication of a continuing sequence of mysteries, up through the "heart-soul," "shadow," etc., is, of course, clear. The sailor tells the captain about his experience of the *Ka*; the serpent tells the sailor about his experience of the star and the daughter; so this presumably gave the serpent something that made him able to survive *his* loss of his relatives, and so on.

What is the effect this has on the sailor? This is to ask, What is the nature of the gift the successful hero obtains in his journey to the unknown place? It is contained in the serpent's words to the sailor: "If you would be brave, regulate your heart. Then you will fill your embrace with your children, you will kiss your wife, and you will see your house again, for this is better than anything." And the sailor paraphrases this to the captain as "The speech of a man can save him, and his words gain indulgence."

These are two interconnected themes common in many Egyptian tales and especially stressed in surviving examples of wisdom literature. The Egyptians ascribed the qualities of psychological awareness and intelligence to the heart and believed it was the center of the emotional self. It was "the seat of the power of life and the fountain of good and evil thoughts (Budge 1895, p. lxi). An encounter with a deeper level, the "double" or *Ka*, thus permits control of a more superficial one, the "heart" or *Ab*. To "regulate the heart" would imply power to regulate the passions, to maintain one's composure in difficult situations, to moderate emotional reactions, and to speak deliberately and effectively.

The desire for this kind of control is understandable to us today. We describe it differently, as ego's desire to rule the complexes and make the psyche obey orders. In ancient Egyptian terms, this is the desire for effective speech. But it is not to be achieved through an act of will by a lower part of the individual on a higher one, but rather by submission of both to a higher mystery still. What the serpent provides is awareness that the *Ka* has been terrified in turn, from the next level up. To continue the sequence, presumably, "regulation" of the serpent's level would only be gained from an experience with the next terror, hinted at by the falling star.

The transformation the sailor goes through is movement from being terrified and speechless before a manifestation from beyond the *Ka*—the serpent—to being able to relate to it and receive its gifts; this is accomplished by being lifted up in the serpent's mouth and hearing its story, for when he is put down, he can speak. To put it another way, an encounter with the personality's inherent structure seems to provide an inclusive framework within which both the sailor's ego-awareness and his fundamentally erratic heart can be contained.

Acceptance of the inherent structure of one's individual personality is something we try to find through psychoanalysis, and the changed awareness it can accomplish seems to resemble what happens to the sailor. Once one knows one's personality, one can accept its strengths, weaknesses, and various quirks as the givens within which one lives, and one ceases to agonize so much over not resembling the given ideal—which, in "The Shipwrecked Sailor," the captain seems to be doing.

This is a considerable gift, and as we know, it can have the effect the sailor describes; for newfound personal authority often results in a new position, a step up in society, wealth and servants, etc.

If we see the story this way, then we can easily explain one of its more puzzling aspects, which is the captain's apparent inability to grasp what his attendant is talking about. The captain's remark at the end of the story suggests that he continues to see his journey as a failure. The view of one's journey as a failure is the depressing situation that often brings people into analysis. Their situation is not unlike the captain's in that, failure notwithstanding, this is the only journey they have. The transformative gesture cannot be a new journey; rather, as the sailor implies, it can be found only in the telling of the story. "Compose yourself," he exhorts the captain, "then you will be able to reply when you are being questioned and speak to the king with presence of mind." It is as though the telling of the captain's story, by itself, will give it meaning for the king as well as for the captain. We have already seen how both the attendant and the serpent found this to be true. The attendant is advising the captain to take seriously the story he has and is suggesting that this alone will make it adequate in the king's eyes.

It doesn't work, of course; the captain doesn't listen. One doesn't believe an analysis is going to work, either, until it does. And afterward, one cannot easily convince other "captains" one encounters that such a process makes any difference at all.

But telling one's story is fundamentally what analysis is about. The reexamination of the events of a life, as well as the inner responses one had to them (probably the *heart's* experience, in Egyptian terminology) clarifies the nature of the personality that experienced those events in a way that the teller finds both acceptable and self-revelatory. It is possible to say this kind of examination of one's life causes the island of the *Ka* to emerge from the sea of the unconscious. Although one is at first terrified to see one's personality this starkly, one discovers in it a connection, like the serpent, to deeper levels of one's self, and it provides the gift of self-acceptance, as one is.

This can be enormously freeing, for lifelong senses of inadequacy and guilt (such as the captain's despair) can lessen dramatically. The awareness of the structure of that island—self-acceptance—enables one to live a richer life.

We end up with a rather surprising theory: if we want to accept the premise that this story is an elaborate metaphor for some kind of inner journey, then it is possible to read it as a Middle Kingdom exhortation to deal with one's existential despair in a way we still employ today, by telling one's story as it is. It depicts an ancient process not unlike a Jungian psychoanalysis.

Here we seem to arrive at the essential meaning of all hero stories. As we noted in the beginning, all of them can be read as elaborations upon the idea of the journey within, to self-knowledge. The peculiar genius of "The Shipwrecked Sailor" is in its concise yet extremely detailed elaboration of this theme, so clearly constructed that it communicates sophisticated psychological attitudes to our own time. In it we find a confirmation from the remote past of the rightness of the psychological journeys upon which we find ourselves embarked, as well as some valuable hints as to how to complete them. Wisdom literature turns out to be rightly named, both for its time and for our own.

## Notes

1. For bibliographical references and commentary, consult Lefebvre (1949, pp. 29–40), and Erman (1966, pp. xxiii–xxiv, 29–35).

## References

Budge, E. A. Wallis, trans. 1895. *The Egyptian Book of the Dead.* New York: Dover Publications, 1967.

DeBuck, A. 1948. *Egyptian Readingbook.* Stichting Nederlandsch Archaeologishch-Philologisch Instituut voor het Nabije Oosten, E. J. Brill.

Erman, A. 1966. *The Ancient Egyptians: A Sourcebook of Their Writings.* New York: Harper Torchbooks.

Lefebvre, G. 1949. *Romans et Contes Egyptiens de l'Epoque Pharaonique.* Paris: Adrien-Maisonneuve.

Simpson, W. K. 1972. *The Literature of Ancient Egypt.* New Haven, Conn.: Yale University Press.

# Book Reviews

**The Borderline Personality: Vision and Healing**
Nathan Schwartz-Salant. Wilmette, Ill.: Chiron Publications, 1988. 256 pages. $16.95

Reviewed by Lionel Corbett

Schwartz-Salant's book is an enormous effort of synthesis. It is surely the prototype and exemplar of an essential and growing movement within analytical psychology, and it makes no easy demands on the reader. Within this work one is confronted with the convergence of many apparently disparate streams of thought. But no splitting is allowed; we simultaneously witness the (holographically) interacting levels of the archetypal, mythic, symbolic, and "purely" (whatever that means) clinical aspects of therapy. All of this incidentally makes Schwartz-Salant foremost in the attempt to render obsolete the traditional distinctions between these different types of Jungian therapy. In this book these different but essential aspects of our work are masterfully woven into a textual richness that illumines our relationships with our most trying patients, in ways which have been most helpful to me. But it must also be said that at times, Schwartz-Salant gives eloquent voice to the difficulty of mixing competing paradigms. To succeed in his synthetic work, he has to describe the same phenomena not only from different perspectives but also in several languages at once. Since their nuances do not always translate happily between each other, the reader is required to be familiar with them in order to grasp the depth of the text.

In this context Schwartz-Salant has given the field of analytical psychology a major gift. Because Jung wrote little on the practical, how-to-do it aspects of therapy, most of us find it necessary to learn from the personalistic writers, so that we have Kleinian, Kohutian, Langsian and other types of Jungians. Not only is Schwartz-Salant at home among many such authors, he is very sensitive to the

---

**Lionel Corbett**, M.D., is an analyst in private practice in Santa Fe, New Mexico.

concomitant archetypal implications of their theories. These implications ensoul and enspirit them immeasurably and render them accessible to a Jungian orientation by placing them in their transpersonal context. Further, Schwartz-Salant stresses the religious dimension and importance of the work, especially by his practical demonstrations of the healing power of the *numinosum* acting as an autonomous agency within the therapy. Schwartz-Salant thereby provides a level of meaning to the suffering and *therapeia* of the borderline patient which I believe is hitherto unequalled. He also delineates the importance of the therapist in the process by which the negatively experienced *numinosum* may transform, and he illustrates how this process can be facilitated.

It is difficult to single out for comment a few of Schwartz-Salant's unique contributions, but surely the idea of an unconscious couple that dominates the interactive field deserves special mention. Schwartz-Salant is forthright in declaring that such phenomena exist within the subtle body, in the psychic field between the two participants. They are seen with imaginal sight, not by means of our usual vision. This example underscores the idea of the reality of the psyche at its most practical level. Schwartz-Salant has a talent for explaining the clinical relevance of what otherwise seems merely an arcane idea. He deserves credit for "going public" with an idea that many people would be shy to discuss. For Schwartz-Salant, the subtle body is a crucial concept; the therapist's ability to "see" processes at this level is the beginning of the work of transforming these phenomena. In the case of the borderline, they consist of very toxic forms of non-union. Such vision, which Schwartz-Salant believes is experienced via projective identification, connects the participants at the level of the objective psyche. Here it acts as an intermediary process linking the time–space world with the pleroma. I am so glad that our cultural climate and his personal courage allow Schwartz-Salant not to be reticent about these important matters.

Schwartz-Salant gives the idea of the *coniunctio* new importance. Many of us knew the notion from Jung's alchemical writing but failed to grasp its direct applicability until we read Schwartz-Salant's work, in which he explains its central importance in healing. The roots of the concept of the inner couple and its relevance for the development of the *coniunctio* are found in Andre Green's (1975, p. 12) notion of the unconscious dyad, in Winnicott's (1971, p. 3) idea of the importance of the intermediate area between inner and outer, and in Bion's stress on the linking function. However, Schwartz-Salant relates this concept to the One Continuum, and its transformative ability, without the usual stress on personalistic interpretation. This insight is indeed new. For Schwartz-Salant, the heart-centered *coniunctio* experience, perceived and accepted at its own irreduceable level, allows the integration of hitherto unmanageable inner figures and overwhelmingly negative archetypal affects. His explanation of how these are Yahweh-like is an unsurpassed piece of amplification. Above all, I am grateful to him for helping to free us from the numbing idea that psychotherapy is only applied developmental psychology. Again and again, Schwartz-Salant indicates how new and unexpected healing potentials may arise from the objective psyche. These are not reduceable to early childhood experience and its cure within a purely interpretive focus, but they are nevertheless highly dependent on an accurate understanding of transference-countertransference dynamics for their constellation and proper management. Schwartz-Salant is courageous in the many revelations of how his own intrapsychic processes enabled such dynamics to occur. Inevitably we will compare our own process with his. Whereas we do not all have his gift of imaginal sight—which may be typological—we can probably all cultivate our personal medium for experiencing the *mundus imaginalis*, which is "where" these processes operate.

There is only one major area in which I feel Schwartz-Salant would have been better to have used a different paradigm, namely in his amplification of Jung's commentary on the Rosarium pictures. My suggestion here may seem like too technical a quibble, but it does have important implications for theory and therapy. Jung (1946) believed that the alchemists were depicting the union of opposite intrapsychic principles in their *coniuntio* imagery. He regarded this union as the archetypal basis of the transference, within which the Self finally emerges as the union of opposites. Schwartz-Salant describes and interprets these woodcuts and the transference situations they depict in terms of the phenomenology of an interactive field between two participants when they are afflicted by projective identification. This mechanism is typical of situations arising in the treatment of borderline states of mind. I feel that a better case can be made for viewing these pictures as depictions of stages in the development of a personal self via the selfobject experience, as described by Kohut (1971). My quibble is that there is no need to see the pictures as necessarily due to borderline dynamics; they might just as well be seen in terms of an intersubjective field between healthier people, or as the depiction of the intrapsychic experience of the selfobject. Projective identification is a psychotic mechanism by means of which an intolerable part of the personality is split off and installed in another, thus impoverishing the psyche. It is normal only in the very young infant, involving loss of self–other differentiation and loss of self-cohesion. By contrast the selfobject experience is a normally occurring phenomenon throughout life, building self structure and cohesion. It creates psychic reality rather than denying it. There is no definitive reason to assume that the Rosarium is depicting a pathological process. There does seem to be a shared psychic field, but the term "projection" implies an experience between whole, separate objects, whereas the selfobject is an experience of wholeness while held together by another who is subjectively experienced as part of the self. Hence the "two-ness" imagery is at the same time a "one-ness." The Rosarium woodcuts may well depict stages in the development of a self via merger with another—the *coniunctio*at an early stage of development. This reformulation in no way detracts from the importance of the *coniunctio*, but defines it differently. The value of this reformulation is for us to realize that the felt sense for the patient is that he is only whole in the presence of the therapist. This wholeness occurs when the two are intrapsychically fused, shown in the early pictures. This state continues until the patient emerges with a separate sense of self. Thus, figure 5 (Schwartz-Salant 1988, p. 118) would represent an unconscious, erotized pre-oedipal yearning for wholeness via the selfobject. Figure 7 (ibid., p. 120) indicates a state of disruption of the self–selfobject bond leading to a feeling of "soul-loss" or despair. Figure 10 (ibid., p. 124) or the lesser *coniunctio*, suggests the establishment of a solid selfobject transference, or wholeness in the presence of the other, while the resurrected Christ (ibid., fig. 20, p. 130) looks like the rebirth of the original self out of the Self, or wholeness in the context of the transpersonal. I feel that Schwartz-Salant is so committed to the importance of the concept of projective identification that he applies it too broadly. This is my only criticism of an otherwise brilliantly original piece of work.

For those of us who are concerned with seeking ways to connect our everyday clinical work with the direct experience of the Self, this book is essential reading.

Schwartz-Salant's insights reflect his commitment to the borderline patient, whom he understands so well and so compassionately.

## References

Green, A. 1975. The analyst, symbolization and absence in the analytic setting. *International Journal of Psycho-analysis*56/1.

Jung, C. G. 1946. The psychology of the transference. *Collected Works* 18:203–323. Princeton, N.J.: Princeton University Press, 1954.

Kohut, H. 1971. *The Analysis of the Self.* New York: International Universities Press.

Winnicott, D. W. 1971. *Playing and Reality*. London: Tavistock.

**The Phallic Quest: Priapus and Masculine Inflation**
James Wyly. Toronto: Inner City Books, 1989. 124 pages. $13.00

Reviewed by Nancy Qualls-Corbett

In light of all the recent publications focusing on feminine psychology, feminine sexuality, feminine spirituality, for the most part from feminine writers, it seems not only suitable and timely but undoubtably refreshing to explore the realm of masculine psychology as it relates to masculine sexuality and masculine spirituality and as told by a man. James Wyly's book, richly illustrated with decorative, classical art images of Priapus, offers such an undertaking.

In the introduction, a critical question is raised: When is the inflated phallus a mechanism for bolstering a sense of male ego aggrandizement, i.e., power, competition, *machismo*, and violence, and when is the inflated phlauus the crucial psychological instrument for male creativity? The mythological image of the god with the unrealistic "inflated" phallus, Priapus, is effectively employed to amplify the former aspects of this question. He personifies the destructive element of an inflation, "a psychological distortion in which masculinity's phallic aspect is separated from its whole" (p. 14). Priapus emerges as a complex split off from consciousness, acting autonomously and commanding conscious attention. More importantly, it is this same god who also embodies that psychological function which demands reintegration; for he carries a pruning knife which punctures "the inflated ego position that seems to accompany the split" (p. 14).

Through stories recounted from mythology and classical literature, the reader is introduced to many lesser known associations with Priapus. The author deftly weaves these myths into psychological implications or understandings. One central theme is the connection of Priapus to castration, quite the opposite from our usual imaging of this god. Paradoxically it is the identical implement, the pruning knife, with which the god cares for the sacred pear trees of Hera. Using a series of associations, Wyly

---

**Nancy Qualls-Corbett, Ph.D.,** is a Jungian analyst in private practice in Birmingham, Alabama. She is a diplomate of the C. G. Jung Institute, Zurich. She is the author of the book, *The Sacred Prostitute: Eternal Aspect of the Feminine*.

links this image with a much broader amplification, the Rites of Cybele. He explains that the male ego, due to an adolescent inflated attitude toward *phallos*, participates in symbolic castration, i.e. sterility or separation from the creative source of the unconscious. A similar theme is related from *The Golden Ass*. After knowing full humiliation and suffering mistreatment, Lucius, as an ass, comes to honor the goddess, Isis. In so doing, he leaves his reckless, former self and is transformed into a competent, dependable, and successful man. The author emphasizes that Priapus does not restore that which he prunes. After the necessary sacrifice of the inflated *phallos*, another deity leads the man, perhaps the initiate, into a new relation with the matrix, the creative unconscious. As the associations with the stories suggest, the phallic quest is an inflated or false search for manhood. It is only in abandoning this quest that the true integrated sense of masculinity is achieved.

Moving from antiquity to modern times, Wyly presents an example of twentieth-century man caught in the priapic complex illustrated by the character of Thomas Mann's tragic hero, Gustave von Aschenbach. From the novel, *Death in Venice*, there is a frightening description of what many men in the second half of life experience today. It reveals a shattering commentary on the collective view of the successful man, "the ego-constructed persona image which is still endemic in our culture" (p. 54). A quote from the novel provides such a pathetic image:

> "Ten years later he had learned to sit at his desk and sustain and live up to his growing reputation . . . for many claims press upon the solid and successful man. At forty, worn down by the strains and stresses of his actual tasks, he had to deal with a daily post heavy with tributes from his own and foreign countries." (p. 53)

The outcome of this story (and likewise the psychological understanding) is different from those related earlier. A product of his time and culture, "Aschenbach is unable to assimilate his obsession [with the beautiful youth, Tadzio]. He is struck impotent because he has not honored or acted upon the phallic component of his masculinity, living instead an inflated life bound by that which ego finds acceptable" (p. 58). He cannot withstand the total loss of his own inflated image to join his classical counterpart, Lucius, in saying, "I am an ass." In this story there is no sacrifice, no humiliation, no dedication to the deity, no reintegration of *phallos*. There is only denial in order to preserve the persona at all cost. The cost is great for it is death. In Mann's story, death comes in form of fatal Asiatic cholera; in man's psychological story, death comes in the form of loss of life's force, impotence in directing one's destiny, and the loss of opportunity for the adult male's inner connection to his masculinity.

The second half of *The Phallic Quest* correlates the mythological, literary, and physical (the medical condition of priapism is also described) metaphors to the masculine, human condition. The author carefully and cleverly constructs a developmental outline by interweaving the different elements found in the previously told tales. These developmental stages whose names define the process are: splitting off, inflation, pruning, quest, abandonment of the quest, divine intervention, and transformation. These stages are demonstrated through the use of dreams and dream interpretations from several male analysands, but not complete in any one man's progress. (However, it was well noted that these stages do not operate sequentially, rather in "psycho-mythical time," i.e., "all of its parts are happening always, and movement occurs as the individual or cultural psyche moves within the perpetual, transpersonal myth" (p. 75).)

At this point I did not have a clear sense of the dreamers or feel connected to their process. The case material of these several men whose dreams were recounted is sketchy. For instance, I wondered how old they were. Was this, in part, a normal adolescent biological development or had they become fixated in an attitude unchanged by aging? I wondered if the cultural influence was the same in each case, or, if different, what impact did early masculine mirroring have on their male image. I wondered if the immature masculine on the phallic quest is not comparable to psychological elements seen in the *puer eternus*. I speculated about what these men's relationships with women (or the feminine in a homosexual relationship) would be. The author does give a theoretical description, writing about *coniunctio*:

> Here we must be careful to make a distinction between the unconscious relationship to the feminine, which is adolescent and matriarchal, and a conscious relationship to the feminine, which is phallic, creative and co-equal. We can now see that it is only the uninflated, adult masculine, with full phallic power, that can achieve it. (p. 113)

Here I wished for more elaboration or explanation of the human element (case material) demonstrating the given theory.

In conclusion Wyly states: "The purpose of the Priapus cycle we have described is to move masculinity from relating to femininity as mother to relating to her as consort. Only in this way can there be a *coniunctio* which will give birth to a viable cultural future" (p. 113). As a woman I applaud that statement, and I think the author for giving men and women this and other essential insights into the realm of male sexuality and masculinity.

**Analytical Psychology: Notes of the Seminar Given in 1925.**
William McGuire, ed. Princeton, N.J.: Princeton University Press, 1989. 179 pages. $24.95.

Reviewed by Peter Mudd

For the reader interested in the history and development of the theory of analytical psychology, *Analytical Psychology: Notes of the Seminar Given in 1925* provides a fascinating glimpse into the mind and motives of its creator, C. G. Jung, while it narrates the evolution of a theory only now coming into its full promise. Some four years after this seminar was given, Jung would write that "every psychology—my own included—has the character of a subjective confession" (*CW* 4, par. 774). This book is a testimony to that statement. Although "reviewed and

---

**Peter Mudd** is a Jungian analyst in private practice in Evanston, Illinois. He is currently the Executive Director of the C. G. Jung Institute of Chicago and Director of Studies of the Institute's Analyst Training Program.

corrected by Dr. Jung" (p. xx), the notes of the seminar were not intended for general publication and provide a more informal, free-wheeling, oral recitation of analytical psychology's foundations and growth.

Throughout the seminar, Jung moves back and forth between an examination/elucidation of major tenets of his theory at that time and a confession of his experiences that were the source of those ideas. He purports to divulge "the weaving about among mistakes, impure thinking, etc., etc., which is always very difficult for a man to make public" (p. 32), and, in fairness, he does reveal himself to a degree, but there is a frustrating absence of truly personal confession in Jung's account. Curiously enough, it bears a resemblance to Freud's *History of the Psycho-analytical Movement* in that it provides a rather sanitized version of the process of theory building by omitting a more complete account of the shadow's role. Darker factors such as psychoanalytic politics with its interpersonal rivalries, intrigues, and alliances, and Jung's dual life with Sabina Spielrein, Toni Wolff, and Emma Jung are notably absent from Jung's version of the history. Realistically, one could not expect this level of confession in a seminar, but it is of vital importance to recognize that Jung's "official history" of analytical psychology is truly a partial history, anticipating his chapter, "Confrontation with the Unconscious," in his autobiography. I was struck by how little his view of these events would change more than 30 years later.

Nonetheless, Jung's account is informative. We learn that he had indeed recognized the profoundly projective element in his appropriation of the so-called "Miller Fantasies" in the *Psychology of the Unconscious*:

> She became an anima figure, a carrier of an inferior function of which I was very little conscious. I was in my consciousness an active thinker accustomed to subjecting my thoughts to the most rigorous sort of direction, and therefore fantasizing was a mental process that was directly repellent to me. As a form of thinking I held it to be altogether impure, a sort of incestuous intercourse, thoroughly immoral from an intellectual viewpoint. Permitting fantasy in myself had the same effect on me as would be produced on a man if he came into his workshop and found all the tools flying about doing things independently of his will. It shocked me, in other words, to think of the possibility of a fantasy life in my own mind; it was against all the intellectual ideals I had developed for myself, and so great was my resistance to it, that I could only admit the fact in myself through the process of projecting my material into Miss Miller's. Or, to put it even more strongly, passive thinking seemed to me such a weak and repellent thing that I could only handle it through a diseased woman. (pp. 27–28)

Here, it seems to me, Jung confirms in himself the inevitability of the projective relationship between observer and observed, theorist and theory, and analyst and analysand, which he asserted over and over throughout his writings and which is among his most important contributions to analytical practice. This point of view permeates every useful theory of countertransference.

In the light of the theory of analytical psychology, however, this excerpt from the seminar illuminates the current controversy over anima/animus theory by revealing Jung's personal proclivity for projecting into "the feminine" aspects of his own shadow and psychological makeup and then encapsulating them in a concept. I have dealt with this subject elsewhere (see *The Archetype of Shadow in a Split*

*World*, Proceedings of the Tenth International Congress for Analytical Psychology, Berlin, 1986) as both an intrapsychic and interpersonal dimension of Jung's personality which had a crucial impact on theory. These "relocations" of personal psychology into theoretical constructs are nowhere more evident than in anima/animus theory, and their effects reverberate throughout the post-Jungian debates over the nature and content of gender.

Throughout the seminar, it is impossible not to notice Jung's tendency to make rather sweeping generalizations on a number of subjects, including female psychology, art, Catholic psychology, etc. These pronouncements are at best ill advised, and one can see in them the forerunners of Jung's tragic blunders with regard to national socialism and the Jews that would occur ten years later. One angle on this tendency to understand things too quickly, and so to injure by oversimplifying, is also evident in the seminar, namely Jung's intense preoccupation with form at the expense of content. Ironically enough, this tendency led Jung, who is undoubtedly the greatest defender of the necessity of being an individual, to ignore the complexity and diversity at play beneath and within the broad, presumably archetypal, forms of being with which he was working. Andrew Samuels, in an insightful paper entitled *Jung, Anti-Semitism and the Führerprinzip* (given in New York at the Lingering Shadows conference, March 1989), makes a related point regarding nationhood and Jung's notion of national psychology.

This fascination with form appears most prominently in the predominance given to typology throughout the seminar. Jung had published *Psychological Types* just four years prior to the seminar, and at the time of the meetings, he undoubtedly saw it as the most comprehensive statement of his views and the best paradigm for understanding the mysteries of the psyche. His frequent explorations of psychological dynamics as essentially typological conflicts, while useful and illuminating, do not have the convincing authority of later theoretical positions put forward in works like *The Relations Between the Ego and the Unconscious* (1928) or *The Psychology of the Transference* (1946). Of particular interest is Jung's notion that the individuative conflict seen in analysis would most often be fought between the auxiliary functions, while the battle between superior and inferior functions would be waged in life (Lecture 11). Since Jung rarely cites case material which might illustrate his points, we are left with a rather abstract set of assertions that beg for elaboration. Again and again, I was drawn into Jung's propositions with interest and curiosity and then found myself frustrated when the lecture ended with many points left teasingly undeveloped.

Among the most interesting and compelling themes that characterize the seminar and which especially caught my attention was that of life and death as the most fundamental and dynamic pairing of opposites. He says in Lecture 10, "We have to learn with effort the negations of our positions, and to grasp the fact that life is a process that takes place between two poles, being only complete when surrounded by death" (p. 79). Jung notes this theme as the basic dualism of psychic life and rightly sees it in all human endeavor. This theme is implicit when Jung gives a resume of his thinking that led to the creation of *The Psychology of the Unconscious* (1911–1912). He states that the splitting of libido into a positive and negative current was the basic thesis of the book. This position, as we know, is imaged throughout that work as the hero's struggle to conquer the devouring mother (the deathly unconscious) from the inside out. It represents quite lucidly Jung's sense of the dangers that can overcome the regressed ego and turn individuative opportunity into destructive psychopathology. In all this we can glimpse just how powerful Jung's own experience with unconscious inundation must have been. It was surely a matter of life and death.

As an interesting, although tangential, point, Jung also tells us, with regard to the split libido thesis, that Freud, whom he viewed as a monist in relation to libido theory, could not accept his (Jung's) dualist proposition. I found it ironic, even tragic, that just five years prior to the seminar Freud had written *Beyond the Pleasure Principle*, where a dualistic conception of libido is proposed, and strangely enough an accusation of monism is levelled against Jung by his former colleague. It seemed from the seminar transcript that Jung had not read this work of Freud's, and I couldn't help but wonder how he might have responded to it. It has always seemed to me that these two geniuses were much more alike than either of them would ever admit.

Where I find Jung at his best in this seminar is when he discusses fantasy as a creative, natural healing process of the psyche. There always seems such tremendous conviction in Jung about this aspect of psychic life that I never fail to be impressed and moved by it. What I especially liked about the various passages dealing with this topic was the quality of balance between healing and destructive potentials and the inestimable importance of the ego's capacity to endure and integrate the symbolic process. The transcendent function, often referred to as the mediatory function throughout, is powerfully presented as a kind of voluntary agony in service of becoming oneself. With all the New Age appropriation of Jung's ideas, listening to Jung address the issue and process of transformation in this seminar refreshingly reminded me again just how practical and realistic he could be.

While many other aspects of this seminar are worthy of some discussion, space does not permit. I would like, however, to say a few words about two of the seminar's participants, whom I found nearly as interesting as Jung himself, namely Charles Aldrich and Cary Fink de Angulo. Mr. Aldrich impressed me as an altogether cultured and articulate person. His discussions of art seemed far more well considered and less judgmental than Jung's. As far as I can recall, he is the only member of the seminar to whom Jung addresses a question. I think this is telling. Dr. de Angulo, who later became one of Jung's better translators, struck me as a challenging person, undaunted by what must have been an imposing figure of C. G. Jung. I found her willingness to question Jung and to reject his formulations (on occasion) admirable and impressive. For me, the other participants remained pale by comparison.

It is always difficult to try to summarize an opinion about anything Jung has produced, and this seminar is no exception. It could be said that the notes represent an extended statement of the theory of analytical psychology in 1925. That would be true, but it would be empty truth. The seminar notes provide a cross-section of a living, creative process as it unfolds, diversifies, and evolves. The value of this particular cross-section is its important placement in time and in its form—the spoken word of Jung addressed to those more trusted than a troublesome reading public. So we receive seldom seen facets of his personality and his theory. This rare opportunity to hear "Jung in private" complicates while it enriches the study of analytical psychology, because we realize all the more that this is the work of a mortal human being, and we have to contend with all the complexities of a subjective confession.

**The Plural Psyche: Personality, Morality and the Father**
Andrew Samuels. London: Routledge, 1989. 253 pages. $25.00

Reviewed by Ruth El Saffar

The Golden Age of depth psychology is over; the second-generation consolidators of psychological theory have also come and gone: thus has Andrew Samuels characterized the situation to which contemporary analytical theorists and practitioners have fallen heir. In his most recent book, Samuels sets himself the task of describing the negotiatory ideology required of the third generation, taking up the role associated astrologically with the sign of Gemini and the spirit of Hermes.

In *The Plural Psyche* it is, in fact, Hermes who leads us and to whom we are led. Although Hermes makes a highly uncharacteristic center-stage appearance midway through Chapter 8 (pp. 135–140) where his nature and genealogy are brought in for brief discussion, his traces are evident in the book from start to finish. Samuels's concerns, as well as his style, the topics he presents, and his methodology, are saturated in Hermes's elusive, transitive nature.

The "ideology of pluralism" within which Samuels explores current analytical thought and practice is itself not so much a system as a way of mediating between systems polarized along such axes as diachrony/synchrony, unity/diversity, determinism/acausality, reduction/synthesis. Rather than choosing sides or seeking forced reconciliations among the whole gamut of possible opposites, Samuels explores ways of maintaining the integrity of the different systems while finding the connectors through which they may couple and mutually fructify one another.

Pluralism is a difficult concept to hold onto. Neither formless nor fixed, neither liquid nor solid, pluralism is best understood not as a concept at all, but rather as an instrument. Like tide water advancing and retreating along a body of land, at once in touch with and distinct from that over which it ebbs and flows, Samuels's pluralism shares with post-structuralism an emphasis on relativity, interaction, and the experiential.

The image of the tide evokes, along with issues of constancy and change, predictability and undecidability, the notion of borders that informs Samuels's discussion of gender. He finds in "gender confusion" opportunities for growth that are thwarted in the presence of gender certainty. He also probes the notion of borderline as a diagnostic category, its place at the edges between consciousness and the unconscious, as well as its place in the fascination of present-day theoreticians.

The pluralist apprcach/method/theory, like the tide waters, brings up an unexpected array of materials: the debates between "nature" and "culture," transmogrified into the post-Jungian division between developmentalists and archtypalists, come up for consideration; so does the question of the father and his role in gender and culture construction; so also do the questions of the nature and function of the archetypes, the role of incest in personality development, the role of

---

**Ruth El Saffar** is an analyst in training at the Jung Institute of Chicago, and research professor of the humanities at the University of Illinois in Chicago. She is the author of several books and numerous articles on various aspects of Spanish literature.

aggression in interpersonal relatedness, and the effect on the collective of the threat of nuclear annihilation.

Diverse though these issues may be, and scattered through the web of argumentation as snippets of an analytic case here, a countertransference survey there, a case colloquium transcript somewhere else, consistent currents can be found acting on the material that is washed ashore. Principal among these is the numerical problem of the one, the two, and the three (the four is referred to, but never really developed).

The questions of fusion, division, and relationship implied in oneness, twoness, and threeness undergirds Samuels's discussion of developmental psychology (Chapter 2) where he proposes a diagnostics based on how the patient's transference manifests. It comes up again in Chapters 4–7 where the question of the role of the father in particular and of parental imagery in general becomes the basis for a discussion of analytic interpretation and of gender identity. Crucially, it reappears in Chapter 8, where primal scene imagery and its relation to psychological health is taken up, and where, not insignificantly, Hermes makes his appearance.

Hermes, it turns out, carries many of the qualities and attributes of pluralism. He is the god who can *celebrate* the primal scene, that is, he can hold the place of the third, needing neither to deny nor to subvert the possibility of union between the one (mother) and the Other (father). Hermes's realm of the in-between can also be found in Samuels's wonderful chapters on countertransference and the *mundus imaginalis* (Chapter 9) and the alchemical metaphor (Chapter 10). In both chapters, what is developed is a sense of the "intermediate dimension" (p. 162) within which analysis takes place. The analysis would constitute not so much the work of interpretation, with all that that implies of patient/analyst hierarchies, but the cultivation of an awareness of the imaginary field constellated between analyst and patient. As the emphasis shifts here from patient to analyst, from transference to countertransference, it will be the body of the analyst that will hold the image of the work, leading to the idea of countertransference as a "religious or mystical experience" (p. 165), and analysis as a "mysticism of persons . . . polyvalent, pluralistic" (p. 167).

Above all, what Samuels has sought in *The Plural Psyche* is to challenge rigidities where systems appear too dominant within a given theoretical landscape and to promote connection when divergent structures appear to have lost the ability to communicate with one another. We of Samuels's third generation are being encouraged to image the "parents"—our theoretical foremothers and forefathers—in bed together, to imagine the often conflictual and frequently contradictory theories of psychology not only as separate and distinct, but capable of ecstatic comingling as well. Further, we are urged to celebrate not simply autonomy, or simply union, but the alternate states, the one in the many, the many in the one, that can be recognized only from a third position. To do this requires neither taking sides nor denying conflict, but dwelling in that in-between place where nothing is sure and all is possible.

The place of the in-between also has its dangers, of course. Playing the role of constant critic leaves it without a place of its own. Devoid of passion, it may lose, in its deconstructive zeal, a grounding on which choice can be made and action taken. After seeing the failings of once passionately embraced systems, the pluralist would rightly be suspicious of numinous ideas. The *numinosum*, however, as Samuels points out in his last chapter, is an essential ingredient in theory: without it, systems lack conviction; with it, they lack flexibility. Samuels dodges this particular conundrum by a characteristic move from content to form:

> Pluralism and the *numinosum* become compatible when *the act of choice is experienced as numinous* and not simply what is chosen. Then we are free to choose, and choose again; conviction and tolerance both flourish. (p. 226, emphasis his)

We are back in the realm of constant motion, constant change, that world of flux where passion, if it surfaces, becomes attached to a form rather than to a substance. It looks uncomfortably like the polymorphous perversity of Hermes—lots of activity, little consistency, no commitment.

My suspicion, however, is that in Samuels's pluralism there is a substance, a substance passionately embraced. The in-between so well described by Samuels is not empty, as becomes clear in his discussion of countertransference and the alchemical metaphor for analysis. The in-between is a place of connection and is populated by images. The very plenitude of the intermediate brings back into pluralism, its post-modern affiliations notwithstanding, the threat of attachment.

Self-reflexivity has finally, therefore, to put its own self into question. When it finds itself caught—by desire? by the numinosum?—it must make itself available to its own deconstructive impulses. That is why it was so important for Hermes to appear in person in Chapter 8—to become himself an object of analysis. Hermes's appearance, with all his shortcomings as well as his strengths, suggests Samuels's own commitment to a continually provisional position in the book, his willingness to place pluralism alongside other theories, as another "system" that has failings and is still developing.

The book challenges many pet notions of Jungian and post-Jungian psychology, including developmental theories of personality formation, the archtypal structuring of the psyche, and the existence of the feminine as an absolute. It also provides many new insights into the work of analysis and the development of personal identity. Its challenge to gender certainty and its liberation of the feminine from the confines of the eternal or the natural seem especially salubrious. Overall, Samuels has worked here to keep boundaries at once functional and permeable, as he asks of our schools and our theories that they keep open the possibility of a third place between them where they might imagine delighting in creative interaction.

**The Unfolding Self**
Mara Sidoli. Boston: Sigo Press, 1990. 203 pages. $15.95

Reviewed by Ronald G. Jalbert

---

**Ronald G. Jalbert**, Ph.D., is a Jungian analyst and child psychotherapist in private practice in Pittsburgh.

Since the final version of Mara Sidoli's *The Unfolding Self* was not yet available at the writing of this review, I am reviewing only the galley proofs. This constraint forces me to review the work without benefit of final editing, pagination, table of contents, or index. In spite of this constraint, I find the book informative, clinically rich, and stimulating both intellectually and analytically. I highly recommend it.

The author is to be commended for this welcome addition to the slowly growing literature on Jungian child psychotherapy. The view she conveys in *The Unfolding Self* is representative of Fordham and his followers who emphasize infant observation and individuation in childhood and who interface Jungian thought with Kleinian and Freudian contributions to child development. The book contains nine chapters that are loosely arranged to follow the developmental order of the child. The beginning chapters report protocols of actual infant–mother observations and cases of preschool and latency-aged children, accompanied by a general overview of some of Fordham's key concept about infancy and childhood. Later chapters discuss preadolescent and adolescent cases. The author additionally emphasizes the value of the developmental approach in work with the "child within" the adult by frequently commenting on adult cases, making the book quite relevant to all analysts and therapists regardless of the age group in which they specialize.

Sidoli highlights Fordham's contributions including:

a) theory—formulation of the concept of the Primal Self as an extension of Jung's understanding of the Self; explication of the convergence of Klein's ideas with those of Jung;
b) methodology—insistence on the importance of direct infant–mother observations, following Bick; application of empirical studies, such as Bowlby's among others, to the clinical setting; and
c) analytic practice—splitting and polarization of archetypal patterns in the process of deintegration/reintegration; appreciation for different levels of symbolization where the first affectively charged rudiments of the "symbol" are embodied—that is, they relate to the child's experience of its own body and that of the mother.

I appreciate Sidoli's book for showing us what the deintegrative/reintegrative process looks like empirically and clinically. In one of the more interesting and intriguing sections of the book, she carefully reminds the reader that the earliest psychic states are in essence "unthinkable" since they are preverbal and preconceptual. "The unrememberable and the unforgettable" (quoted by Mahler 1975, p. 197) are inscribed in the emotions, in the body (in its vulnerability to somatization), and in the proto-images that populate the infant psyche. From the beginning, the human infant (from the Latin *infans*, one incapable of speech) is as "hungry" for words as it is for mother's milk. Since the child's ego is primarily a body-ego, the infant uses the body, its openings and parts, to "speak" its distress. In the potential, transitional space between itself and the mother and in the mother's ministerings and reverie, the infant is exposed to the symbol in its nascent form.

In agreement with Fordham's thought, Sidoli sees the Primal Self as a psychosomatic unity that undertakes a cyclic process of deintegration and reintegration. In normal development, this process is in concert with the maternal figure. In the theoretical discussion as well as in the case material, Sidoli points out how the psyche's inability to deintegrate leads to autism while a disruption in its ability to deintegrate properly brings on disintegration. Prolonged disintegration that is not responded to by the maternal figure in such a way as to reintroduce the rhythm of deintegration/reintegration puts the child at risk for serious emotional disorders. This reintroduction requires of the mother the capacity to empathize with the child's psychic experience. This capacity is based upon access to her own "inner child" with its specific history of the deintegration/reintegration cycle that is reawakened by her pregnancy and the birth of her actual child.

The author highlights the role parents and therapists play in mediating the archetypal world. Parents function in this capacity in the everyday life of the child. They serve as "carriers" of the child's projections of archetypal images, while "humanizing" the instinctual pole of the archetype in the way they respond to the child. Therapists mitigate the "all or nothing" effects of the archetypes upon patients in the context of the transference-countertransference by means of "holding" and interpretation. In its nonmediated state, the archetype can be terrifying and overwhelming, particularly for fragile ego states. In this way, parents and therapists are called upon to metabolize into thought what the infant, the child, or the regressed adult was unable to make sense of previously.

Richly detailed case material is used to illustrate theoretical points, such as in the case of Miss S in Chapter 2; at other times, the case may stand on its own—for example, the case of Mary in Chapter 3—to demonstrate the value of an overall approach to the psyche. In all, there are eighteen cases. Some of them are lengthy reports of treatment, others are vignettes. All serve to add texture to the book and bring developmental theories closer to the consulting room. On occasion, the author tends to lapse into a "she/he said–I said" type of format, which can make reading difficult. It would facilitate the reader's task if there were more discussion explaining and summarizing the therapeutic interaction rather than simply reporting it.

The candor with which the author speaks to the transference-countertransference issues is part of the strength of the case narratives. Sidoli does not shy away from giving an account of a failed case (case of John in Chapter 8). Our failures are in part a measure of the limits of the therapeutic instrument—ourselves and our own psyche. At deeper levels, the therapeutic instrument is the healing capacity of the psyche itself which is made available to patients.

To support the developmental approach to psychotherapy, Sidoli frequently cites Jung's writings and illustrates how Jung's ideas anticipated later discoveries and key concepts relevant to child development. The author's concern is to give shape to a particularly Jungian approach to child therapy. While some might object that she and others from the developmental school borrow too heavily from Kleinian or Freudian thinking, I would like to point out that she is doing exactly what Jung did in his time, borrowing from her predecessors and contemporaries. Truth has no favorites. Sidoli acknowledges that Jung left us with an approach to the psyche that is different and distinct from that of Sigmund or Anna Freud and from Klein and her followers. I would add that Jung's approach approximates, as Humbert (1988) has pointed out, an epistemology and a phenomenology that respects psychic phenomenon prior to its being thematized into a particular theoretical framework. If it is generally agreed, as Sidoli reminds us, that Jung's psychology is so much better suited to the understanding of pre-oedipal and borderline states than Freud's, it might also be that there is something of the child that Jung implicitly grasped which others, more explicitly centered on child development, failed to grasp at all. The assumption is that the levels of regression apparent in severe pathologies reach back to the earliest phases of infantile and childhood development.

The book did leave me with a couple of questions pertaining to Sidoli's use of interpretation in treatment. Does an interpretation need to be understood in order to be effective? Does it even need to be "correct"? If not, at least if not always, what makes it work? Or, to put it differently, what might distinguish interpretations that need to be understood from those that do not, or that need to be "correct" from those that are not? The question comes to mind about whose language the therapist speaks—that of the therapist? that of the patient? Unconscious fantasies that appear in child's play or in the behavior of children and adult patients can be "read" *semiotically*, that is, as signs that have a particular, usually well-known meaning. One has the impression of directly "decoding" the unconscious. However, there are unconscious fantasies and images that do have a life of their own, those that are more symbolic—images, universal as they may be, that bear the stamp of the idiosyncratic and allow for the on-going life of the psyche. In other words, where is the tension between the need to take the fantasy as a sign, to reduce it to an already known, and the need to respect the integrity of the fantasy in whatever form it might appear? I often see fantasy as a psychic phenomenon whose meaning for the patient and the analyst has yet to be discovered in the analytic work. An overreliance upon any pre-set "code" hampers rather than facilitates analytic understanding.

## References

Humbert, Elie. 1988. *C. G. Jung: Fundamentals of Theory and Practice*. Wilmette, Ill.: Chiron Publication.

Mahler, M., et al. 1975. *The Psychological Birth of the Human Infant: Symbiosis and Individuation*. New York: Basic Books.

## Sex in the Forbidden Zone

Peter Rutter, M.D. Los Angeles: Jeremy P. Tarcher, Inc., 1989. 240 pages. $17.95

Reviewed by James Wyly

Peter Rutter has written an important, pathfinding, courageous, and disturbing book. "Sex in the forbidden zone" is his term for sexual contact "within professional relationships of trust" (p. 11), which, of course, include psychother-

---

**James Wyly**, Psy.D., is a clinical psychologist and a member of the Chicago Society of Jungian Analysts. He is the author of *The Phallic Quest: Priapus and Masculine Inflation*. He is in private practice in Chicago.

apy. The book demonstrates beyond doubt both that this kind of sexual contact does great harm and that our culture makes it difficult to avoid. For these reasons alone, *Sex in the Forbidden Zone* is essential reading for psychotherapists, lawyers, teachers, clergy, physicians, and their clients.

The book is clear, straightforward, and deliberately written in nontechnical language. It initially establishes three points that, taken together, demonstrate the seriousness of the issues. First, approximately 10 percent of professionals engage in sexual relationships with their clients. Second, there are almost always adverse effects upon the clients which last for years, profoundly disturbing their lives. And finally, not only have professional organizations and publications ignored this issue until very recently, many have actively suppressed the surprisingly few efforts that have been made to bring it to general awareness.

For his raw material, Rutter has relied heavily upon interviews he conducted with participants in this kind of sexual relationship, as well as with people in positions to know about them. He provides a great many quotes. The accumulation of firsthand accounts is horrifying. Rutter's professionals are all men and all the victims are women, reflecting the sex roles in the overwhelming majority of the cases he studied. One reads of professional men with the highest aspirations deluded and overwhelmed by erotic fantasies they could not avoid enacting. One also sees the lives of already fragile women ruined as their professions, marriages, therapies, and educations are subverted by the very relationships they entered with hopes of healing and furthering themselves. "I found it both striking and sad," writes Rutter, "that although all the women interviewed for this book have spent years trying to find their way back to recovery from their injuries, not one of them has yet borne a child since her experience of sex in the forbidden zone" (p. 89). Apparently their experiences closed this form of creative expression for these women.

This is appalling, and I am presenting it this way in hopes of conveying the powerful effect Rutter's work had on me. To be honest, I hated reading it. I kept looking for evidence that he has overstated his case and had great difficulty finding any. Indeed, women in my own practice who have told me of sex with earlier therapists have confirmed all Rutter says. I turned anxiously to Rutter's analysis of how this situation has come to pass and avidly read his suggestions as to what we can do about it. Like the rest of the book, they are clearly stated, simple, and persuasive; but they did not entirely relieve my bad feeling.

Now I should like to say a word or two about why I continued to feel this way.

To explain why this feeling persisted, I must first summarize the remainder of the book—too briefly to do it justice. Rutter is a Jungian analyst and a psychiatrist. Without technical language, he discusses the way men in our culture learn to project intimacy and the ability to heal upon women from childhood, and how women learn to project strength, independence, and autonomy on men. Ignorant of the function of fantasy, these "wounded" men and "wounded" women see their own latent qualities in one another. These qualities could heal them if they had intrapsychic access to them; instead they desperately grasp for them by means of sexual enactment. Rutter's evidence suggests that this almost never succeeds; the result is disillusion and despair as both fail to live up to that which is projected upon them. Rutter then concludes with chapters of psychologically based advice for men and women who are in such relationships, who have had them, who are in danger of having them, and who are parents.

All of this is accomplished, as I have said, with hardly a hint of psychological language, let alone Jungian terminology. Rutter uses exactly eleven semitechnical terms on the level of "boundaries," "sexual behavior," "fantasy," "wounds," and so on, for which he provides totally accessible definitions (pp. 39 ff). This incredible *tour de force* accomplishes the very desirable goal of increasing the possible audience for this book. However, this language has a somewhat weird effect on important arguments. I should like to illustrate how Rutter's use of language influences the overall effect of the book.

One example is found in the section called "The Masculine Myth of the Feminine: Deference, Sexuality, and Destructiveness" (pp. 64 ff). In explaining myth, Rutter differentiates "family myths" from "cultural myths" and attributes the view of women as inherently "deferential, sexual, and destructive" to cultural mythology. So far so good; but by leaving myth here, Rutter gives it a negative cast: the "masculine myth of the feminine" is something to be moved through. There is no mention of myth on a larger, deeper scale. Where is ongoing mythic development as the way cultures evolve? Where is myth as the way the psyche communicates its meditations to us?

Of course in asking this, I have gone beyond the limits of the language Rutter has chosen to employ; and I admit he has chosen his language with good reason. The thing that disturbs me is that I really don't see how we can hope for significant change in the awful situation regarding the feminine that has led to the atrocities this book documents unless we make exactly this transcultural move with mythology. We must try to understand the new mythology the psyche is now trying to show us. If we are deploring an outdated, bankrupt, and destructive mythology, I fear that solutions for its evil effects proposed from within will be little more than bandages. Any vocabulary that is limited by a bankrupt mythology is ultimately going to be subverted by it. Yet it is just such a vocabulary that this book necessarily employs.

This is one example of the subversive effect of deliberately nonpsychological language on psychological material. Rutter's tendency to generalize is another. I know we talk in generalizations now; but the truth is that *all* men don't subscribe to the myth we have just discussed, and *all* men and *all* women don't do many of the things the book attributes to them. It is easy to read this language as suggesting that masculinity itself is inherently psychopathically heterosexual, and femininity inherently helpless and passive, although we know otherwise. Again, if we employ language that excludes the exceptions to the problems we are trying to solve, how will we gain access to the alternative attitudes we so desperately need?

In a way, I am quibbling. This is a brilliantly executed book, while I am asking for another book altogether; and mine is a book Rutter consciously chose not to write, for reasons with which I can concur. Our culture needs the book Rutter wrote. But as I am writing this for a Jungian journal, about a book by a Jungian, I think I can also say we need more.

Rutter's book implies what this "more" is. The masculine myth he shows us is more than destructive; it is exhausted. The exhausted myth is grounded in assumptions Rutter gives us: they are the idea of sexuality as "the ultimate symbol of intimate human relationship" and the idea that "the act of intercourse can allow us to experience in the most intense way possible our deepest biological, emotional, and spiritual strivings, and at the same time allow us to share these feelings with anther person" (pp. 54–55). We know this is a cultural myth, because not all cultures accept it; and it inflates sexuality in a way that may well have to be eliminated.

Are we ready for this? Here is where the implications of Rutter's book begin to get painful, for we all grew up in the patriarchal, sexually abusive culture he describes. Our early aspirations, affections, and sexual ambitions were determined by it. Most of us committed greater or lesser abuses, if not in our offices, then in the back seats of our parents' cars or somewhere; for we were children in a culture that called what we were doing love. Now we are waking up, and our new awareness of our past is excruciating, especially as other ways of being are still unclear to us.

Jungian psychology and Jungian language give us what is probably the best intellectual framework we have yet found for addressing very difficult transcultural issues such as this one. Now I wish Rutter would write another book, using his Jungian conceptual framework uninhibitedly. This work certainly qualifies him to take the next step toward a sexuality that can replace this worn-out ruin of which he has made us so painfully aware.

**The Ability to Mourn: Disillusionment and the Social Origins of Psychoanalysis**
Peter Homans. Chicago: The University of Chicago Press, 1989. 390 pages.

Reviewed by Donald E. Kalsched

This tightly argued scholarly book stands as a creative milestone along the path formed by that growing literature which is attempting to explore the "third space" between the inner world of the self and the outer world of our common culture. In developing his ideas about this complicated subject, Homans makes creative use of two psychoanalytic theories which "locate" the psyche in this intermediate area, i.e., Kohut's ideas about this intermediate field as the domain of the "self-object," and Winnicott's "transitional space" filled with "transitional objects" including the symbolic "objects" of culture. Chiron's readers will be aware that long before Winnicott or Kohut, C. G. Jung also located the psyche in this space describing it as an "*anima media natura*, capable of uniting the opposites [which is] never complete in the individual unless related to another individual" (Jung 1946, par. 454). While it is apparent that Homans is not especially familiar with Jung's "cultural texts," (among which Jung's essay on transference would be included), his emphasis on such issues as the constructive aspects of illusion, the reality of a "self" beyond the ego, and his focus on mythic and religious structures which sustain the ego in its "object-relations," should find a sympathetic readership among those interested in Jung's ideas. To Jung's paradoxical statements about self–world relations, Homans prefers the dialectical conceptions of Kohut moving from disillu-

---

**Donald E. Kalsched,** Ph.D., is a Jungian analyst and faculty member at the C. G. Jung Institute of New York. He is also director of the Institute of Depth Psychology at Wainwright House, Rye, New York, and has a private practice in New York City and Ridgefield, Connecticut.

sionment or de-idealization to internal psychic structure. Midway through this sequence, Homans adds "mourning" as an important intermediate stage and believes that the ability to mourn is essential if the modern self is to find its way both to interior depth *and* to a meaningful life in society.

Homans develops his thesis about this intermediate "third" space by first exploring two large bodies of scholarly work which fail to acknowledge it. First are psychoanalytic studies of society, religion, art, and history, which purport to see through the illusions of culture to the primary instinctual entities underneath; second, social and cultural criticism of psychoanalysis, which emphasizes the secularizing influence of Freud's thought and the idea that modernity represents a total break with the past leading to "negative communities" (Rieff), "disenchantment" (Weber), or "anomie" (Durkheim). Both the psychoanalysis of culture and the cultural critique of psychoanalysis, Homans feels, neglect the deeper mythic dimensions of unconscious fantasy which structure the very language of their purportedly "scientific" and "rational" claims. Both, in other words, neglect what Jung would call the religious or mythic dimension of the psyche thus leaving the ego cut off from its true sources of sustainment.

While this review focuses primarily on Homans's psychological analysis, the author emphasizes again and again that without a theory of social reality, psychology becomes solipsistic. For example, the process of "mourning" is not just directed individually to lost "objects" but is a process that extends, for all modern men and women, to the symbolic "objects" of culture as well. Yet this "cultural" mourning, while just as critical to the individual's development in depth, is generally neglected. All psychology, Homans believes, begins with a rupture (disillusionment) to the fabric of an individual's religio-cultural beliefs; but this should not lead either to an inwardness intolerant of illusion (psychoanalysis) or to the secularization of modern culture (sociological theory). Both create an impenetrable barrier between the inner and social worlds of the individual. Instead, this mourning of a lost culture "can stimulate the desire to become who one is" (p. 9) and lead to the creation of meaning:

> the conception of meaning which I now wish to propose is an interpsychical one in which the products of one's own subjectivity (unconscious fantasies) are synthesized with the world's products of objectivity in a fresh and unique way. Meaning consists in inserting the unconscious products of subjectivity into the space between the self and the social other. (p. 328)

> Because . . . this intermediate space . . . is already filled, by definition with symbolic structures, a new and actually ego-enhancing pattern of dependence upon the social world and upon the past can also come into being. In such cases, the ego is both more independent from the past and more dependent upon it than it thought, before the process of individuation began. The reality and recognition of interdependence is the point at which a structure within the organism deeper than the ego begins to take shape. It is best to call this structure the self. (p. 334)

For the psychoanalytic reader, *The Ability to Mourn* will be of interest because it continues the author's creative project (begun 10 years ago with his first book, *Jung in Context*) of applying Kohut's dialect of disillusionment to the personal relations among the early psychoanalysts and to the unusually sectarian "movement" they created. Whereas the focus of his first book was Jung and his "narcissistic" relationship to Freud, the focus here is on Freud and his narcissistic relationship to his psychoanalytic "child" including the various followers to whom Freud entrusted that child. Readers of Homans's first book who were offended by his simplistic and reductionistic characterization of Jung's *Symbols of Transformation* as a "grandiose, and narcissistic idealization" of Jung's own fantasies (Homans 1979, p. 67) will find a more balanced treatment here. For example, he shows how *all* the early analysts, including Freud, suffered a profound disillusionment with their Judeo-Christian roots and were forced to turn inward in their own "creative illnesses." Indeed, the entire psychoanalytic enterprise, beginning with Freud's self-analysis, can be seen as a creative response to this loss of a religiously structured "common culture" and an introverted effort to gain "analytic access" to the inner world instead.

But what psychoanalysis accomplished, says Homans, was one-sided. Classical psychoanalysis got stuck in the inner world, reified it in the metapsychology, and failed to "return" to the cultural interface whose "illusions" it purported to see through. Only recently, with the advent of British object-relations theory and self-psychology, do we see the collapse of a metapsychology based upon instinct and a recognition of how profoundly vulnerable and dependent the human individual is on his or her "object-relations." This leads to an investigation of the intermediate area defined by the self–world boundary, a "space" which is filled, according to Homans, with the products of unconscious fantasy, movement, and narrative (always social). Hence it is here that both the psychoanalyst and the sociologist must look for an understanding of those pathologies of selfhood which define the modern experience.

Among the valuable contributions of the book are Homans's trenchant observations about the primitive and cultlike "culture" of early psychoanalysis—its authoritarianism, splitting, and its "group illusion" of being a culture that transcends culture or "sees through" it. By failing to mourn their loss of a sustaining cultural and religious mythos, says Homans, the early analysts found themselves in the grip of this same forsaken energy returning in the form of an authoritarian religiosity (return of the repressed). In other words, in the hubris of these assumptions, Homans sees an unconscious effort, albeit an extremely creative one, to recover the very symbolic "illusions" that were destroyed by the reductive assumptions of the theory in the first place. This is not far from Jung's reminder that any theoretical attempt at explanation, including science, is always the creation of a new myth.

The early analysts' failure to mourn also made them especially vulnerable to primitive idealizations and de-idealizations of each other. Homans demonstrates very convincingly how much of early psychoanalytic theorizing was interwoven with painful "de-idealizations" in Freud's early circle and how each time, there was a failure to adequately mourn these losses and retain the values they represented. Among the many fascinating "ancestor stories" in Homans's well-researched book is the following story which emerges as the author places Freud's correspondence with Karl Abraham side by side with the correspondence between Freud and Jung.

As the break with Jung grew more imminent, Freud wrote increasingly about Jung to Abraham. While Jung was in America, delivering his Fordham University lectures, Freud confessed to Abraham that he had "no more friendly thoughts for him" and three months later, after reading Jung's "Symbols of Transformation" he wrote "Jung is crazy, but I have no desire for a separation and should like to let him wreck himself first" (p. 38). Then, while struggling with his famous paper on narcissism, Freud became more expressive of his love for Abraham: "I think of you a great deal, because I am writing the paper on narcissism" (p. 39) and, finally cementing the new merger, "Tomorrow I am sending you the 'Narcissism,' which was a difficult birth and bears all the marks of it. . . . Your picture will return tomorrow from the framer's and will then take the place of Jung's" (p. 40). As Homans demonstrates, de-idealization without mourning leads to denegration and primitive "splitting of the object." Freud's scorn and bitterness in follow-up letters to Abraham, demonstrate this: "Good wishes for the new Jungless era" and in a final example, "So we are at last rid of them, the brutal, sanctimonious Jung and his disciples!" (p. 40).

The early break between Freud and Jung is still something we psychoanalysts are trying to recover from—especially because each of these great pioneers had such profound respect for the unconscious and such profoundly different theories about it. This split is slowly coming together in the work of self-psychologists and object-relations theory, and Homans acknowledges that Jung was the first real self-psychologist. Like Jung, Homans very clearly wants to "locate" the unconscious not only in the instinctual nature of man as Freud did, but also, and primarily, in those deeper aspects of human experience recorded in the "monuments" of culture itself. "It makes good sense," he says "to think that the unconscious is that universal intermediate area of human life experience which has its existence and reality midway between nature and culture" (p. 341). Although Homans gives hardly any recognition to Jung's "revisioning" of psychoanalysis as a source of his own thinking, this statement, and many others like it, are decidedly "Jungian." As Jung once said, in a letter to James Kirsch, "In the deepest sense we all dream not out of ourselves but out of what lies between us and the other" (Jung 1973, p. 172).

## References

Peter Homans. 1979. *Jung in Context: Modernity and the Making of a Psychology*. Chicago: University of Chicago Press.

Jung, C. G. 1946. The psychology of the transference. *Collected Works* 16: 163–323. Princeton, N.J.: Princeton University Press, 1966.

Jung, C. G. 1973. *Letters*, vol. 1. R. F. C. Hull, trans. Gerhard Adler, ed. Princeton, N.J.: Princeton University Press.